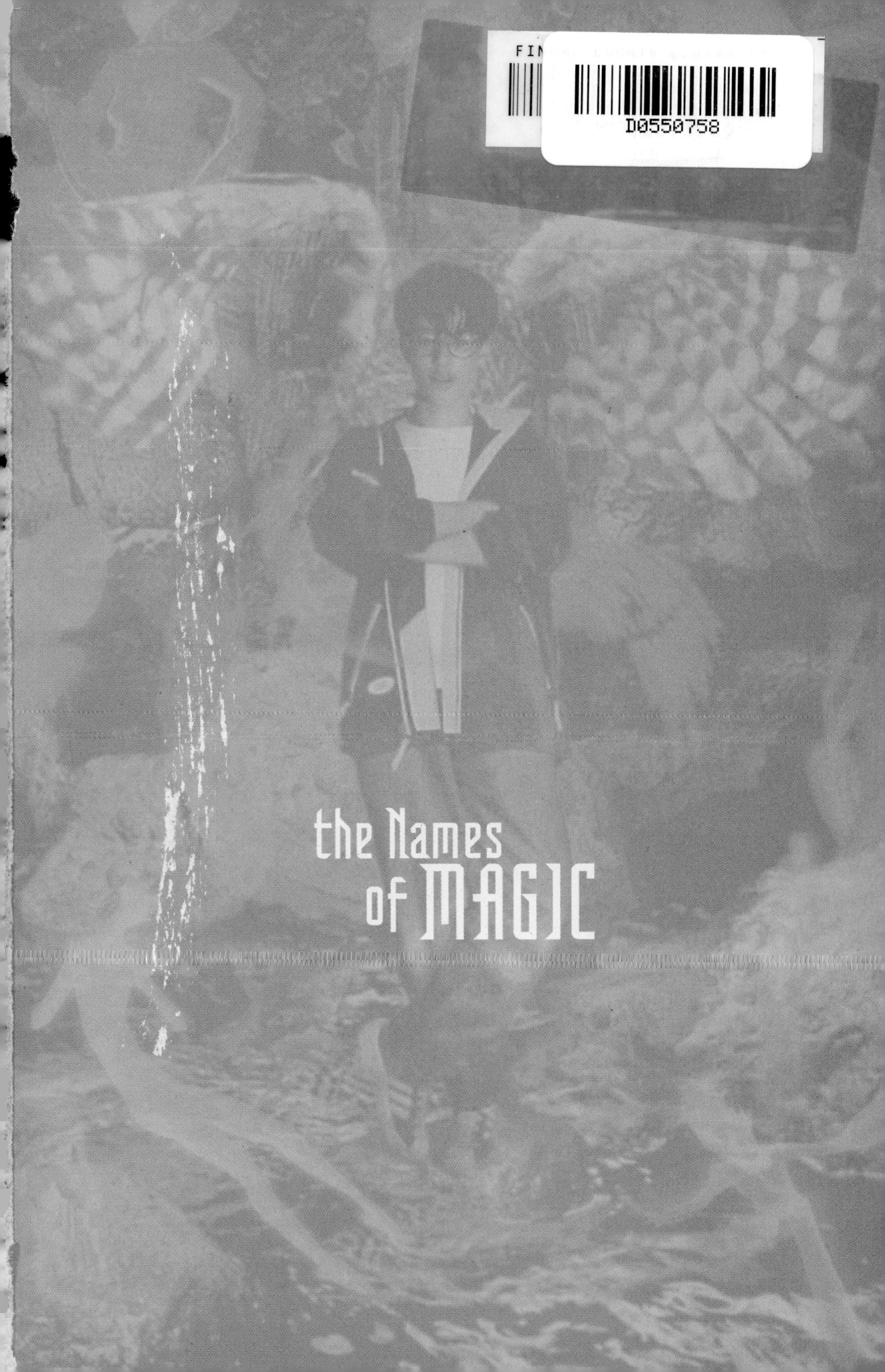
the Names
of MAGIC

Dylan Horrocks *WRITER*

Richard Case *ARTIST*

Sherilyn van Valkenburgh *COLORIST*

Digital Chameleon/Jamison *SEPARATORS*

Comicraft *LETTERING*

John Bolton *ORIGINAL SERIES COVERS*

**Timothy Hunter and
The Books of Magic
created by Neil Gaiman
and John Bolton**

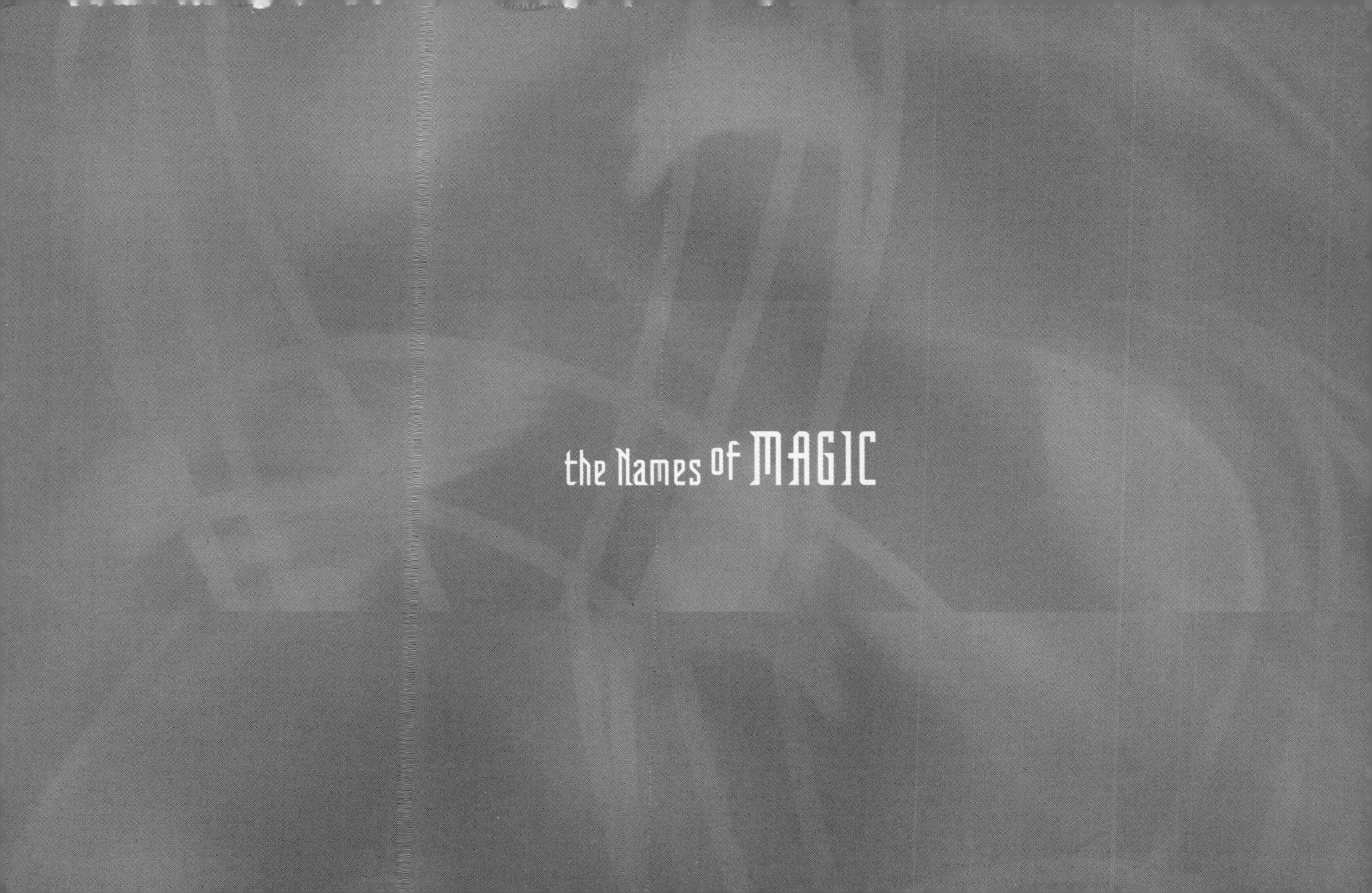

the Names of MAGIC

THE NAMES OF MAGIC. Published by DC Comics. Cover and compilation copyright © 2002 DC Comics. All Rights Reserved.
Originally published in single magazine form as THE NAMES OF MAGIC 1-5. Copyright © 2001 DC Comics. All Rights Reserved. DC, VERTIGO, and
all characters, their distinctive likenesses and related indicia featured in this publication are trademarks of DC Comics. The stories, characters, and
incidents featured in this publication are entirely fictional. DC Comics does not read or accept unsolicited submissions of ideas, stories or artwork.
DC Comics, 1700 Broadway, New York, NY 10019. A division of Warner Bros. - An AOL Time Warner Company. Printed in Canada. First Printing.
ISBN: 1-56389-888-8

John Bolton Cover Illustration
Maria Cabardo Publication Design

Scotland
Ireland
England
Wales
London
Bude
High Cliff
Boscastle
Tintagel
Launceston
DEVON
Tamar
Padstow
Camelford
BODMIN
MOOR
CORNWALL
Plymouth
St Ives
ENGLISH
CHANNEL
Lands
End
0 10 20 30 km
0 6 12 18 miles

What Has Gone Before...

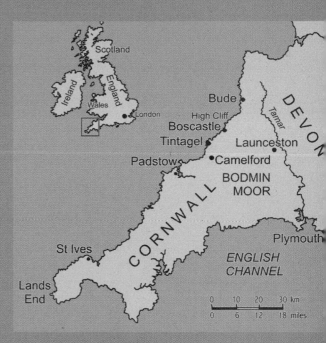

Timothy Hunter has lived more than his few years would suggest. But then, Tim is no ordinary teenager. He is destined to be the world's most powerful magician, and that destiny has cost him dearly.

Following a car crash which left his mother dead and his father despondent, Tim grew up intimate with hardship. Then one day, four men in trenchcoats appeared from the shadows and took Tim on a journey – a journey that showed him what was hidden behind the everyday and mundane.

It was magic. And for Tim, it was a liberation. But as he began to follow the path that magic had opened for him, Tim quickly learned that it was less of a path and more of a gauntlet. His relationship with his first love, neighbor Molly O'Reilly, brought her first to Hell and then to Faerie, from which she emerged carrying a seemingly unbreakable curse. Then, in a belated effort to shield Molly from his magic's dangers, Tim managed to alienate her completely.

But worse was to come. Tim's massive power and inexperience, coupled with the machinations of a host of power-hungry demons, angels, faeries, and magicians, eventually brought the world to the edge of destruction – first in the form of a war between Heaven and Hell, and then in the form of a second Tim Hunter, twisted and corrupted from feeding on the energies of a thousand murdered versions of himself. On both occasions Tim rose to meet the challenge, paying a terrible price for each victory. They have left him homeless and alone, but with his person and his magic whole and complete for the first time in his life.

Now, he is finally ready to claim his birthright.

...magic.

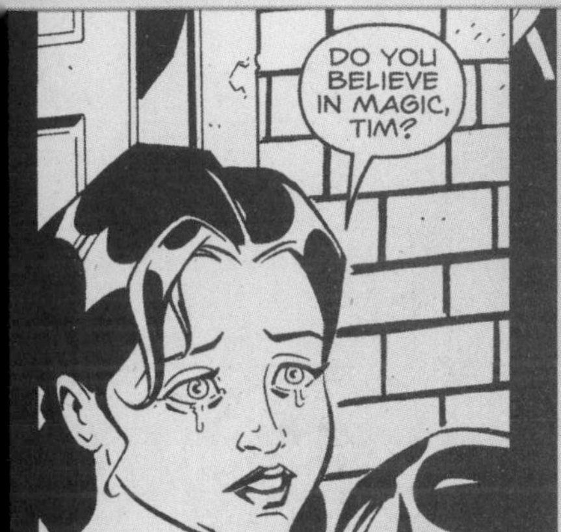
DO YOU BELIEVE IN MAGIC, TIM?

has a price.

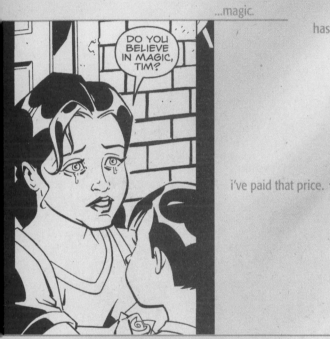

i've paid that price.

everything i cared about is

gone.

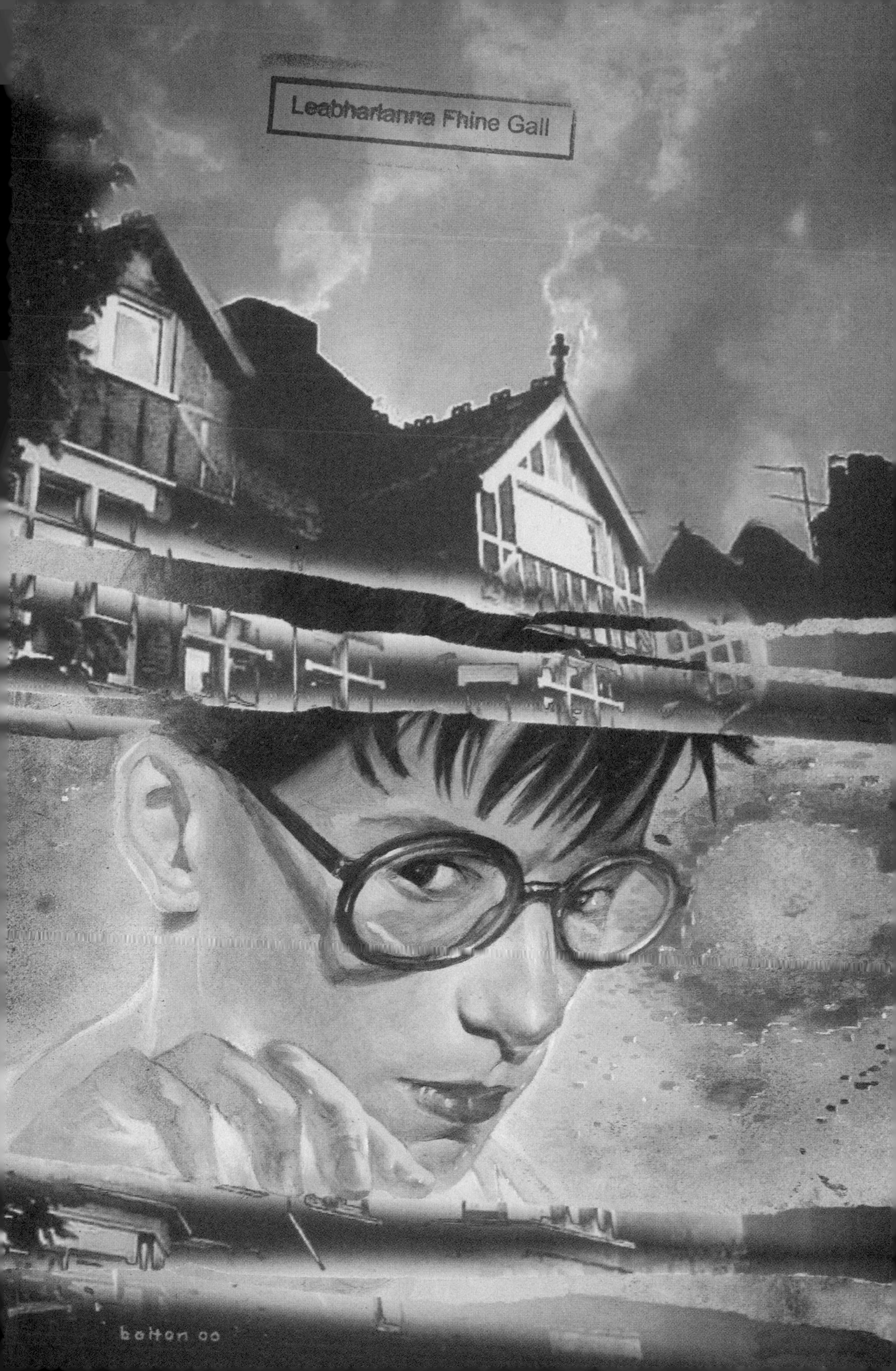
bolton 00

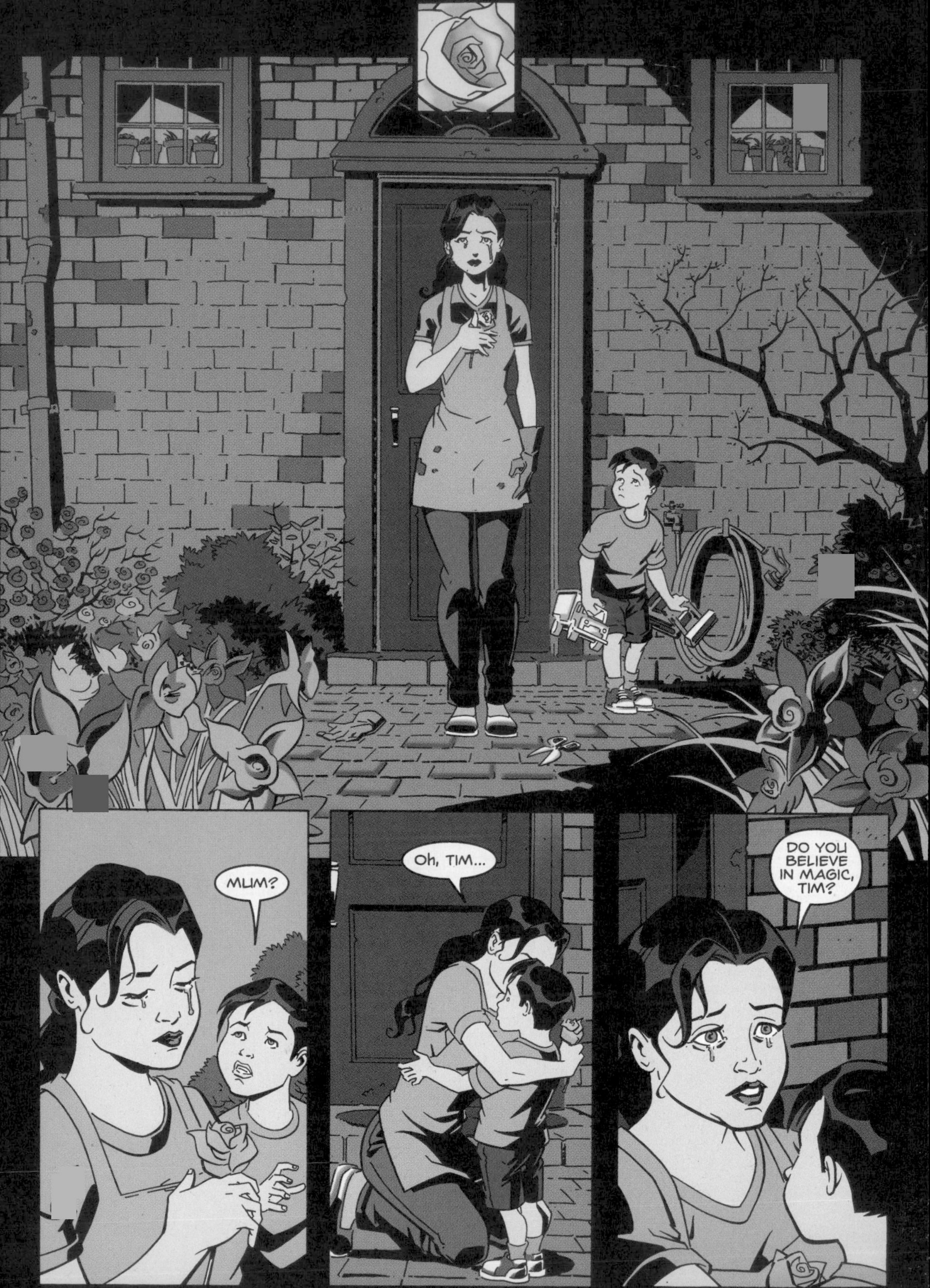
MUM?
Oh, TIM...
DO YOU BELIEVE IN MAGIC, TIM?

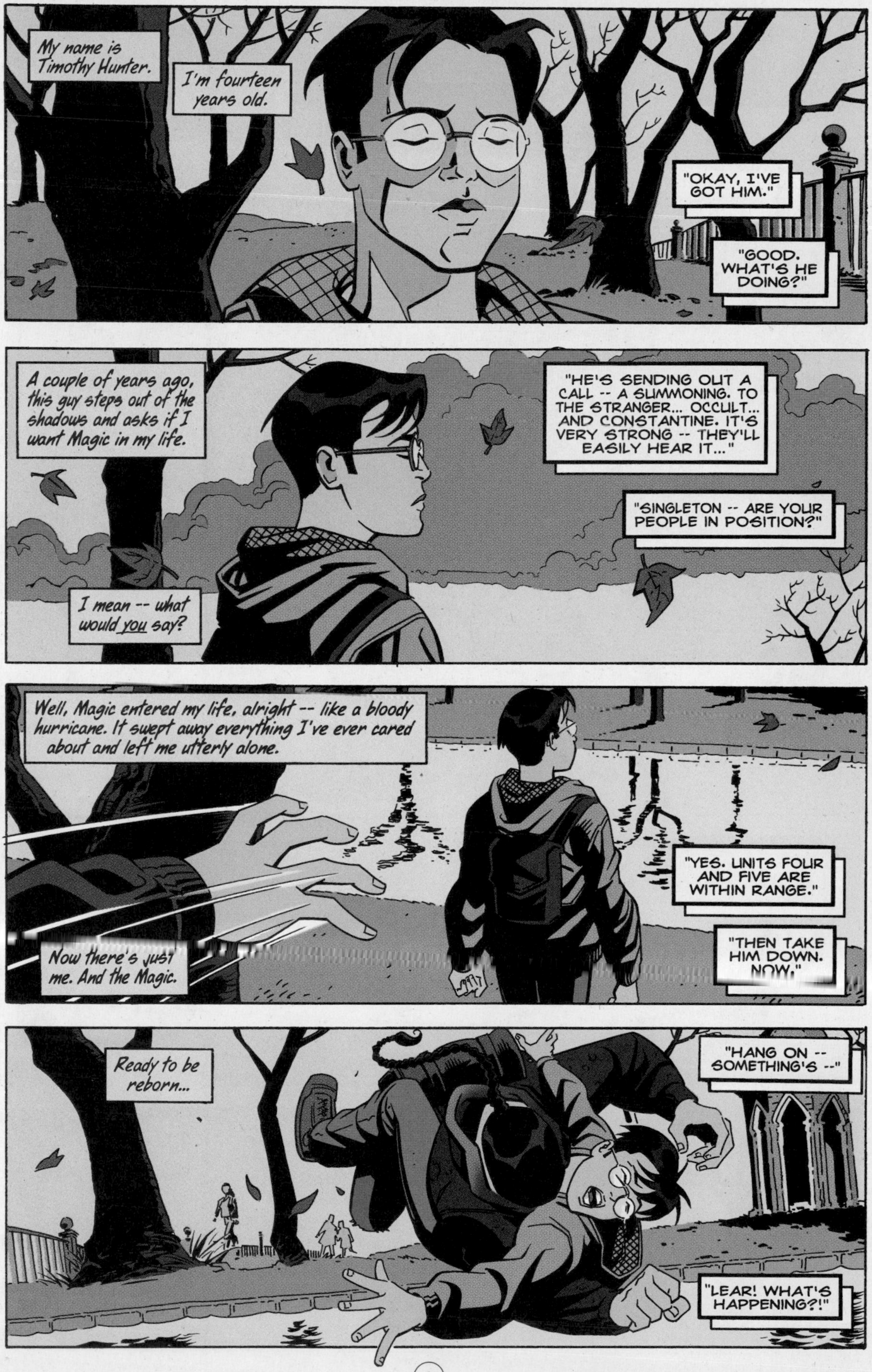

My name is Timothy Hunter.
I'm fourteen years old.
"OKAY, I'VE GOT HIM."
"GOOD. WHAT'S HE DOING?"
A couple of years ago, this guy steps out of the shadows and asks if I want Magic in my life.
"HE'S SENDING OUT A CALL -- A SUMMONING. TO THE STRANGER... OCCULT... AND CONSTANTINE. IT'S VERY STRONG -- THEY'LL EASILY HEAR IT..."
"SINGLETON -- ARE YOUR PEOPLE IN POSITION?"
I mean -- what would you say?
Well, Magic entered my life, alright -- like a bloody hurricane. It swept away everything I've ever cared about and left me utterly alone.
"YES. UNITS FOUR AND FIVE ARE WITHIN RANGE."
Now there's just me. And the Magic.
"THEN TAKE HIM DOWN. NOW."
Ready to be reborn...
"HANG ON -- SOMETHING'S --"
"LEAR! WHAT'S HAPPENING?!"

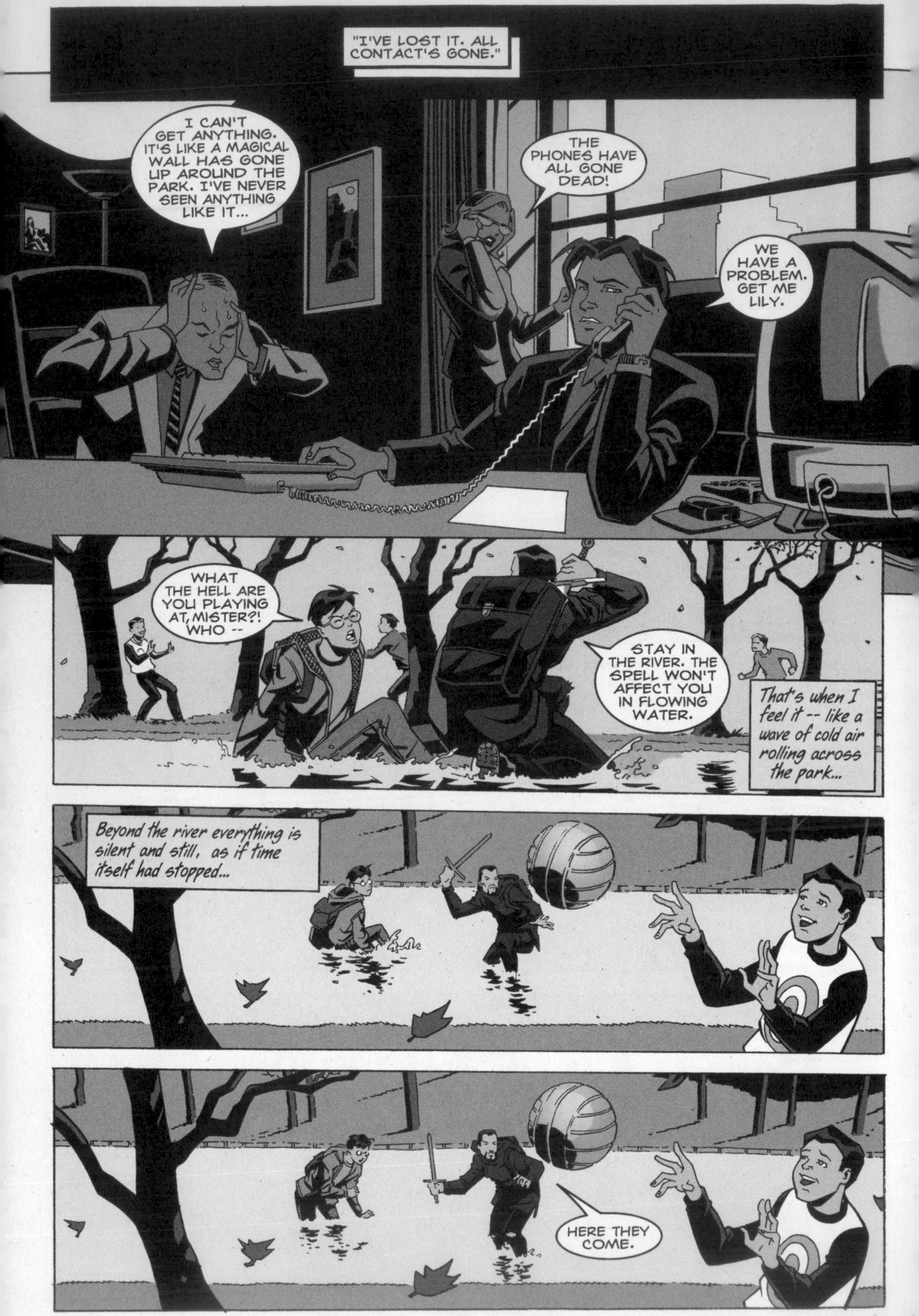
"I'VE LOST IT. ALL CONTACT'S GONE."
I CAN'T GET ANYTHING. IT'S LIKE A MAGICAL WALL HAS GONE UP AROUND THE PARK. I'VE NEVER SEEN ANYTHING LIKE IT...
THE PHONES HAVE ALL GONE DEAD!
WE HAVE A PROBLEM. GET ME LILY.
WHAT THE HELL ARE YOU PLAYING AT, MISTER?! WHO --
STAY IN THE RIVER. THE SPELL WON'T AFFECT YOU IN FLOWING WATER.
That's when I feel it -- like a wave of cold air rolling across the park...
Beyond the river everything is silent and still, as if time itself had stopped...
HERE THEY COME.

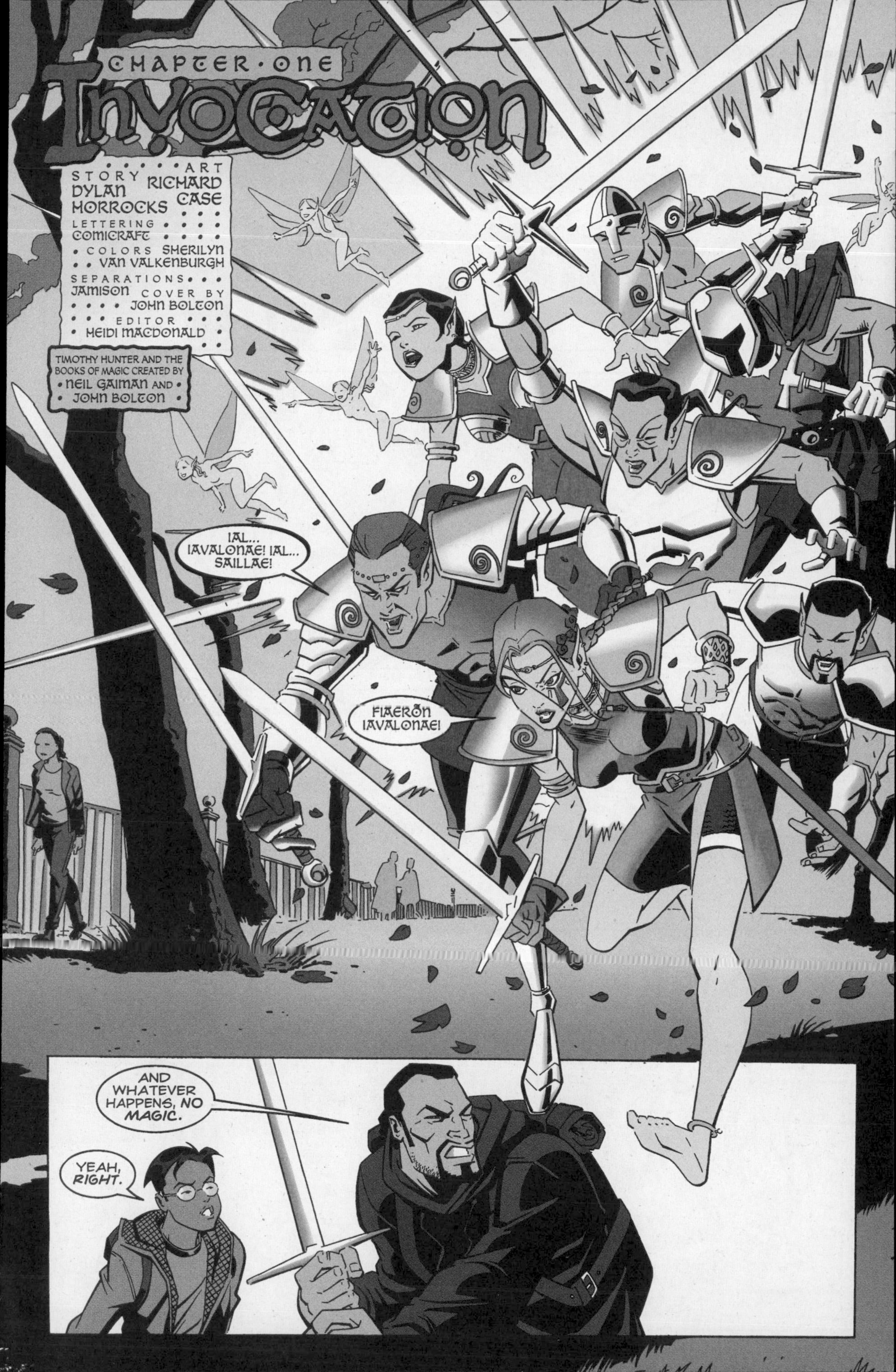
CHAPTER • ONE
INVOCATION
STORY DYLAN HORROCKS
ART RICHARD CASE
LETTERING COMICRAFT
COLORS SHERILYN VAN VALKENBURGH
SEPARATIONS JAMISON
COVER BY JOHN BOLTON
EDITOR HEIDI MACDONALD
TIMOTHY HUNTER AND THE BOOKS OF MAGIC CREATED BY NEIL GAIMAN AND JOHN BOLTON
¡AL... ¡AVALONAE! ¡AL... SAILLAE!
FIAERŌN ¡AVALONAE!
AND WHATEVER HAPPENS, NO MAGIC.
YEAH, RIGHT.

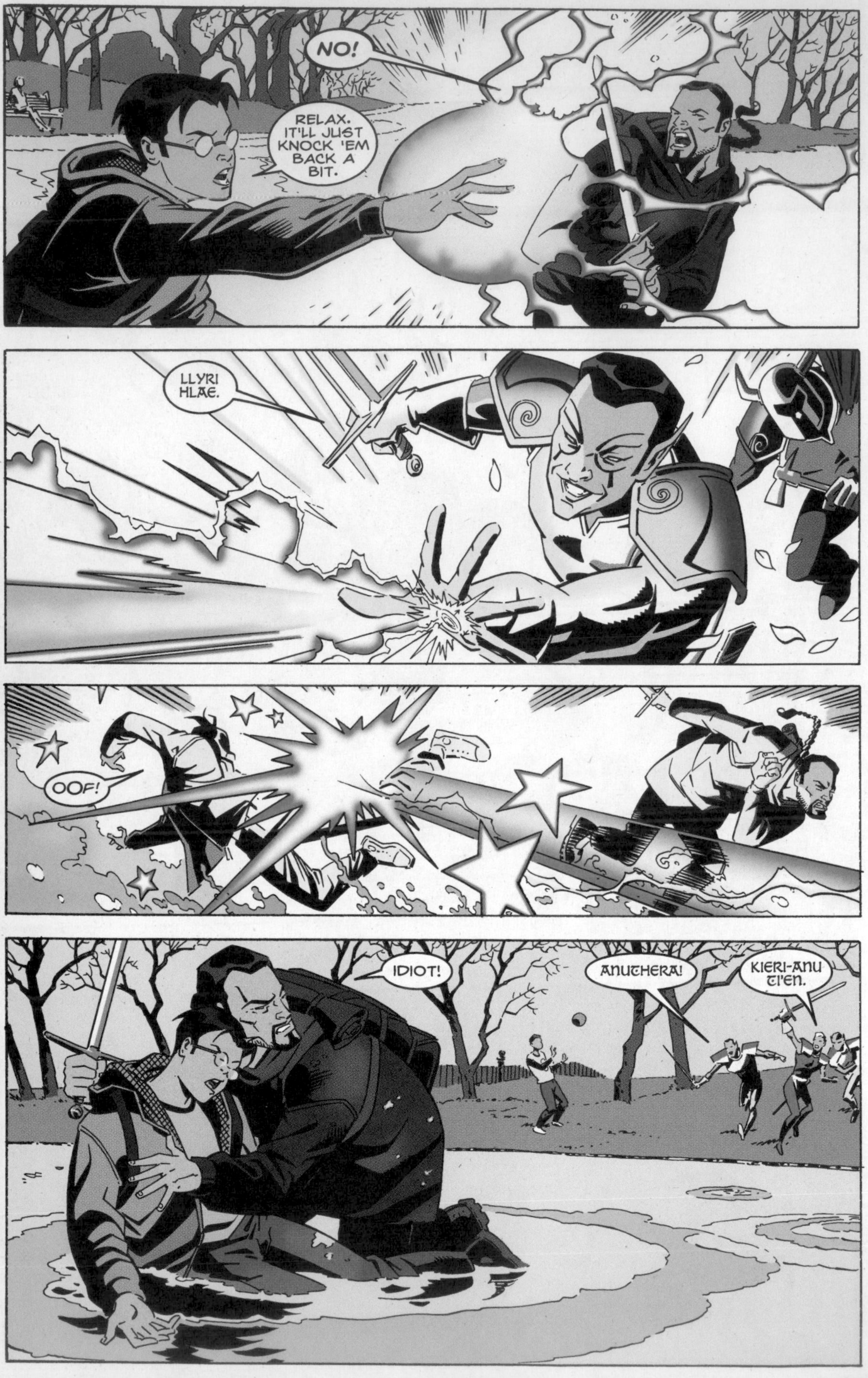
NO!
RELAX. IT'LL JUST KNOCK 'EM BACK A BIT.
LLYRI HLAE.
OOF!
IDIOT!
ANUTHERA!
KIERI-ANU TI'EN.

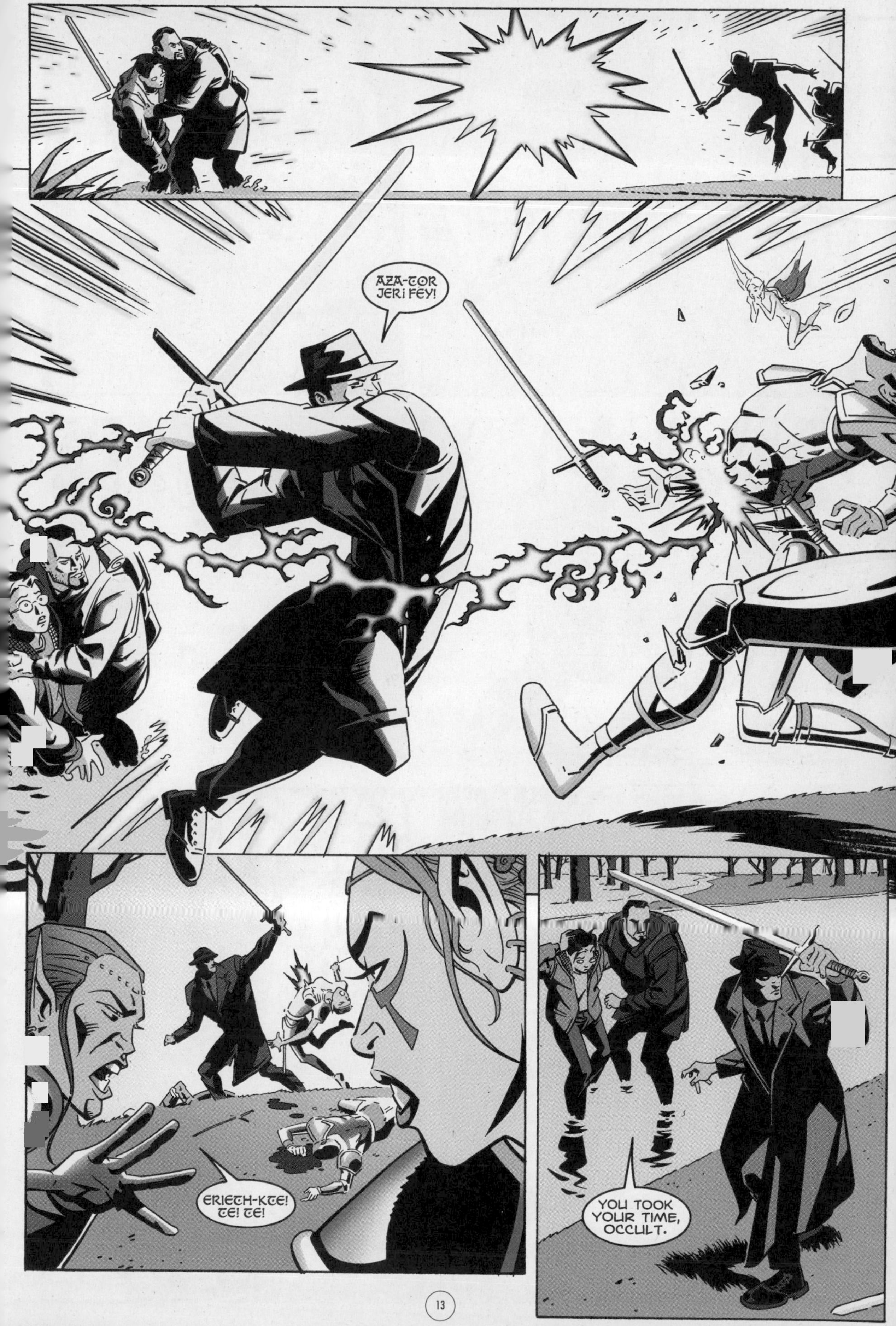
AZA-TOR JERi FEY!
ERIETH-KTE! TE! TE!
YOU TOOK YOUR TIME, OCCULT.

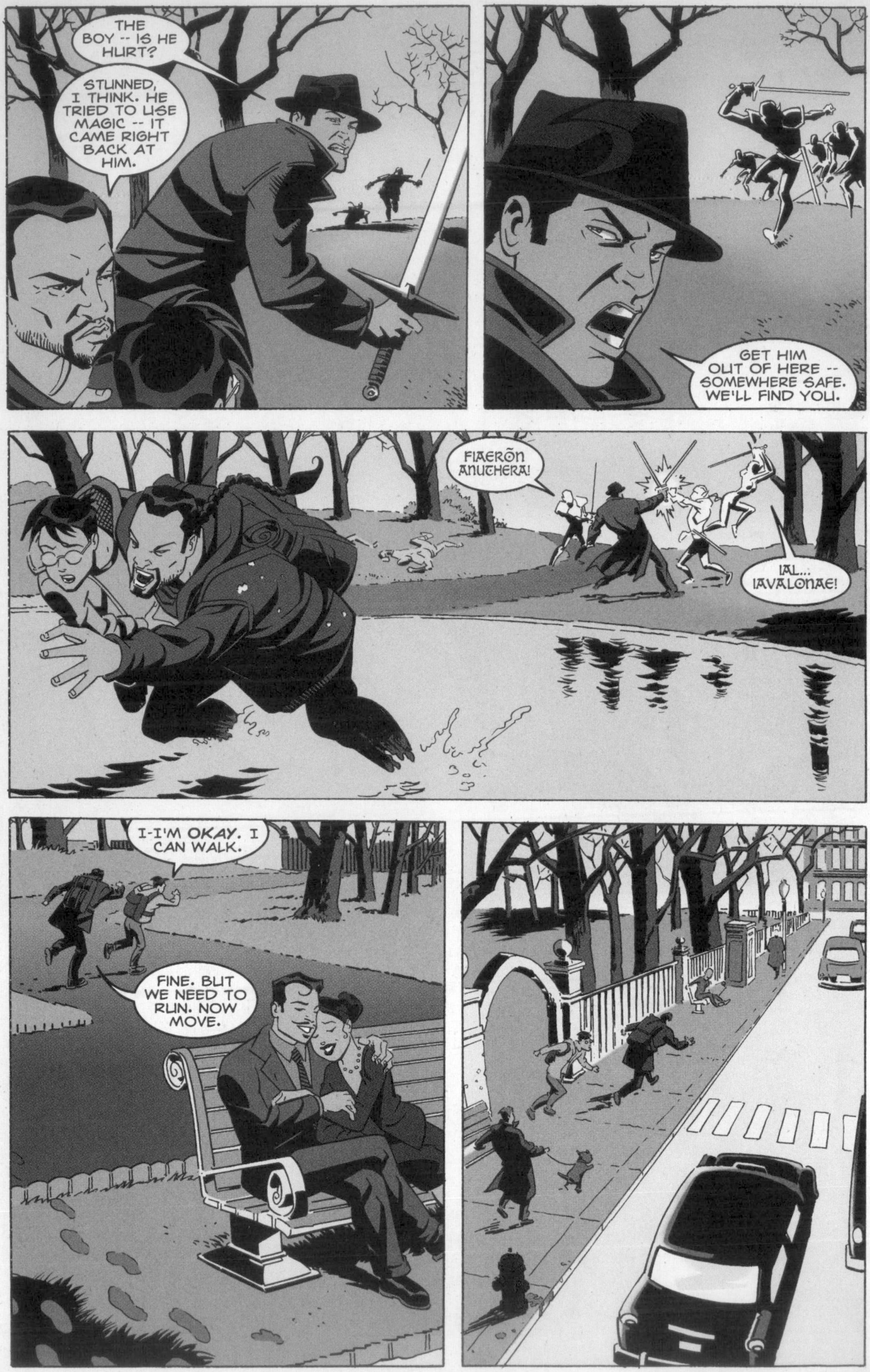
THE BOY -- IS HE HURT?
STUNNED, I THINK. HE TRIED TO USE MAGIC -- IT CAME RIGHT BACK AT HIM.
GET HIM OUT OF HERE -- SOMEWHERE SAFE. WE'LL FIND YOU.
FIAERÕN ANUTHERA!
¡AL... ¡AVALONAE!
I-I'M OKAY. I CAN WALK.
FINE. BUT WE NEED TO RUN. NOW MOVE.

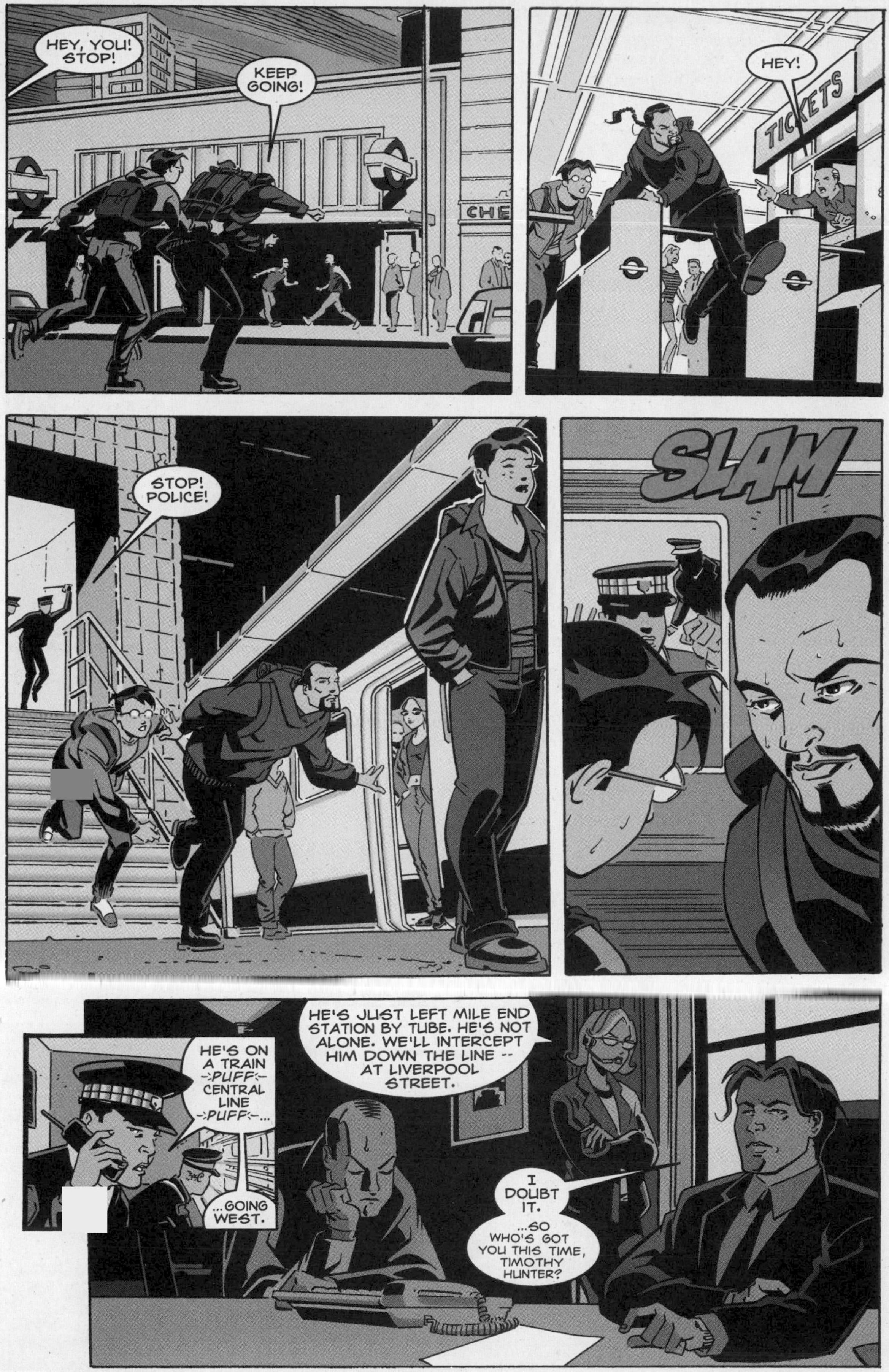

HEY, YOU! STOP!
KEEP GOING!
HEY!
TICKETS
STOP! POLICE!
SLAM
HE'S ON A TRAIN -PUFF- CENTRAL LINE -PUFF-...
HE'S JUST LEFT MILE END STATION BY TUBE. HE'S NOT ALONE. WE'LL INTERCEPT HIM DOWN THE LINE -- AT LIVERPOOL STREET.
...GOING WEST.
I DOUBT IT.
...SO WHO'S GOT YOU THIS TIME, TIMOTHY HUNTER?

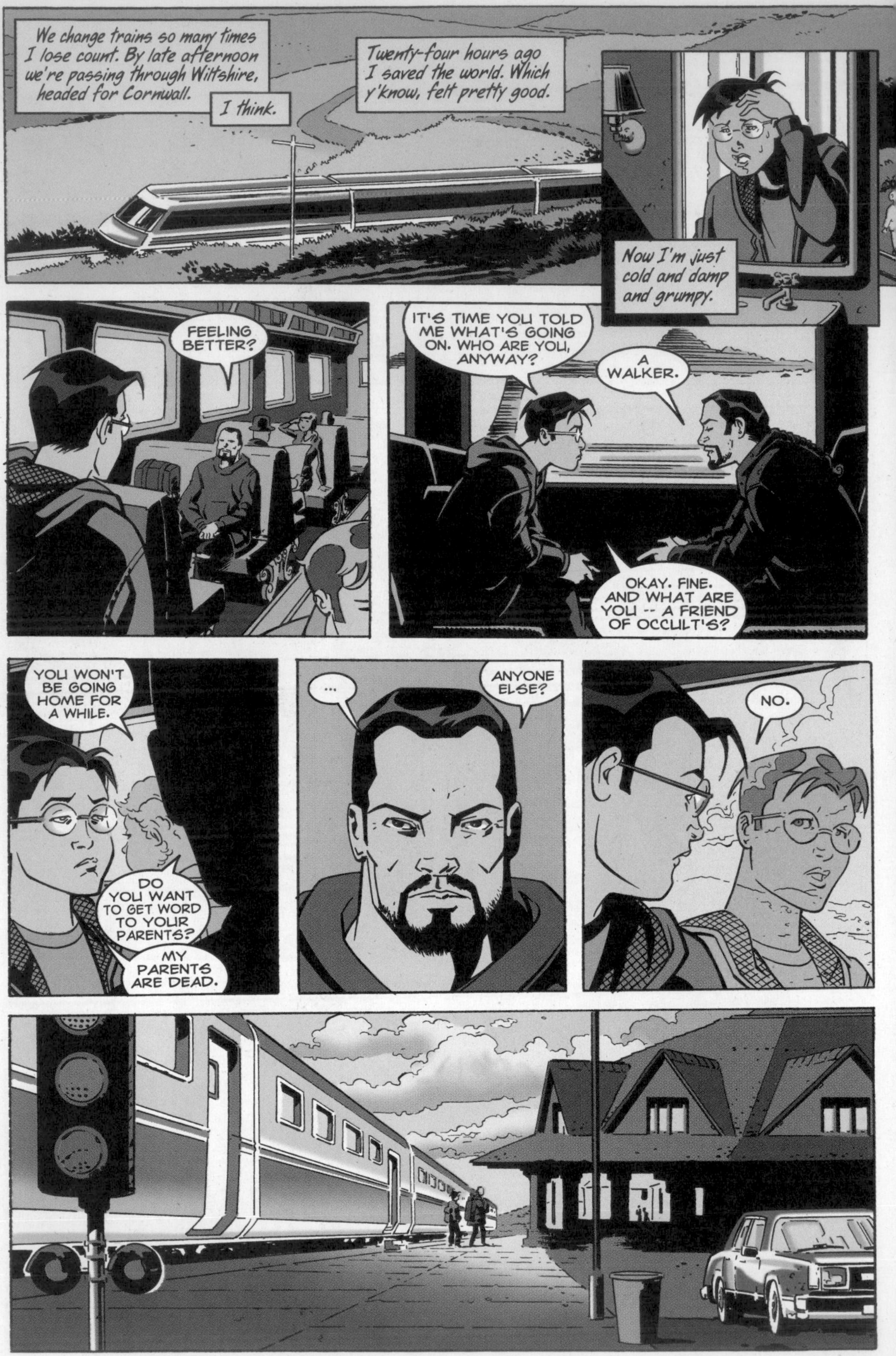
We change trains so many times I lose count. By late afternoon we're passing through Wiltshire, headed for Cornwall.
I think.
Twenty-four hours ago I saved the world. Which y'know, felt pretty good.
Now I'm just cold and damp and grumpy.
FEELING BETTER?
IT'S TIME YOU TOLD ME WHAT'S GOING ON. WHO ARE YOU, ANYWAY?
A WALKER.
OKAY. FINE. AND WHAT ARE YOU -- A FRIEND OF OCCULT'S?
YOU WON'T BE GOING HOME FOR A WHILE.
DO YOU WANT TO GET WORD TO YOUR PARENTS?
MY PARENTS ARE DEAD.
...
ANYONE ELSE?
NO.

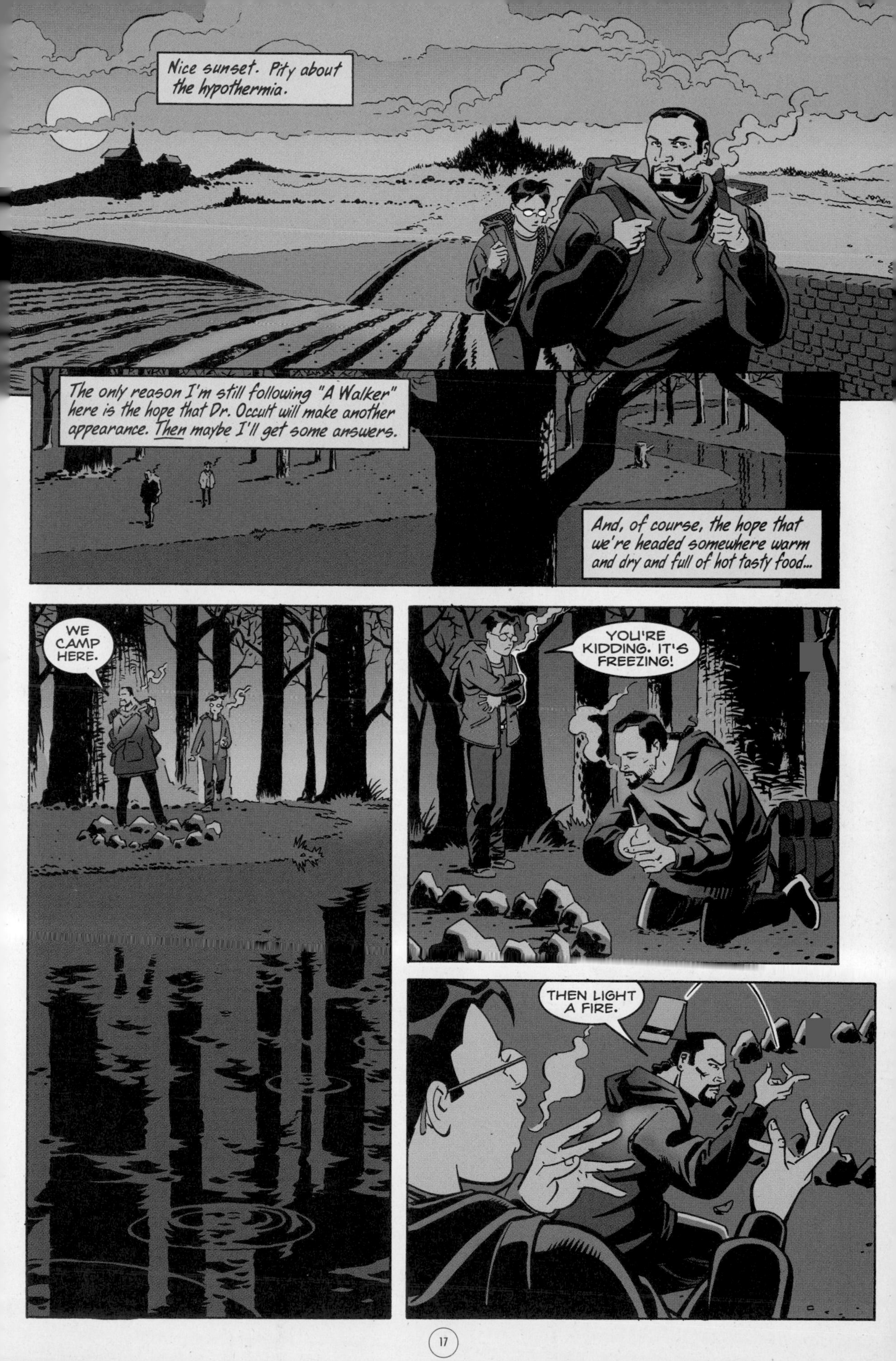
Nice sunset. Pity about the hypothermia.
The only reason I'm still following "A Walker" here is the hope that Dr. Occult will make another appearance. Then maybe I'll get some answers.
And, of course, the hope that we're headed somewhere warm and dry and full of hot tasty food...
WE CAMP HERE.
YOU'RE KIDDING. IT'S FREEZING!
THEN LIGHT A FIRE.

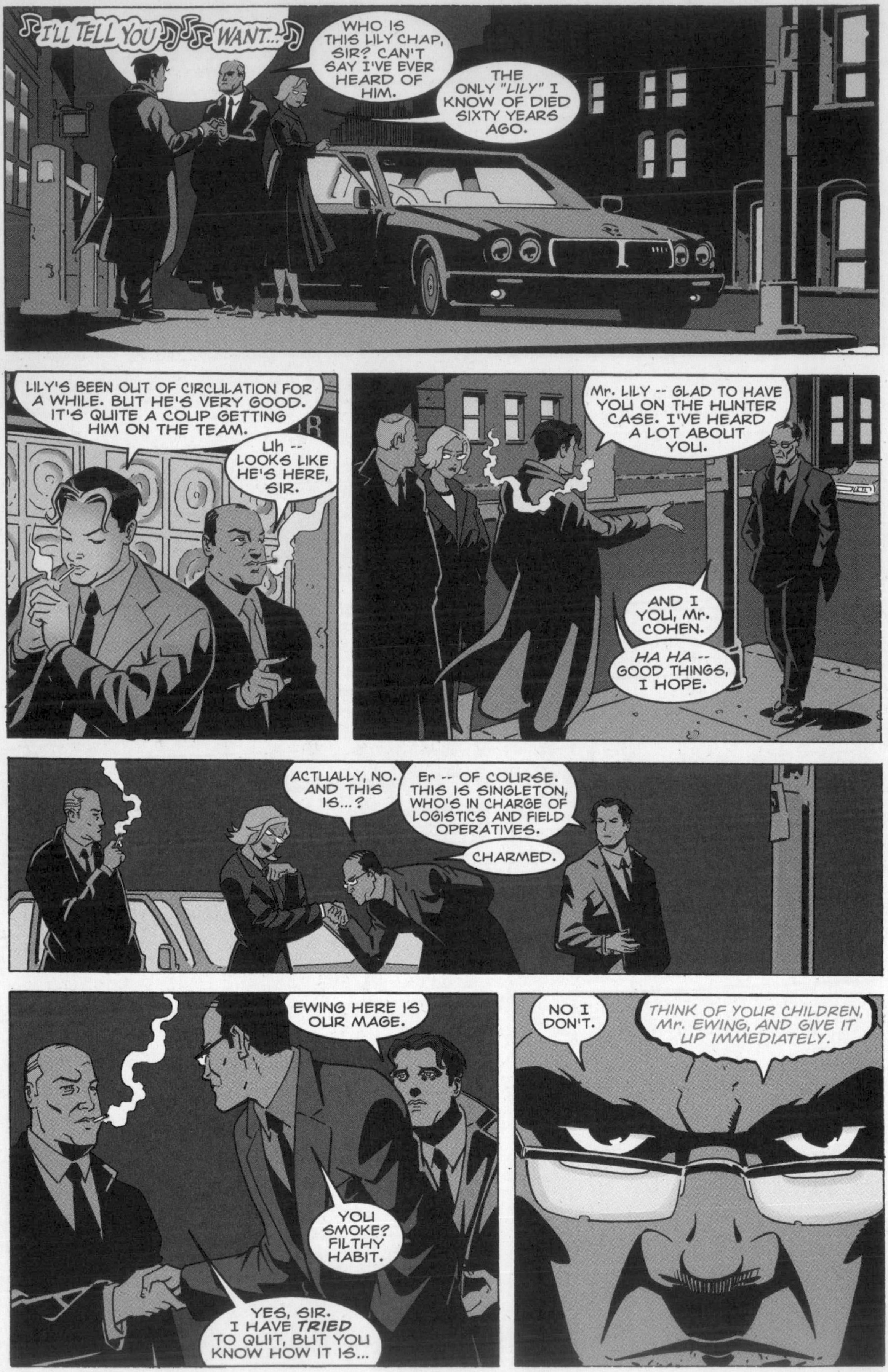
I'LL TELL YOU WANT...
WHO IS THIS LILY CHAP, SIR? CAN'T SAY I'VE EVER HEARD OF HIM.
THE ONLY "LILY" I KNOW OF DIED SIXTY YEARS AGO.
LILY'S BEEN OUT OF CIRCULATION FOR A WHILE. BUT HE'S VERY GOOD. IT'S QUITE A COUP GETTING HIM ON THE TEAM.
Uh -- LOOKS LIKE HE'S HERE, SIR.
Mr. LILY -- GLAD TO HAVE YOU ON THE HUNTER CASE. I'VE HEARD A LOT ABOUT YOU.
AND I YOU, Mr. COHEN.
HA HA -- GOOD THINGS, I HOPE.
ACTUALLY, NO. AND THIS IS...?
Er -- OF COURSE. THIS IS SINGLETON, WHO'S IN CHARGE OF LOGISTICS AND FIELD OPERATIVES.
CHARMED.
EWING HERE IS OUR MAGE.
YOU SMOKE? FILTHY HABIT.
YES, SIR. I HAVE TRIED TO QUIT, BUT YOU KNOW HOW IT IS...
NO I DON'T.
THINK OF YOUR CHILDREN, Mr. EWING, AND GIVE IT UP IMMEDIATELY.

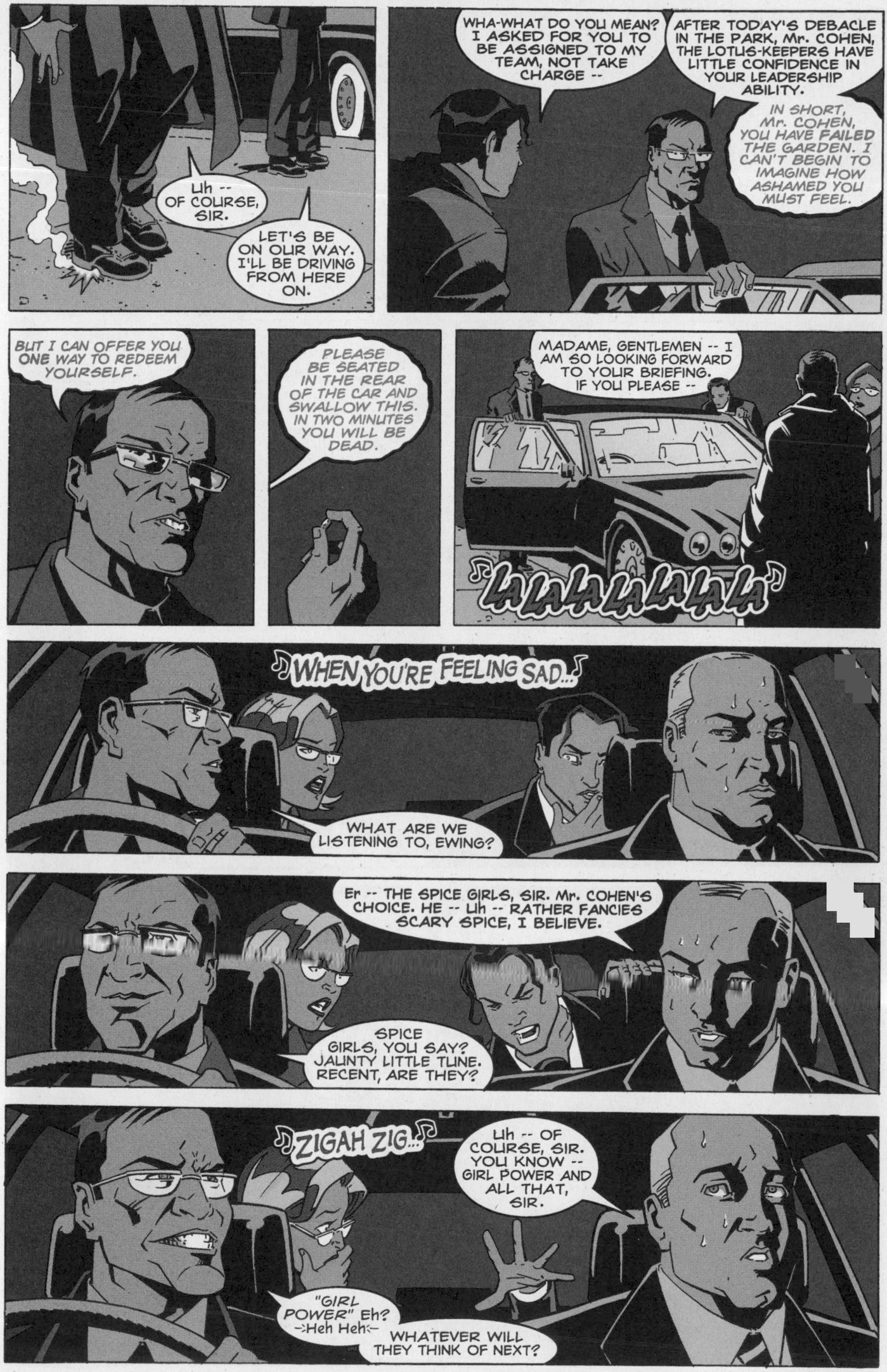
Uh -- OF COURSE, SIR.
LET'S BE ON OUR WAY. I'LL BE DRIVING FROM HERE ON.
WHA-WHAT DO YOU MEAN? I ASKED FOR YOU TO BE ASSIGNED TO MY TEAM, NOT TAKE CHARGE --
AFTER TODAY'S DEBACLE IN THE PARK, Mr. COHEN, THE LOTUS-KEEPERS HAVE LITTLE CONFIDENCE IN YOUR LEADERSHIP ABILITY.
IN SHORT, Mr. COHEN, YOU HAVE FAILED THE GARDEN. I CAN'T BEGIN TO IMAGINE HOW ASHAMED YOU MUST FEEL.
BUT I CAN OFFER YOU ONE WAY TO REDEEM YOURSELF.
PLEASE BE SEATED IN THE REAR OF THE CAR AND SWALLOW THIS. IN TWO MINUTES YOU WILL BE DEAD.
MADAME, GENTLEMEN -- I AM SO LOOKING FORWARD TO YOUR BRIEFING. IF YOU PLEASE --
LA LA LA LA LA LA LA LA
WHEN YOU'RE FEELING SAD...
WHAT ARE WE LISTENING TO, EWING?
Er -- THE SPICE GIRLS, SIR. Mr. COHEN'S CHOICE. HE -- Uh -- RATHER FANCIES SCARY SPICE, I BELIEVE.
SPICE GIRLS, YOU SAY? JAUNTY LITTLE TUNE. RECENT, ARE THEY?
ZIGAH ZIG...
Uh -- OF COURSE, SIR. YOU KNOW -- GIRL POWER AND ALL THAT, SIR.
"GIRL POWER" Eh? -Heh Heh-
WHATEVER WILL THEY THINK OF NEXT?

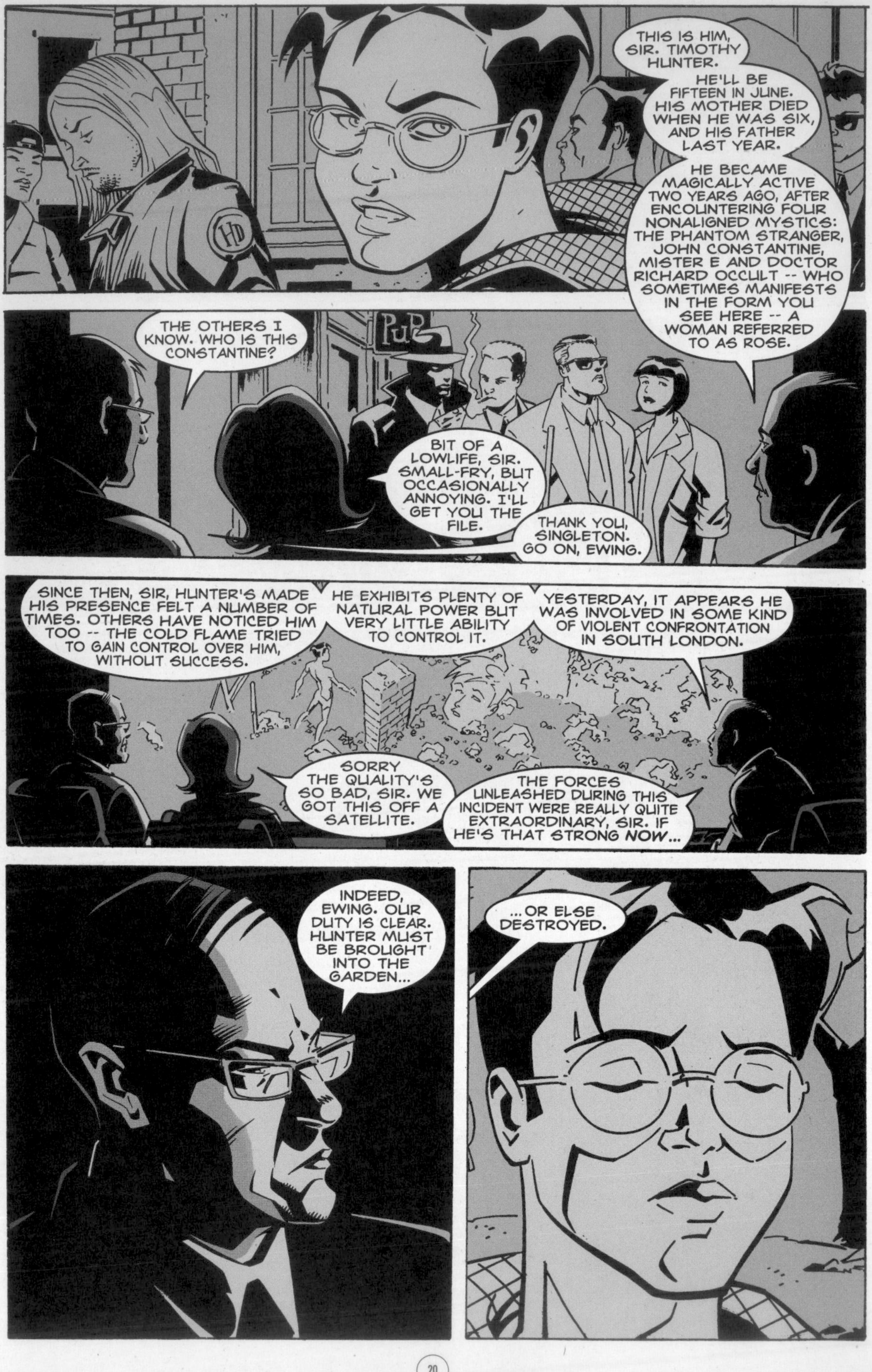

THIS IS HIM, SIR. TIMOTHY HUNTER.
HE'LL BE FIFTEEN IN JUNE. HIS MOTHER DIED WHEN HE WAS SIX, AND HIS FATHER LAST YEAR.
HE BECAME MAGICALLY ACTIVE TWO YEARS AGO, AFTER ENCOUNTERING FOUR NONALIGNED MYSTICS: THE PHANTOM STRANGER, JOHN CONSTANTINE, MISTER E AND DOCTOR RICHARD OCCULT -- WHO SOMETIMES MANIFESTS IN THE FORM YOU SEE HERE -- A WOMAN REFERRED TO AS ROSE.
THE OTHERS I KNOW. WHO IS THIS CONSTANTINE?
PUB
BIT OF A LOWLIFE, SIR. SMALL-FRY, BUT OCCASIONALLY ANNOYING. I'LL GET YOU THE FILE.
THANK YOU, SINGLETON. GO ON, EWING.
SINCE THEN, SIR, HUNTER'S MADE HIS PRESENCE FELT A NUMBER OF TIMES. OTHERS HAVE NOTICED HIM TOO -- THE COLD FLAME TRIED TO GAIN CONTROL OVER HIM, WITHOUT SUCCESS.
HE EXHIBITS PLENTY OF NATURAL POWER BUT VERY LITTLE ABILITY TO CONTROL IT.
YESTERDAY, IT APPEARS HE WAS INVOLVED IN SOME KIND OF VIOLENT CONFRONTATION IN SOUTH LONDON.
SORRY THE QUALITY'S SO BAD, SIR. WE GOT THIS OFF A SATELLITE.
THE FORCES UNLEASHED DURING THIS INCIDENT WERE REALLY QUITE EXTRAORDINARY, SIR. IF HE'S THAT STRONG *NOW*...
INDEED, EWING. OUR DUTY IS CLEAR. HUNTER MUST BE BROUGHT INTO THE GARDEN...
...OR ELSE DESTROYED.

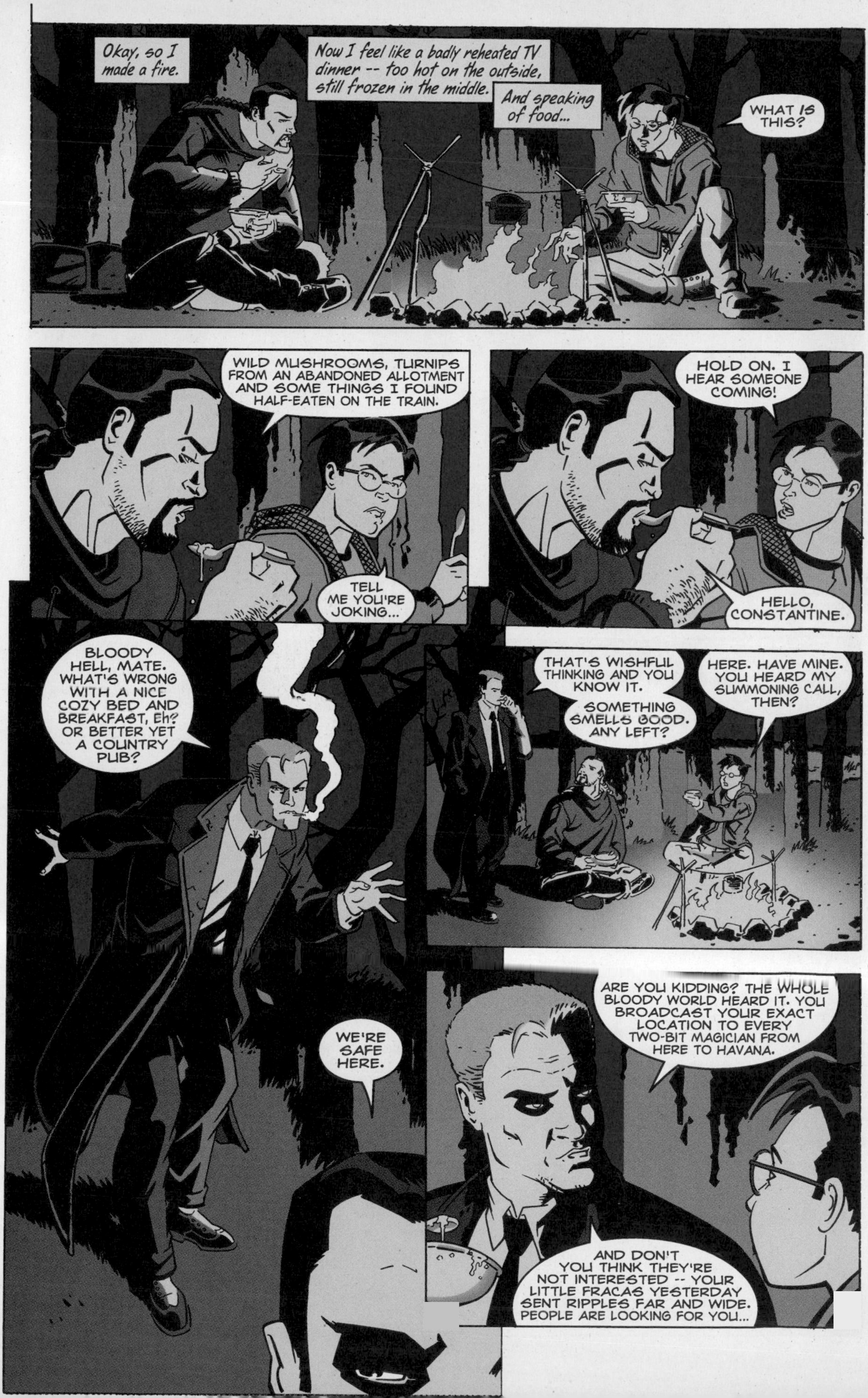
Okay, so I made a fire.
Now I feel like a badly reheated TV dinner -- too hot on the outside, still frozen in the middle.
And speaking of food...
WHAT IS THIS?
WILD MUSHROOMS, TURNIPS FROM AN ABANDONED ALLOTMENT AND SOME THINGS I FOUND HALF-EATEN ON THE TRAIN.
TELL ME YOU'RE JOKING...
HOLD ON. I HEAR SOMEONE COMING!
HELLO, CONSTANTINE.
BLOODY HELL, MATE. WHAT'S WRONG WITH A NICE COZY BED AND BREAKFAST, Eh? OR BETTER YET A COUNTRY PUB?
THAT'S WISHFUL THINKING AND YOU KNOW IT.
SOMETHING SMELLS GOOD. ANY LEFT?
HERE. HAVE MINE. YOU HEARD MY SUMMONING CALL, THEN?
WE'RE SAFE HERE.
ARE YOU KIDDING? THE WHOLE BLOODY WORLD HEARD IT. YOU BROADCAST YOUR EXACT LOCATION TO EVERY TWO-BIT MAGICIAN FROM HERE TO HAVANA.
AND DON'T YOU THINK THEY'RE NOT INTERESTED -- YOUR LITTLE FRACAS YESTERDAY SENT RIPPLES FAR AND WIDE. PEOPLE ARE LOOKING FOR YOU...

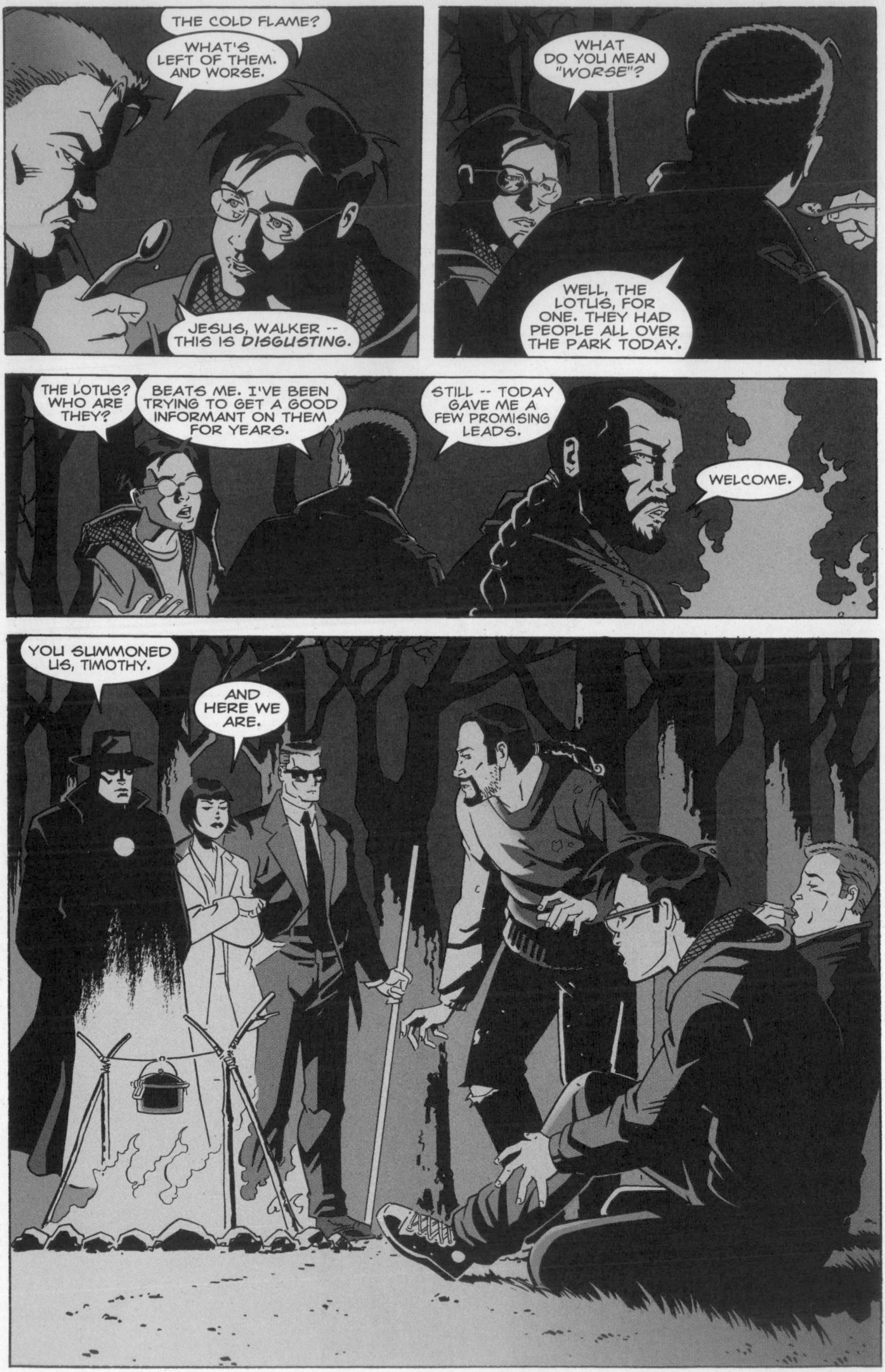
THE COLD FLAME?
WHAT'S LEFT OF THEM. AND WORSE.
JESUS, WALKER -- THIS IS DISGUSTING.
WHAT DO YOU MEAN "WORSE"?
WELL, THE LOTUS, FOR ONE. THEY HAD PEOPLE ALL OVER THE PARK TODAY.
THE LOTUS? WHO ARE THEY?
BEATS ME. I'VE BEEN TRYING TO GET A GOOD INFORMANT ON THEM FOR YEARS.
STILL -- TODAY GAVE ME A FEW PROMISING LEADS.
WELCOME.
YOU SUMMONED US, TIMOTHY.
AND HERE WE ARE.

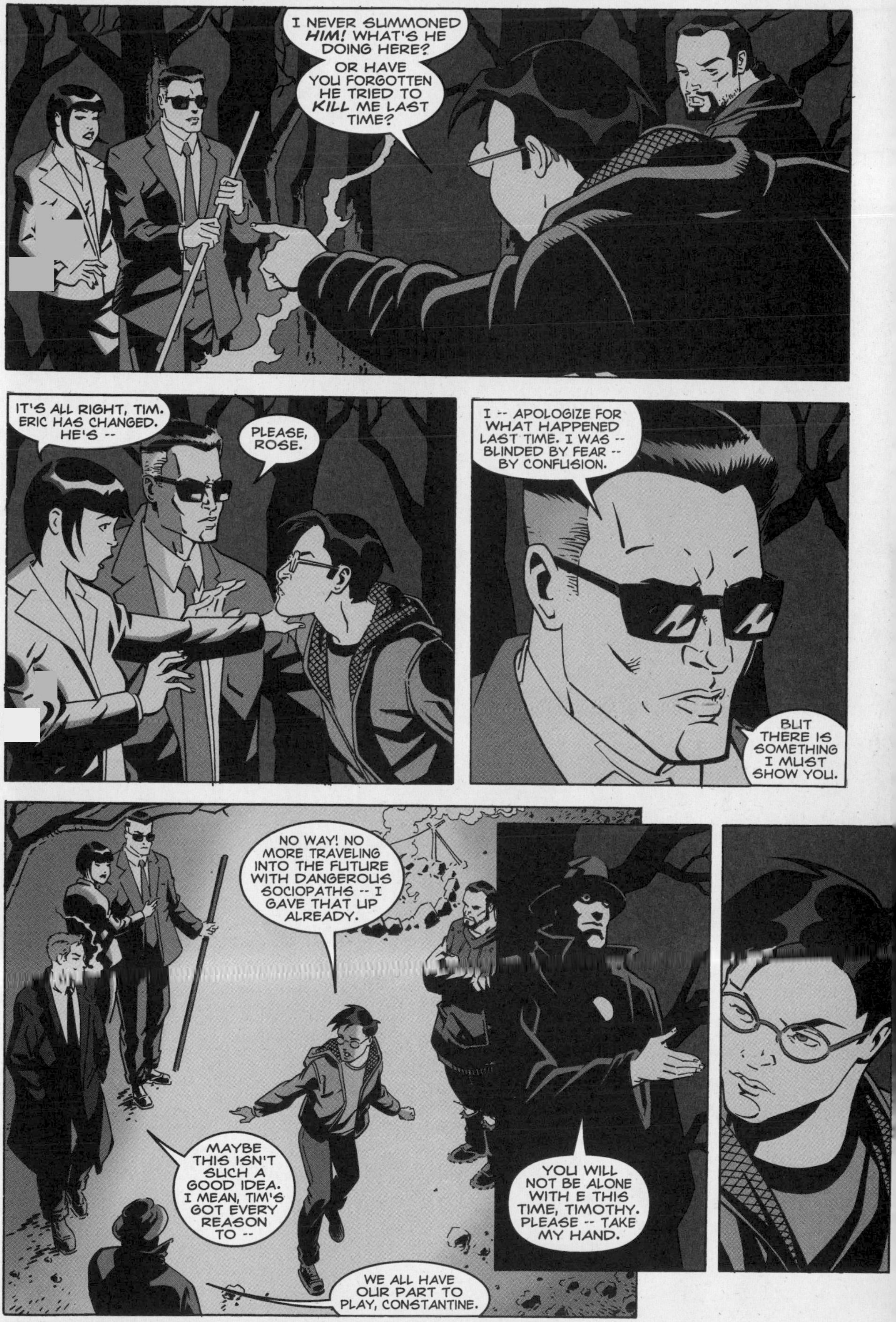
I NEVER SUMMONED *HIM!* WHAT'S HE DOING HERE?
OR HAVE YOU FORGOTTEN HE TRIED TO *KILL* ME LAST TIME?
IT'S ALL RIGHT, TIM. ERIC HAS CHANGED. HE'S --
PLEASE, ROSE.
I -- APOLOGIZE FOR WHAT HAPPENED LAST TIME. I WAS -- BLINDED BY FEAR -- BY CONFUSION.
BUT THERE IS SOMETHING I MUST SHOW YOU.
NO WAY! NO MORE TRAVELING INTO THE FUTURE WITH DANGEROUS SOCIOPATHS -- I GAVE THAT UP ALREADY.
MAYBE THIS ISN'T SUCH A GOOD IDEA. I MEAN, TIM'S GOT EVERY REASON TO --
WE ALL HAVE OUR PART TO PLAY, CONSTANTINE.
YOU WILL NOT BE ALONE WITH E THIS TIME, TIMOTHY. PLEASE -- TAKE MY HAND.

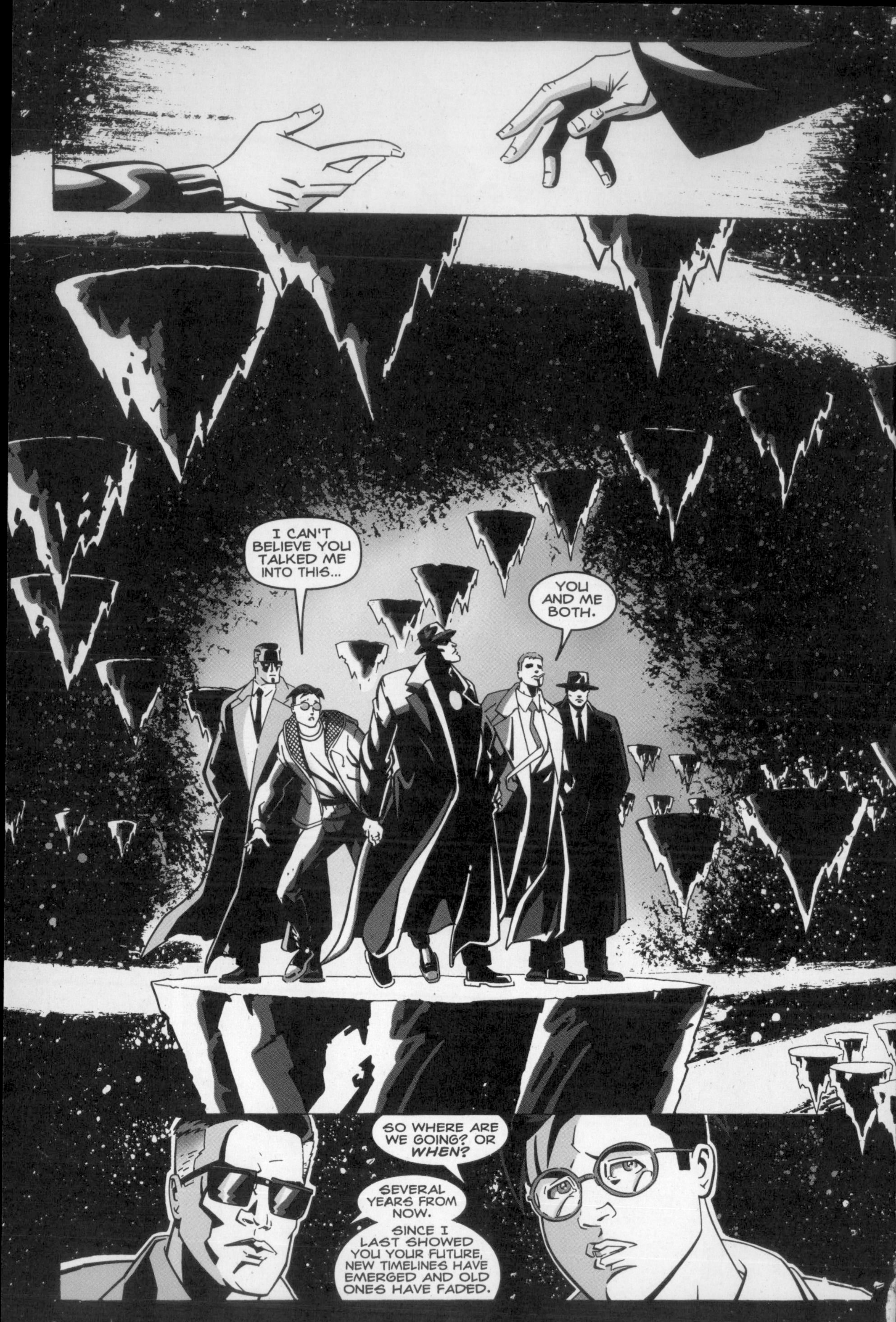
I CAN'T BELIEVE YOU TALKED ME INTO THIS...
YOU AND ME BOTH.
SO WHERE ARE WE GOING? OR *WHEN?*
SEVERAL YEARS FROM NOW.
SINCE I LAST SHOWED YOU YOUR FUTURE, NEW TIMELINES HAVE EMERGED AND OLD ONES HAVE FADED.

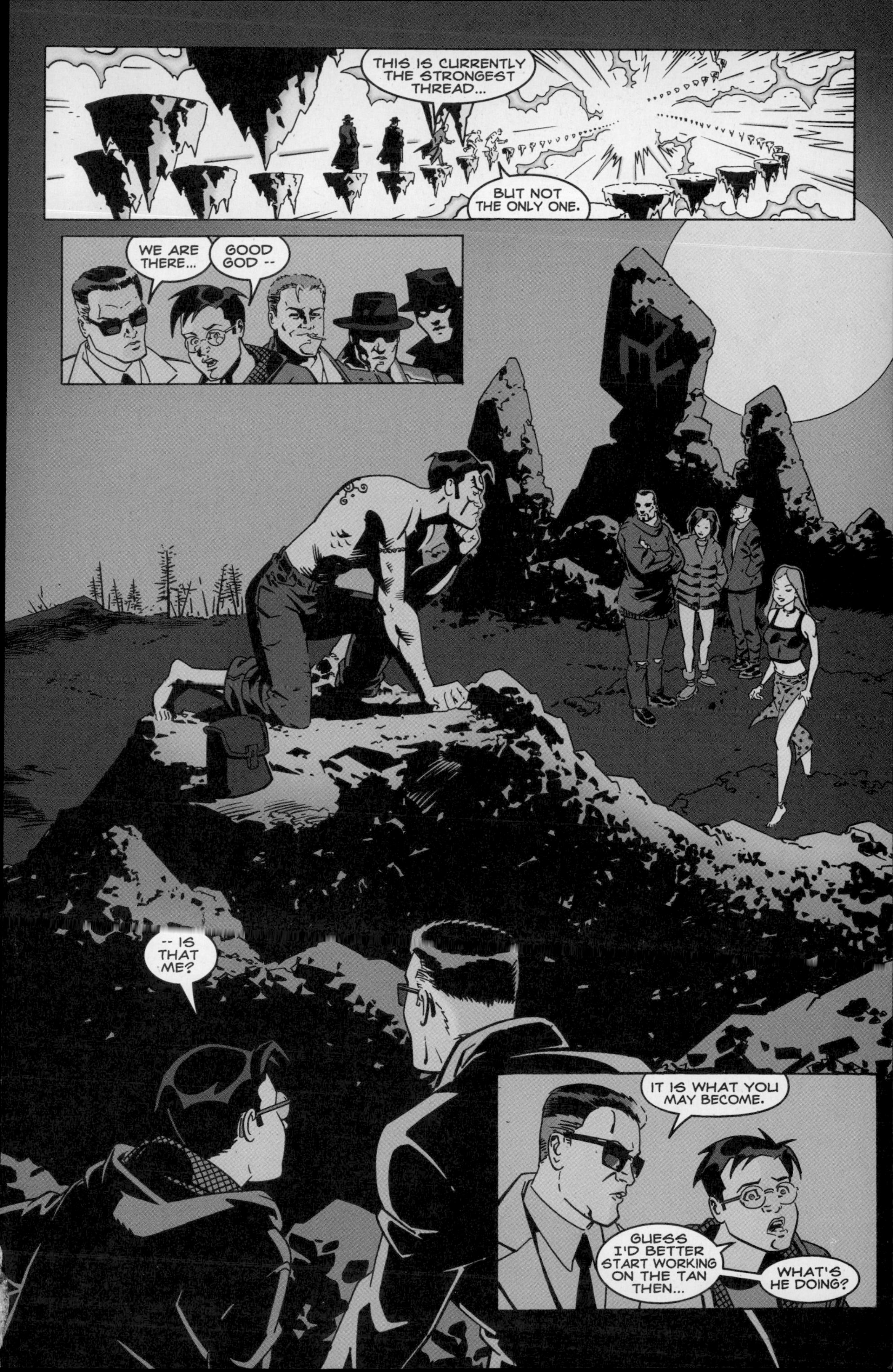
THIS IS CURRENTLY THE STRONGEST THREAD...
BUT NOT THE ONLY ONE.
WE ARE THERE...
GOOD GOD --
-- IS THAT ME?
IT IS WHAT YOU MAY BECOME.
WHAT'S HE DOING?
GUESS I'D BETTER START WORKING ON THE TAN THEN...

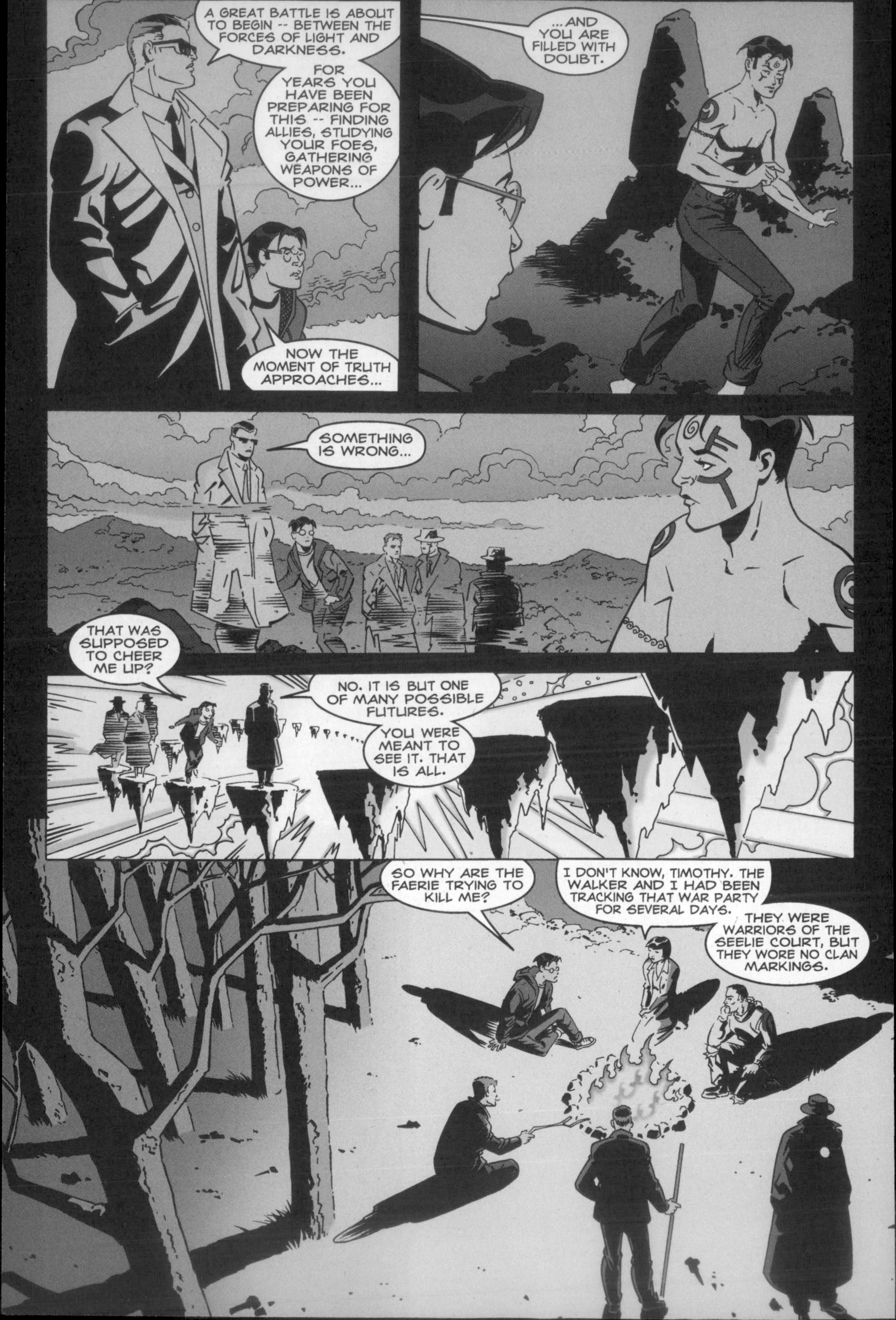
A GREAT BATTLE IS ABOUT TO BEGIN -- BETWEEN THE FORCES OF LIGHT AND DARKNESS.
FOR YEARS YOU HAVE BEEN PREPARING FOR THIS -- FINDING ALLIES, STUDYING YOUR FOES, GATHERING WEAPONS OF POWER...
NOW THE MOMENT OF TRUTH APPROACHES...
...AND YOU ARE FILLED WITH DOUBT.
SOMETHING IS WRONG...
THAT WAS SUPPOSED TO CHEER ME UP?
NO. IT IS BUT ONE OF MANY POSSIBLE FUTURES.
YOU WERE MEANT TO SEE IT. THAT IS ALL.
SO WHY ARE THE FAERIE TRYING TO KILL ME?
I DON'T KNOW, TIMOTHY. THE WALKER AND I HAD BEEN TRACKING THAT WAR PARTY FOR SEVERAL DAYS.
THEY WERE WARRIORS OF THE SEELIE COURT, BUT THEY WORE NO CLAN MARKINGS.

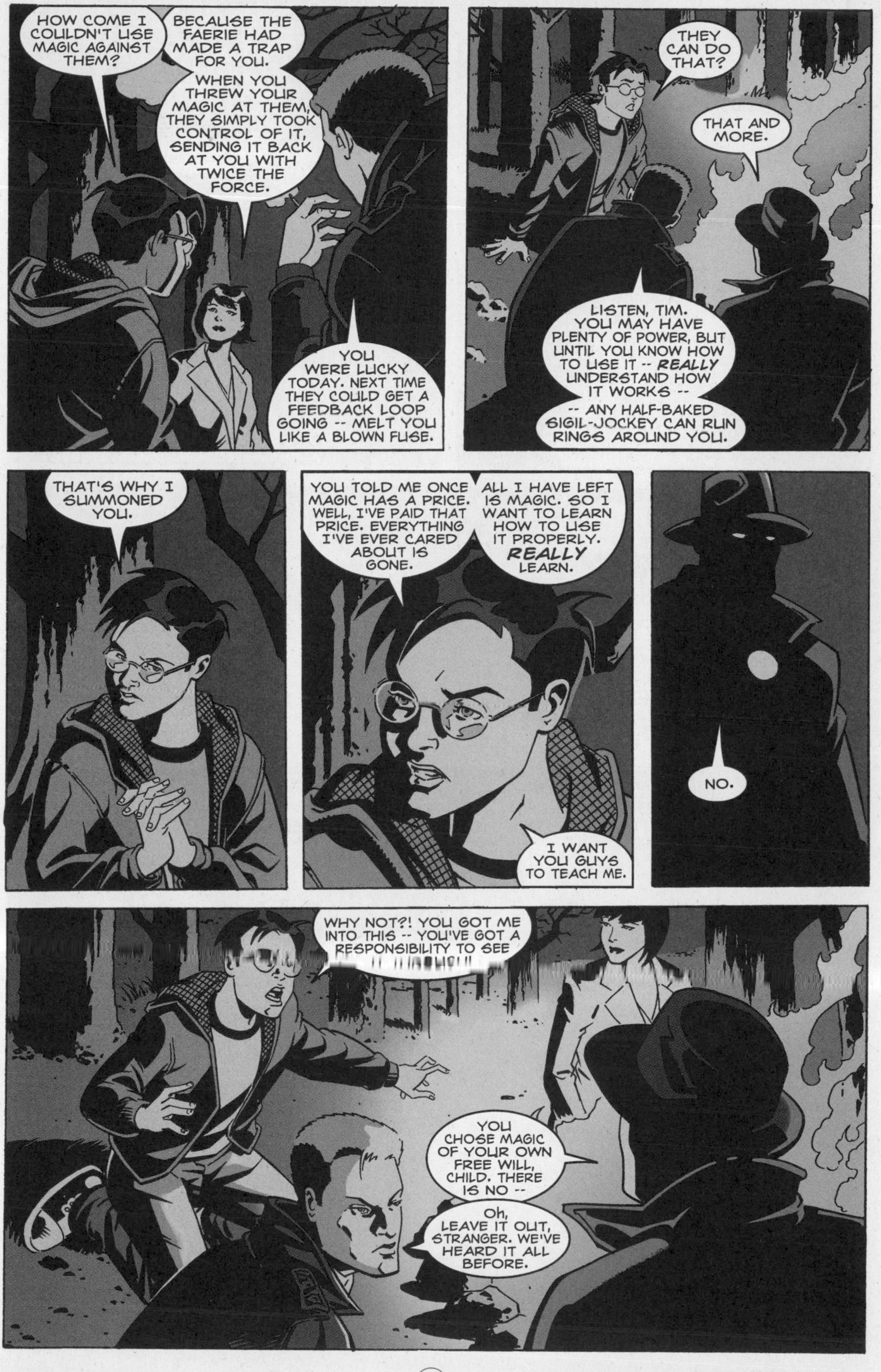
HOW COME I COULDN'T USE MAGIC AGAINST THEM?
BECAUSE THE FAERIE HAD MADE A TRAP FOR YOU.
WHEN YOU THREW YOUR MAGIC AT THEM, THEY SIMPLY TOOK CONTROL OF IT, SENDING IT BACK AT YOU WITH TWICE THE FORCE.
YOU WERE LUCKY TODAY. NEXT TIME THEY COULD GET A FEEDBACK LOOP GOING -- MELT YOU LIKE A BLOWN FUSE.
THEY CAN DO THAT?
THAT AND MORE.
LISTEN, TIM. YOU MAY HAVE PLENTY OF POWER, BUT UNTIL YOU KNOW HOW TO USE IT -- REALLY UNDERSTAND HOW IT WORKS --
-- ANY HALF-BAKED SIGIL-JOCKEY CAN RUN RINGS AROUND YOU.
THAT'S WHY I SUMMONED YOU.
YOU TOLD ME ONCE MAGIC HAS A PRICE. WELL, I'VE PAID THAT PRICE. EVERYTHING I'VE EVER CARED ABOUT IS GONE.
ALL I HAVE LEFT IS MAGIC. SO I WANT TO LEARN HOW TO USE IT PROPERLY. REALLY LEARN.
I WANT YOU GUYS TO TEACH ME.
NO.
WHY NOT?! YOU GOT ME INTO THIS -- YOU'VE GOT A RESPONSIBILITY TO SEE
YOU CHOSE MAGIC OF YOUR OWN FREE WILL, CHILD. THERE IS NO --
Oh, LEAVE IT OUT, STRANGER. WE'VE HEARD IT ALL BEFORE.

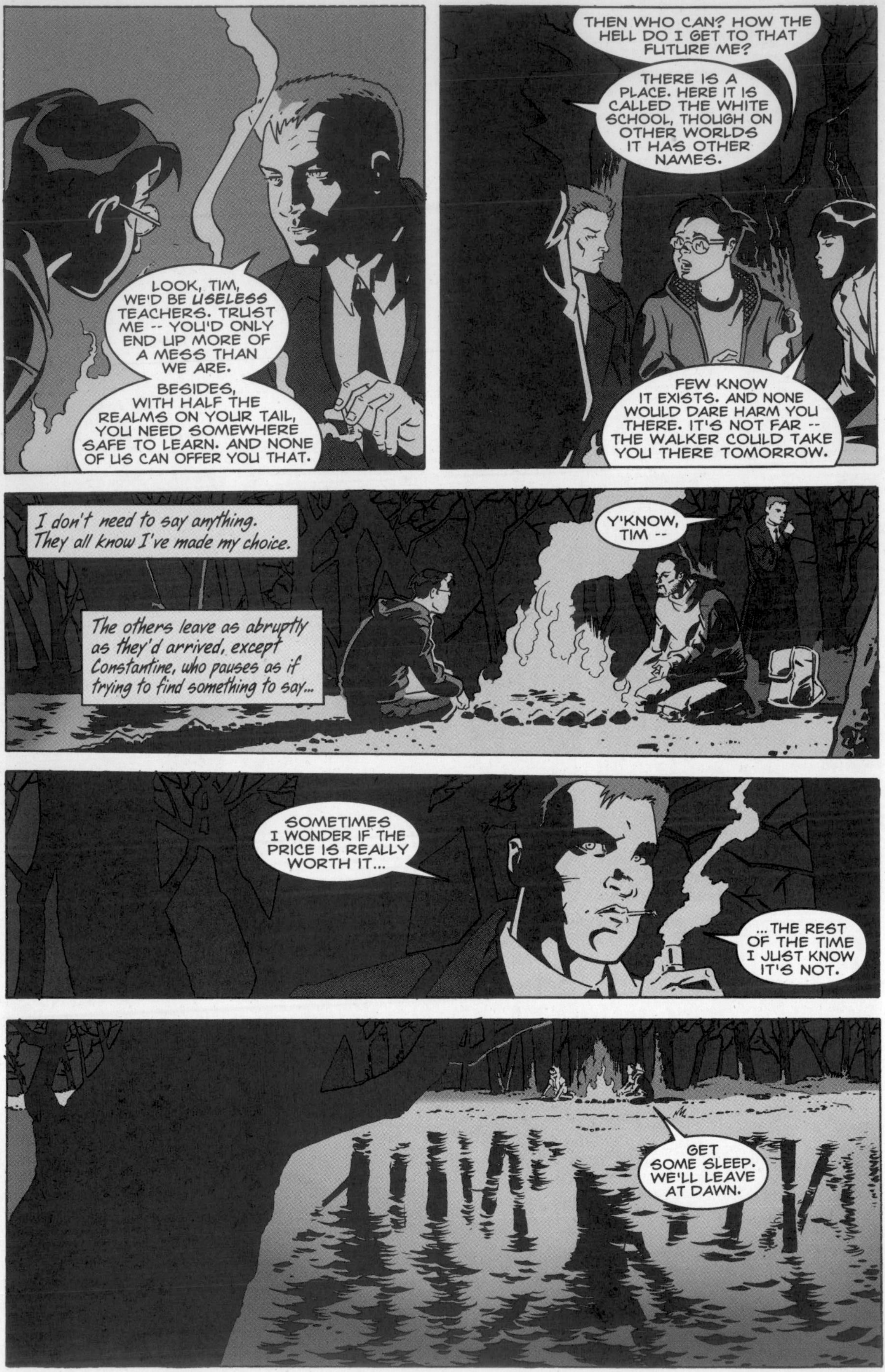
LOOK, TIM, WE'D BE USELESS TEACHERS. TRUST ME -- YOU'D ONLY END UP MORE OF A MESS THAN WE ARE.
BESIDES, WITH HALF THE REALMS ON YOUR TAIL, YOU NEED SOMEWHERE SAFE TO LEARN. AND NONE OF US CAN OFFER YOU THAT.
THEN WHO CAN? HOW THE HELL DO I GET TO THAT FUTURE ME?
THERE IS A PLACE. HERE IT IS CALLED THE WHITE SCHOOL, THOUGH ON OTHER WORLDS IT HAS OTHER NAMES.
FEW KNOW IT EXISTS. AND NONE WOULD DARE HARM YOU THERE. IT'S NOT FAR -- THE WALKER COULD TAKE YOU THERE TOMORROW.
I don't need to say anything. They all know I've made my choice.
Y'KNOW, TIM --
The others leave as abruptly as they'd arrived, except Constantine, who pauses as if trying to find something to say...
SOMETIMES I WONDER IF THE PRICE IS REALLY WORTH IT...
...THE REST OF THE TIME I JUST KNOW IT'S NOT.
GET SOME SLEEP. WE'LL LEAVE AT DAWN.

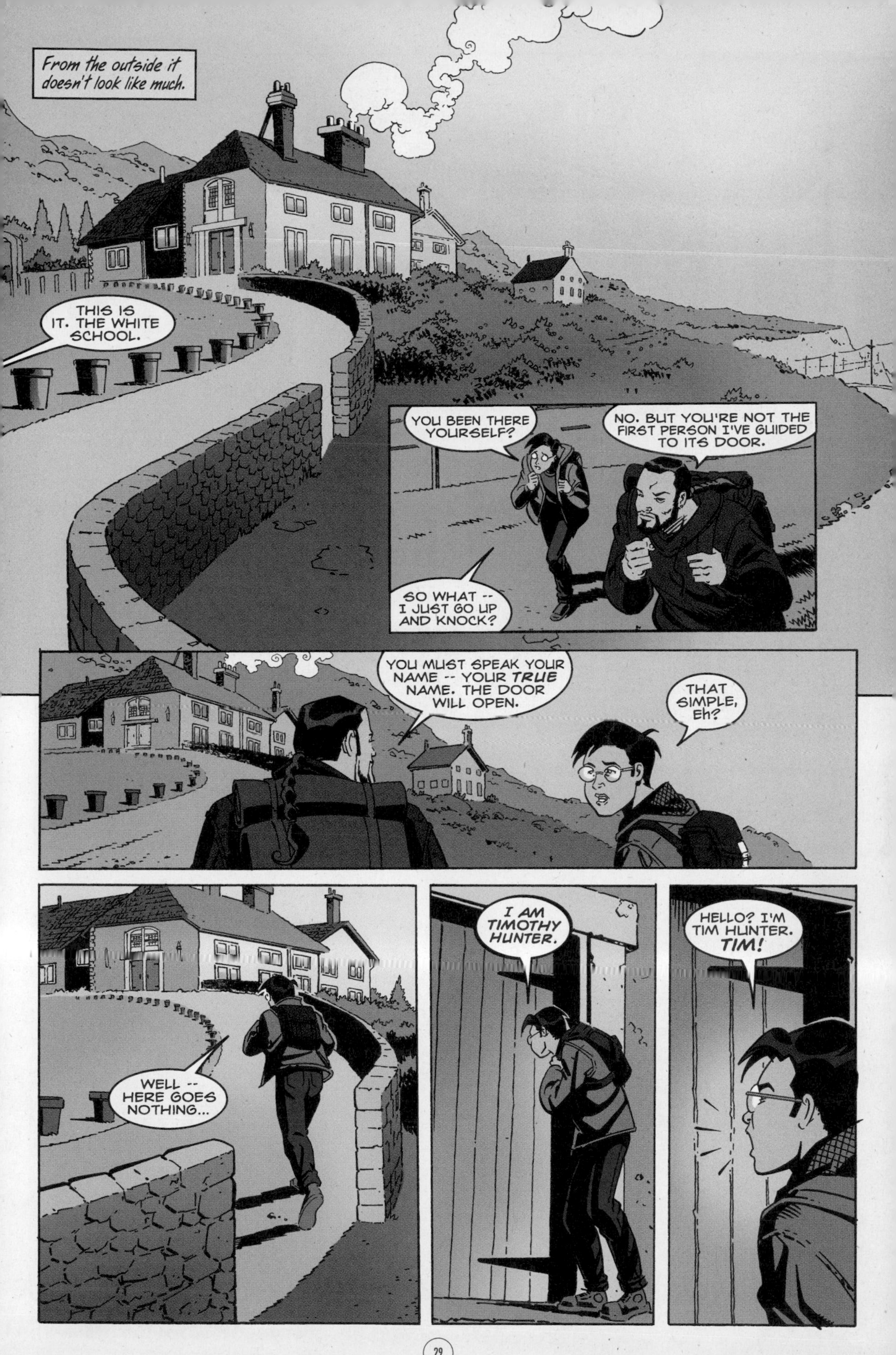
From the outside it doesn't look like much.
THIS IS IT. THE WHITE SCHOOL.
YOU BEEN THERE YOURSELF?
NO. BUT YOU'RE NOT THE FIRST PERSON I'VE GUIDED TO ITS DOOR.
SO WHAT -- I JUST GO UP AND KNOCK?
YOU MUST SPEAK YOUR NAME -- YOUR *TRUE* NAME. THE DOOR WILL OPEN.
THAT SIMPLE, Eh?
WELL -- HERE GOES NOTHING...
I AM TIMOTHY HUNTER.
HELLO? I'M TIM HUNTER. *TIM!*

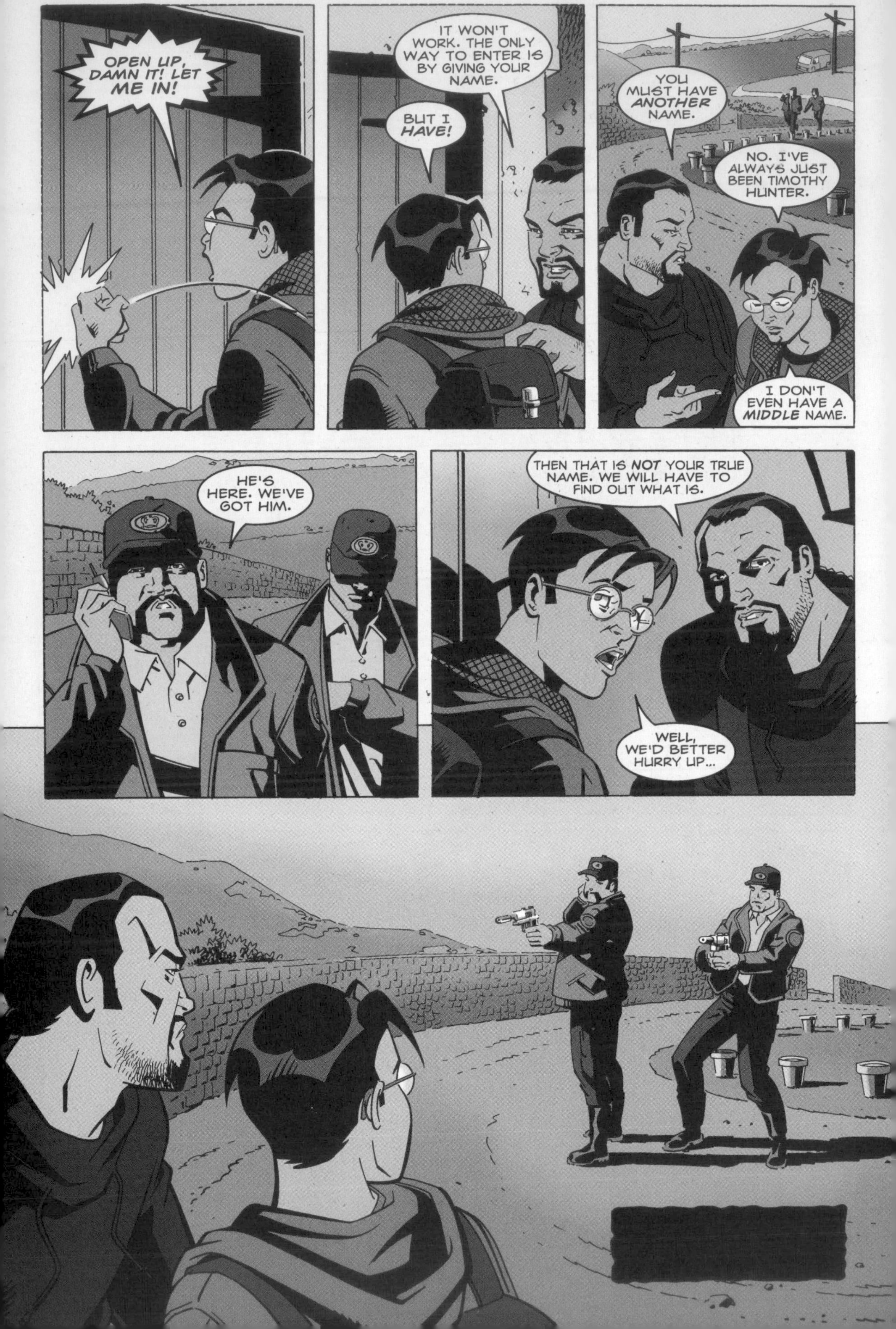
OPEN UP, DAMN IT! LET ME IN!
IT WON'T WORK. THE ONLY WAY TO ENTER IS BY GIVING YOUR NAME.
BUT I HAVE!
YOU MUST HAVE ANOTHER NAME.
NO. I'VE ALWAYS JUST BEEN TIMOTHY HUNTER.
I DON'T EVEN HAVE A MIDDLE NAME.
HE'S HERE. WE'VE GOT HIM.
THEN THAT IS NOT YOUR TRUE NAME. WE WILL HAVE TO FIND OUT WHAT IS.
WELL, WE'D BETTER HURRY UP...
[redacted]

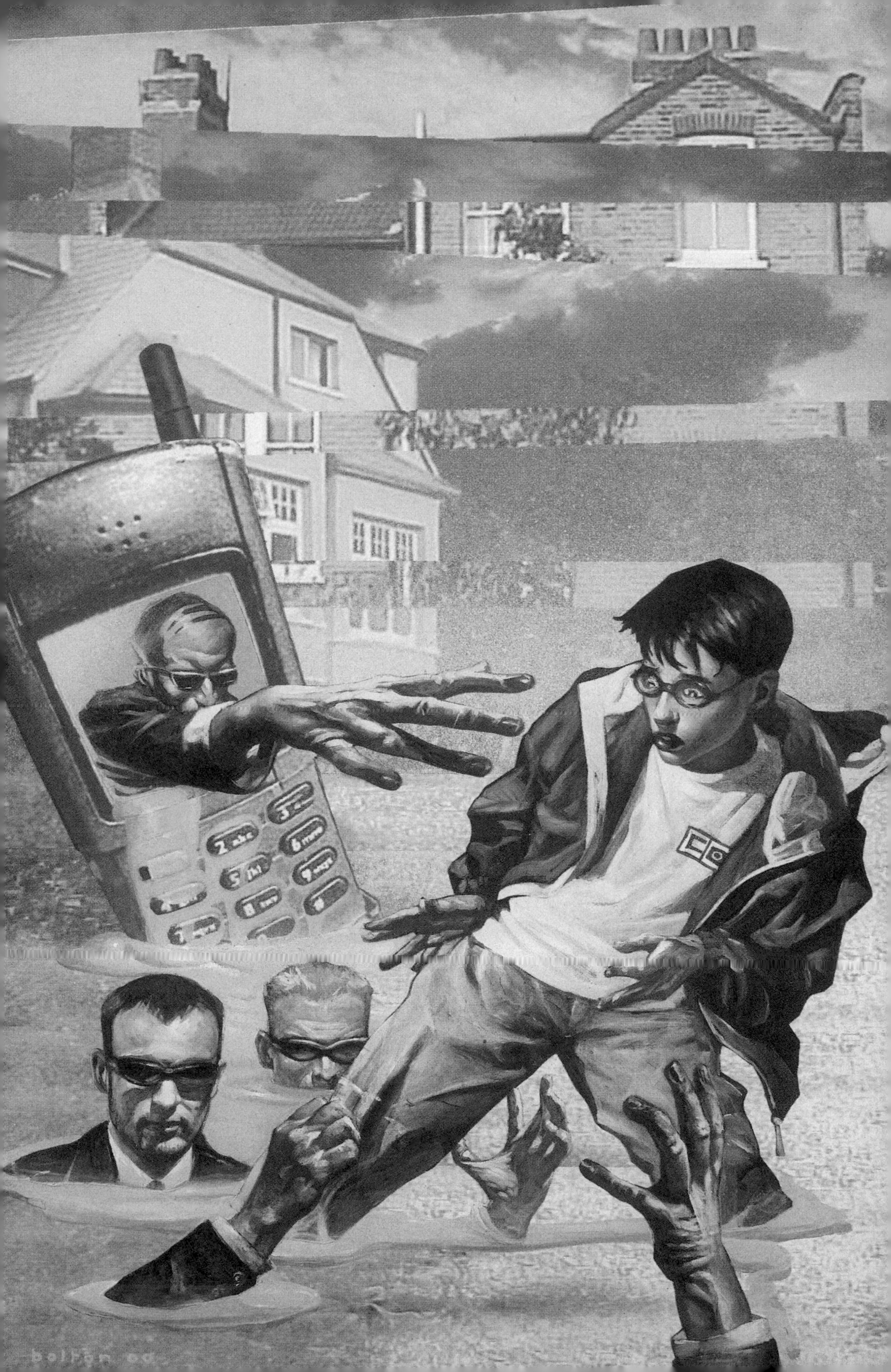

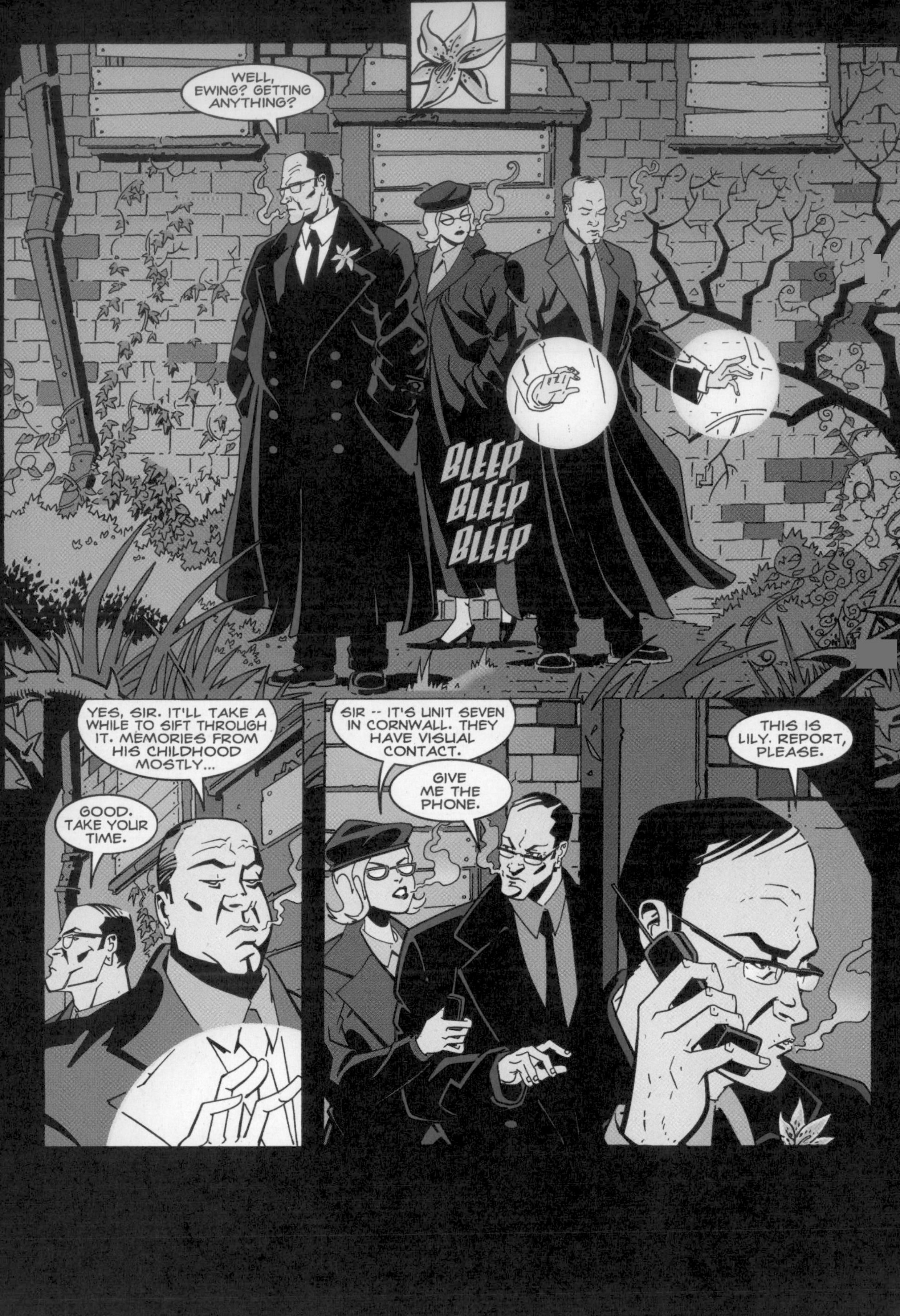
WELL, EWING? GETTING ANYTHING?
BLEEP BLEEP BLEEP
YES, SIR. IT'LL TAKE A WHILE TO SIFT THROUGH IT. MEMORIES FROM HIS CHILDHOOD MOSTLY...
GOOD. TAKE YOUR TIME.
SIR -- IT'S UNIT SEVEN IN CORNWALL. THEY HAVE VISUAL CONTACT.
GIVE ME THE PHONE.
THIS IS LILY. REPORT, PLEASE.

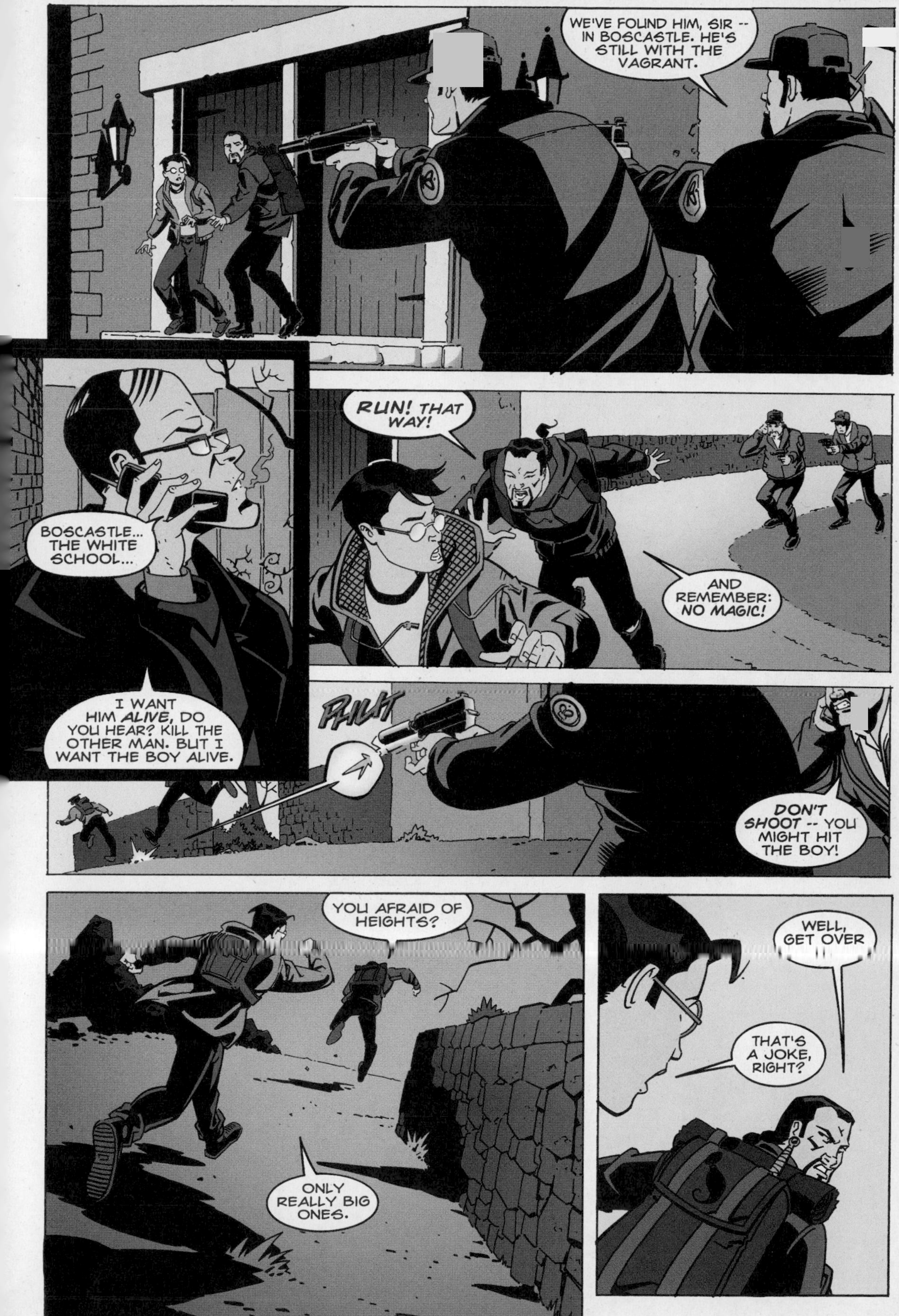
WE'VE FOUND HIM, SIR -- IN BOSCASTLE. HE'S STILL WITH THE VAGRANT.
BOSCASTLE... THE WHITE SCHOOL...
RUN! THAT WAY!
AND REMEMBER: NO MAGIC!
I WANT HIM ALIVE, DO YOU HEAR? KILL THE OTHER MAN. BUT I WANT THE BOY ALIVE.
DON'T SHOOT -- YOU MIGHT HIT THE BOY!
YOU AFRAID OF HEIGHTS?
ONLY REALLY BIG ONES.
WELL, GET OVER
THAT'S A JOKE, RIGHT?

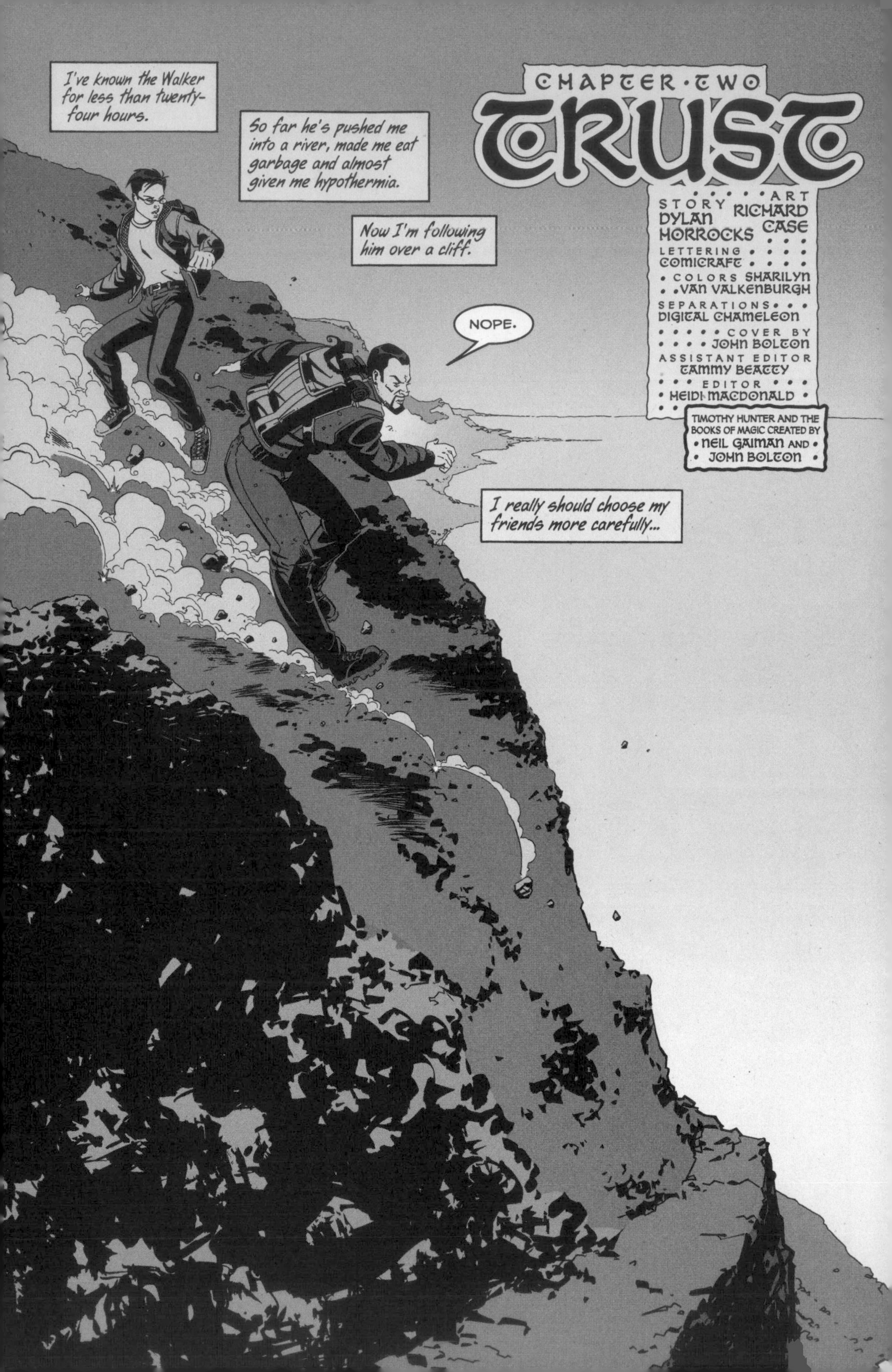

I've known the Walker for less than twenty-four hours.
So far he's pushed me into a river, made me eat garbage and almost given me hypothermia.
Now I'm following him over a cliff.
CHAPTER·TWO
TRUST
STORY DYLAN HORROCKS
ART RICHARD CASE
LETTERING COMICRAFT
COLORS SHARILYN VAN VALKENBURGH
SEPARATIONS DIGITAL CHAMELEON
COVER BY JOHN BOLTON
ASSISTANT EDITOR TAMMY BEATTY
EDITOR HEIDI MACDONALD
TIMOTHY HUNTER AND THE BOOKS OF MAGIC CREATED BY NEIL GAIMAN AND JOHN BOLTON
NOPE.
I really should choose my friends more carefully...

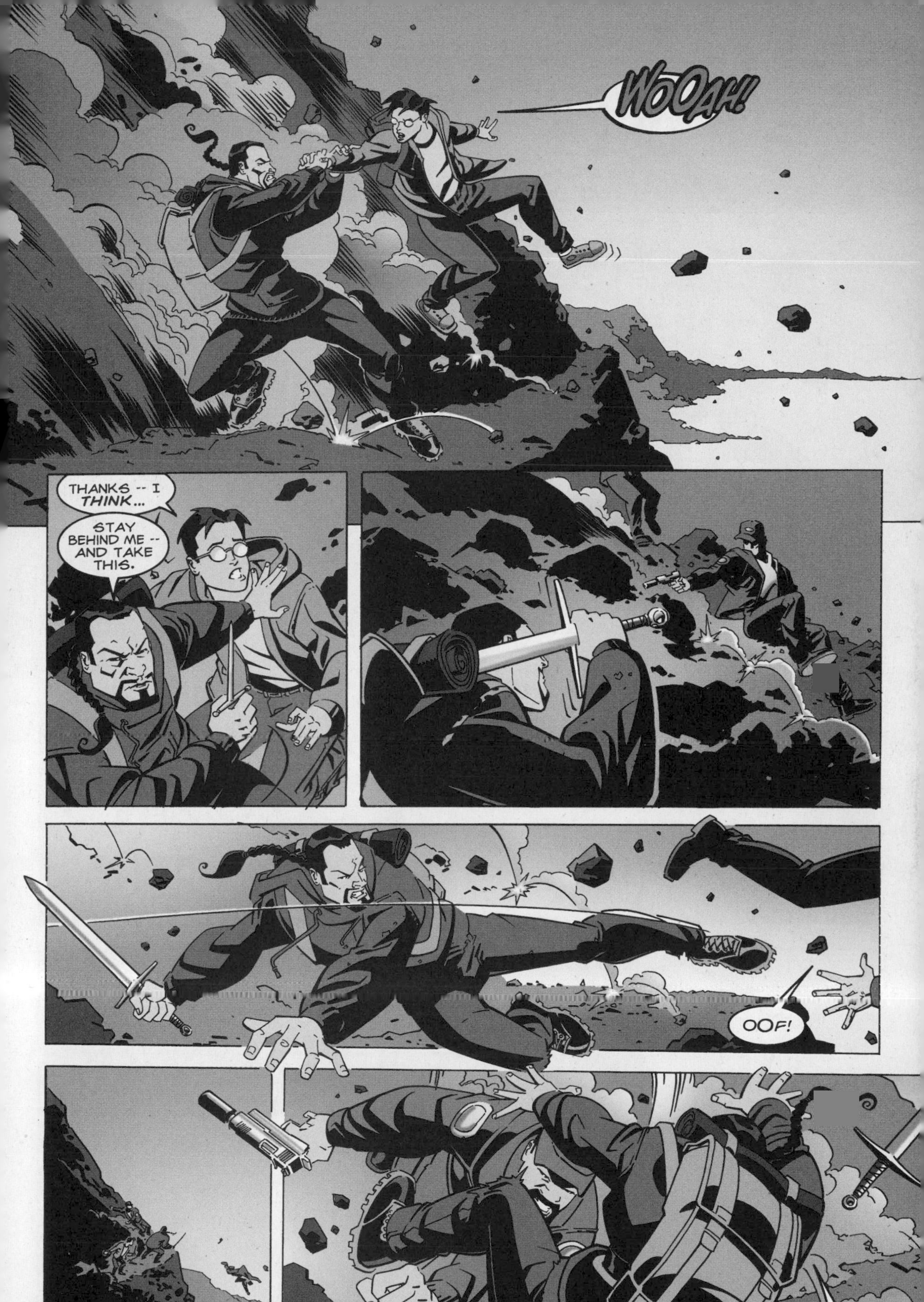
WOOAH!
THANKS -- I THINK...
STAY BEHIND ME -- AND TAKE THIS.
OOF!
UHF!

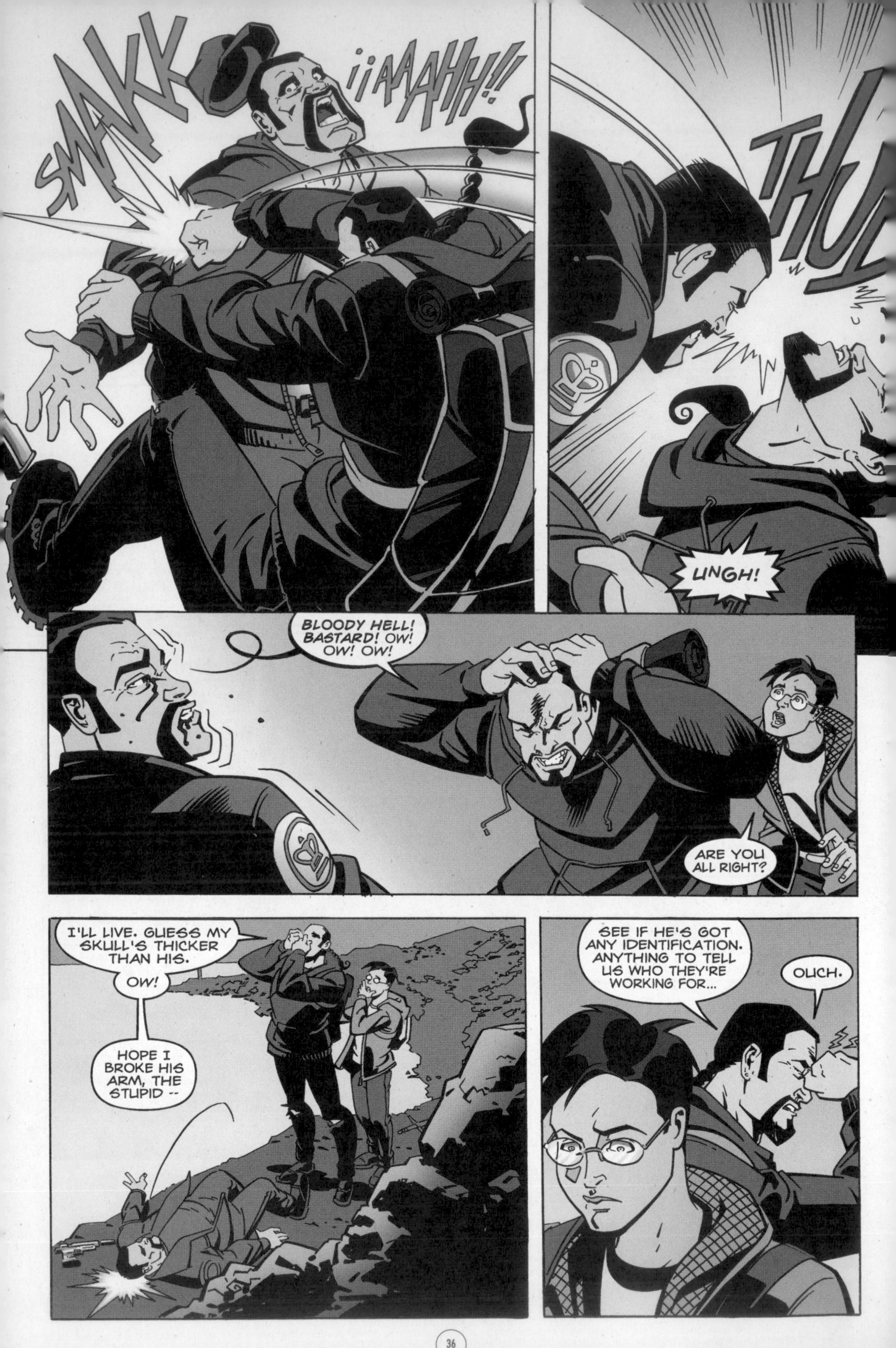
SMAKK
¡¡AAAAHH!!
THU
UNGH!
BLOODY HELL! BASTARD! OW! OW! OW!
ARE YOU ALL RIGHT?
I'LL LIVE. GUESS MY SKULL'S THICKER THAN HIS.
OW!
HOPE I BROKE HIS ARM, THE STUPID --
SEE IF HE'S GOT ANY IDENTIFICATION. ANYTHING TO TELL US WHO THEY'RE WORKING FOR...
OUCH.

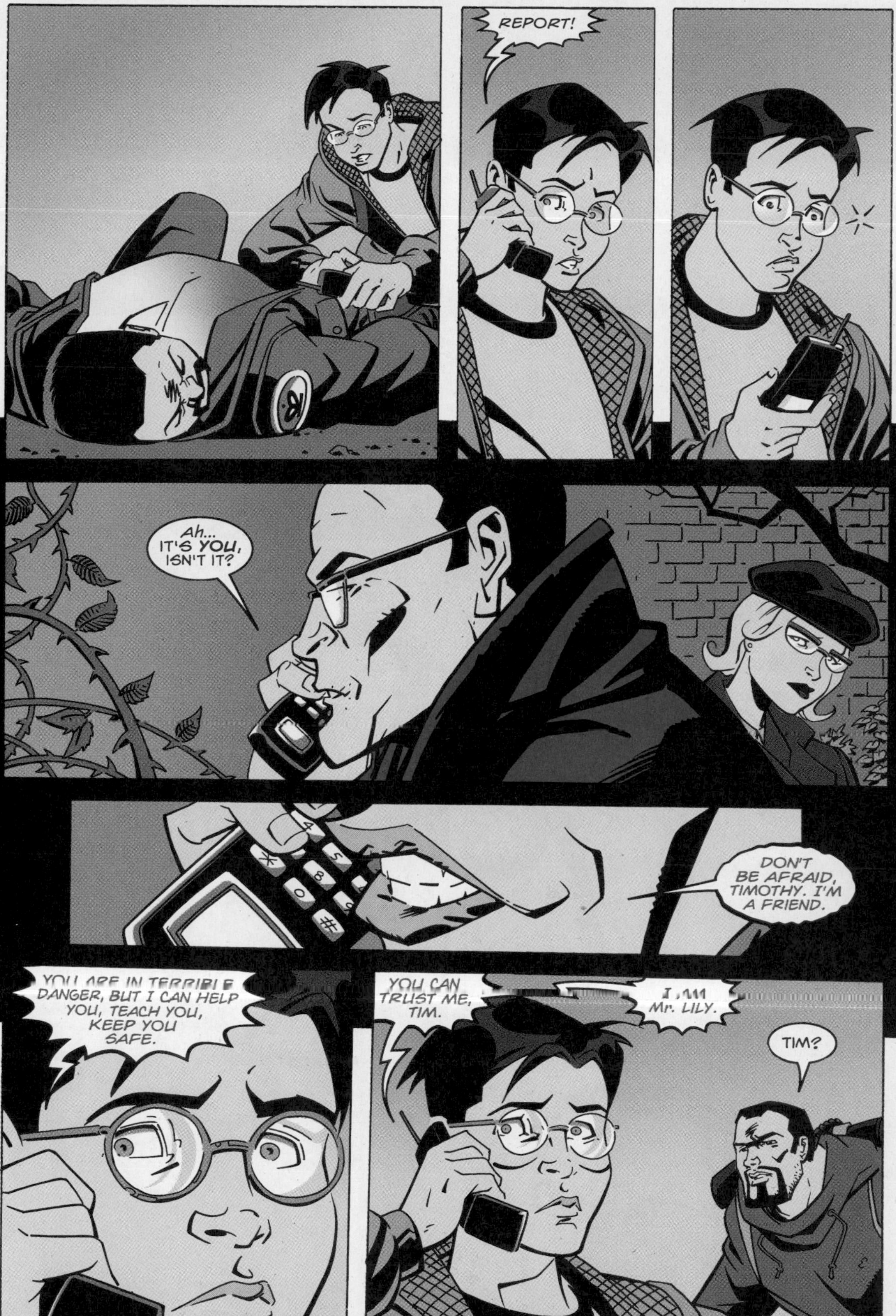
REPORT!
Ah... IT'S YOU, ISN'T IT?
DON'T BE AFRAID, TIMOTHY. I'M A FRIEND.
YOU ARE IN TERRIBLE DANGER, BUT I CAN HELP YOU, TEACH YOU, KEEP YOU SAFE.
YOU CAN TRUST ME, TIM.
Mr. LILY.
TIM?

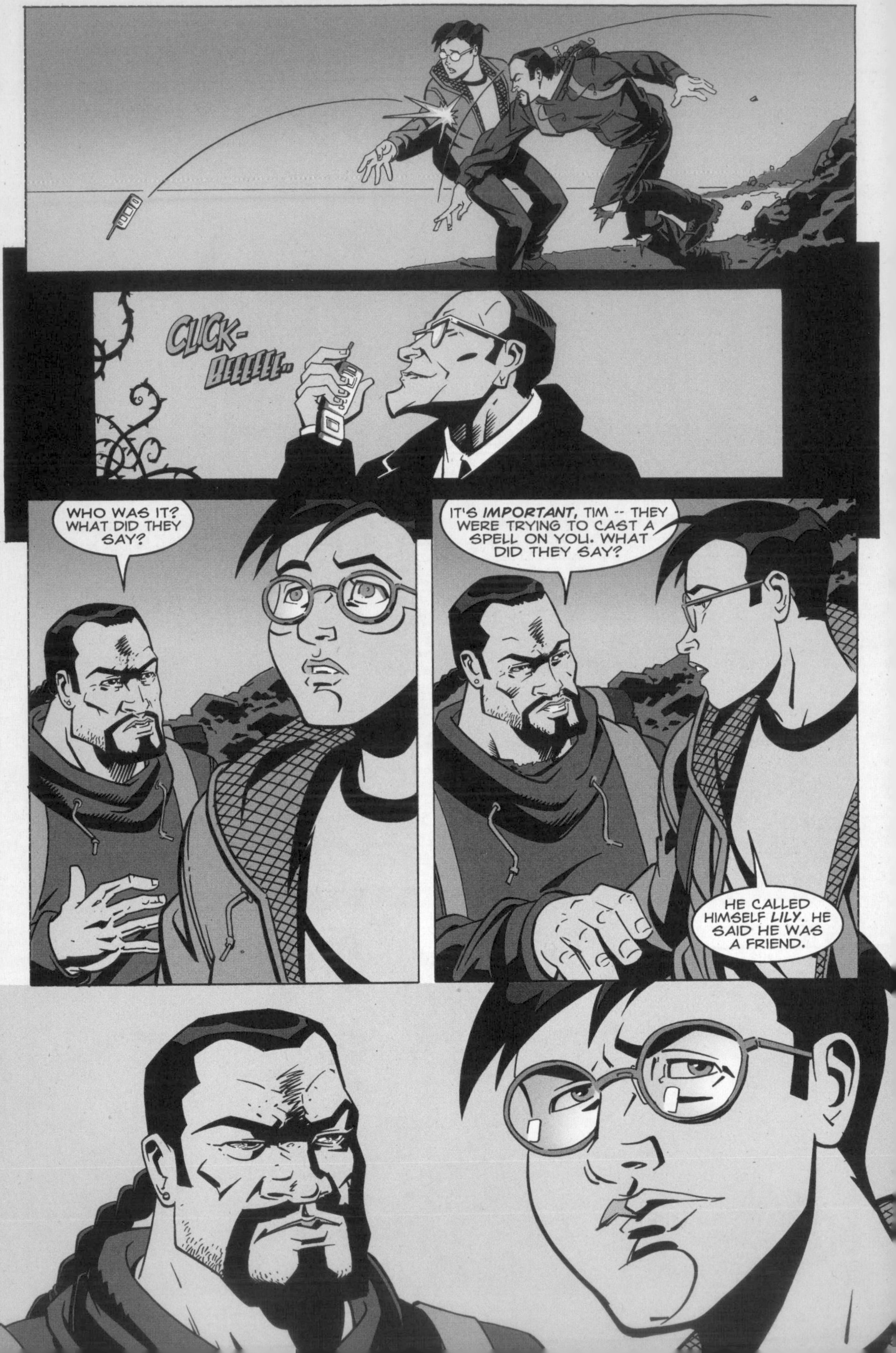
CLICK-
BEEEEEE..
WHO WAS IT? WHAT DID THEY SAY?
IT'S IMPORTANT, TIM -- THEY WERE TRYING TO CAST A SPELL ON YOU. WHAT DID THEY SAY?
HE CALLED HIMSELF LILY. HE SAID HE WAS A FRIEND.

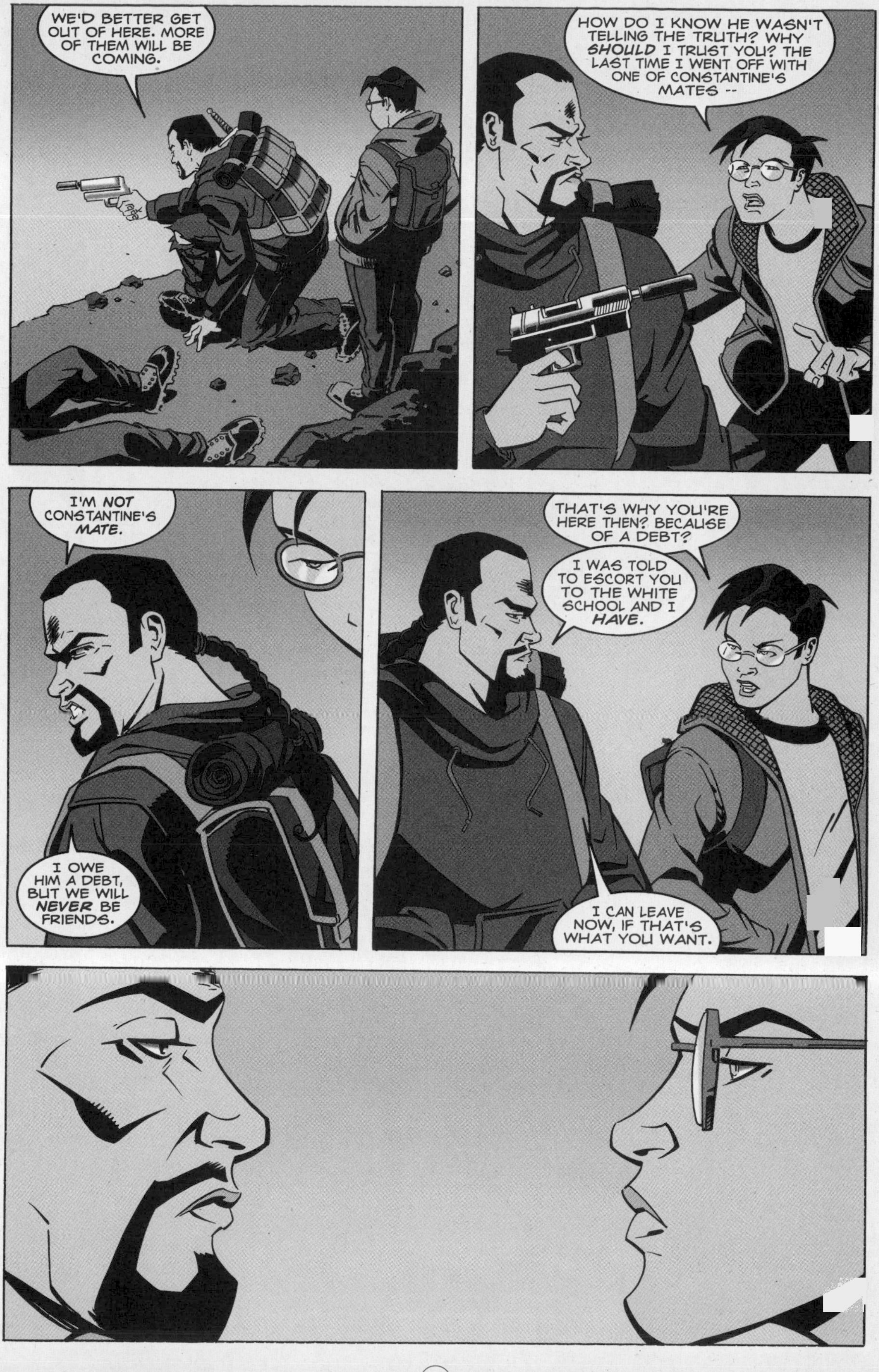
WE'D BETTER GET OUT OF HERE. MORE OF THEM WILL BE COMING.
HOW DO I KNOW HE WASN'T TELLING THE TRUTH? WHY SHOULD I TRUST YOU? THE LAST TIME I WENT OFF WITH ONE OF CONSTANTINE'S MATES --
I'M NOT CONSTANTINE'S MATE.
I OWE HIM A DEBT, BUT WE WILL NEVER BE FRIENDS.
THAT'S WHY YOU'RE HERE THEN? BECAUSE OF A DEBT?
I WAS TOLD TO ESCORT YOU TO THE WHITE SCHOOL AND I HAVE.
I CAN LEAVE NOW, IF THAT'S WHAT YOU WANT.

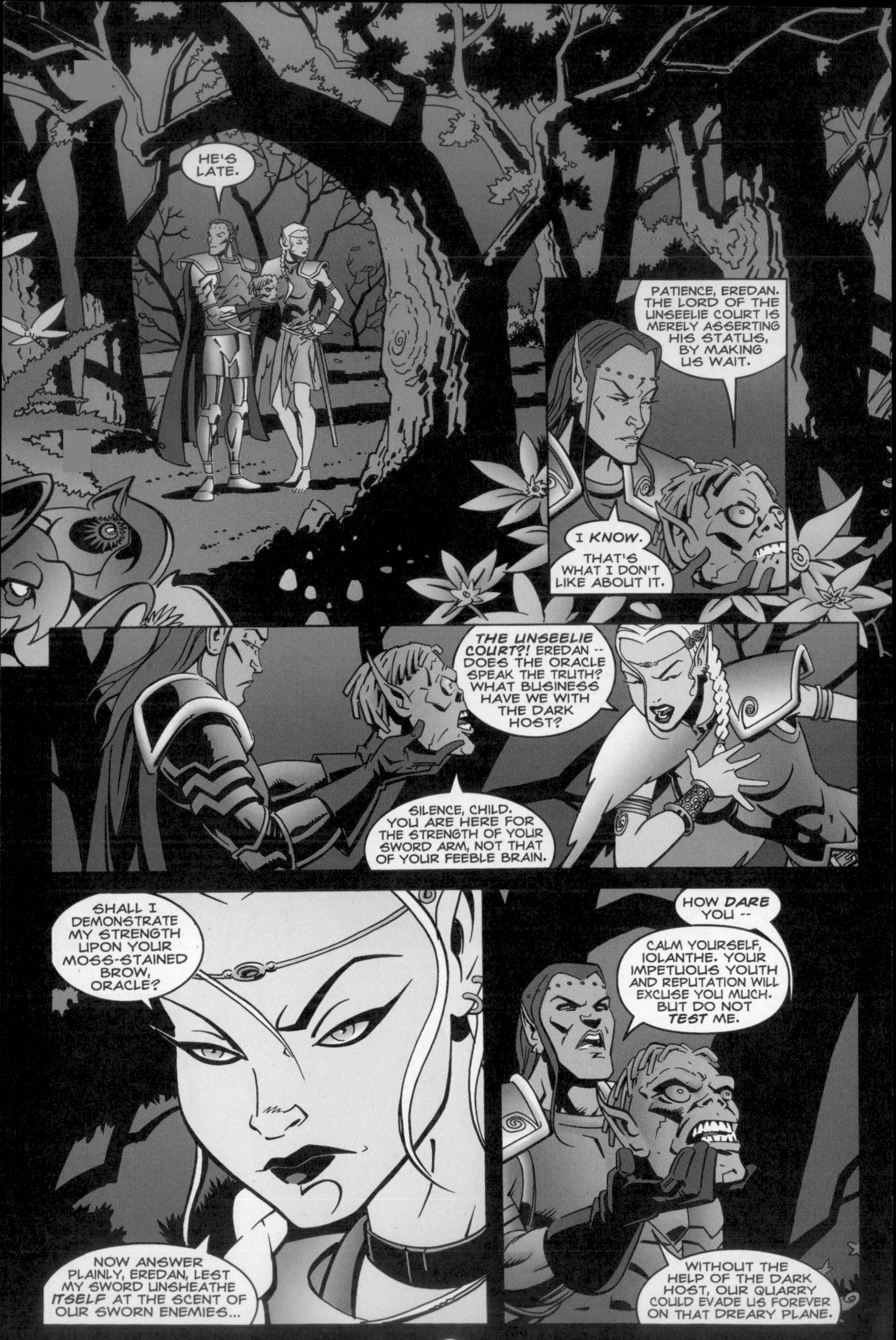
HE'S LATE.
PATIENCE, EREDAN. THE LORD OF THE UNSEELIE COURT IS MERELY ASSERTING HIS STATUS, BY MAKING US WAIT.
I *KNOW.*
THAT'S WHAT I DON'T LIKE ABOUT IT.
THE UNSEELIE COURT?! EREDAN -- DOES THE ORACLE SPEAK THE TRUTH? WHAT BUSINESS HAVE WE WITH THE DARK HOST?
SILENCE, CHILD. YOU ARE HERE FOR THE STRENGTH OF YOUR SWORD ARM, NOT THAT OF YOUR FEEBLE BRAIN.
SHALL I DEMONSTRATE MY STRENGTH UPON YOUR MOSS-STAINED BROW, ORACLE?
NOW ANSWER PLAINLY, EREDAN, LEST MY SWORD UNSHEATHE *ITSELF* AT THE SCENT OF OUR SWORN ENEMIES...
HOW *DARE* YOU --
CALM YOURSELF, IOLANTHE. YOUR IMPETUOUS YOUTH AND REPUTATION WILL EXCUSE YOU MUCH. BUT DO NOT *TEST* ME.
WITHOUT THE HELP OF THE DARK HOST, OUR QUARRY COULD EVADE US FOREVER ON THAT DREARY PLANE.

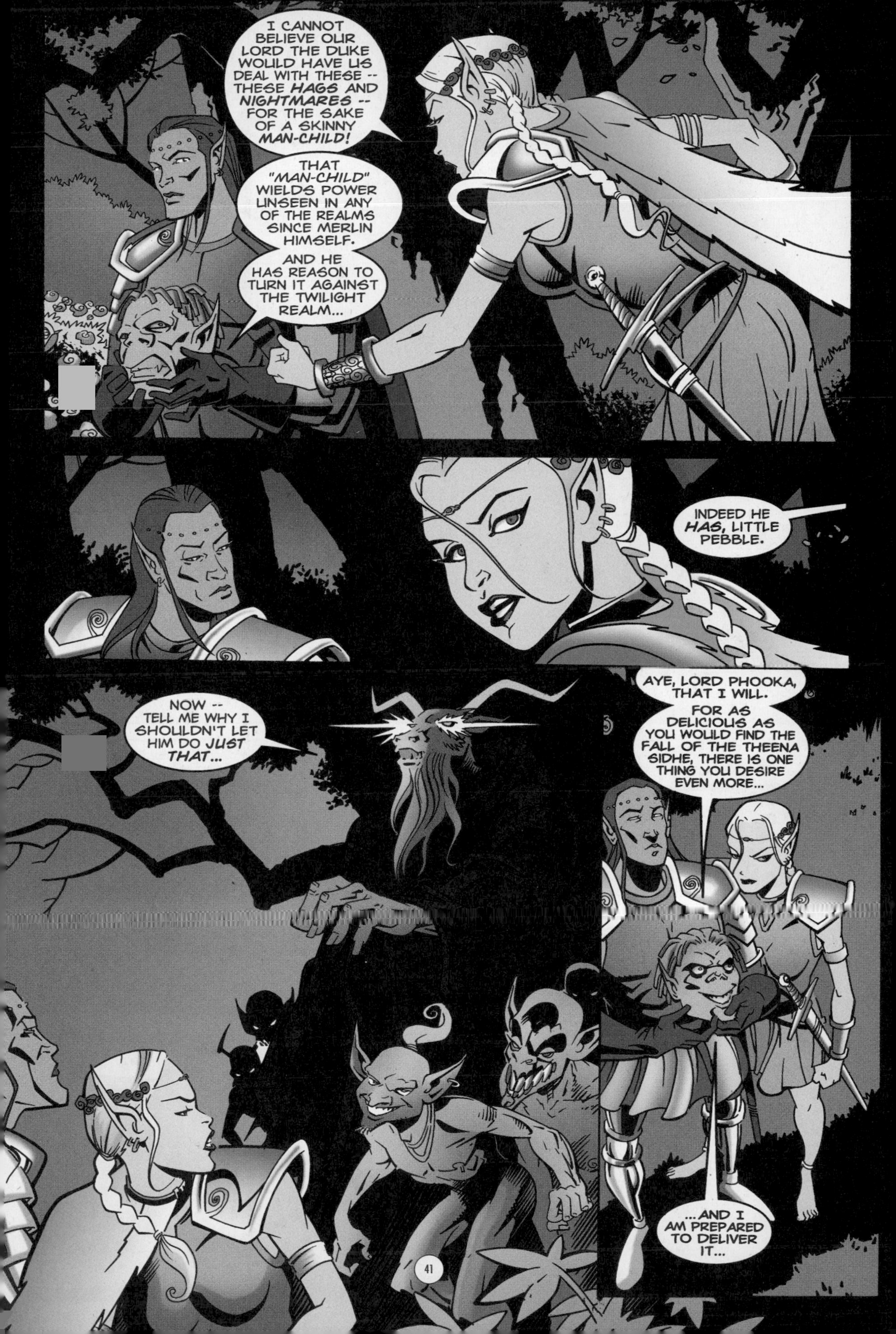
I CANNOT BELIEVE OUR LORD THE DUKE WOULD HAVE US DEAL WITH THESE -- THESE HAGS AND NIGHTMARES -- FOR THE SAKE OF A SKINNY MAN-CHILD!
THAT "MAN-CHILD" WIELDS POWER UNSEEN IN ANY OF THE REALMS SINCE MERLIN HIMSELF.
AND HE HAS REASON TO TURN IT AGAINST THE TWILIGHT REALM...
INDEED HE HAS, LITTLE PEBBLE.
NOW -- TELL ME WHY I SHOULDN'T LET HIM DO JUST THAT...
AYE, LORD PHOOKA, THAT I WILL.
FOR AS DELICIOUS AS YOU WOULD FIND THE FALL OF THE THEENA SIDHE, THERE IS ONE THING YOU DESIRE EVEN MORE...
...AND I AM PREPARED TO DELIVER IT...

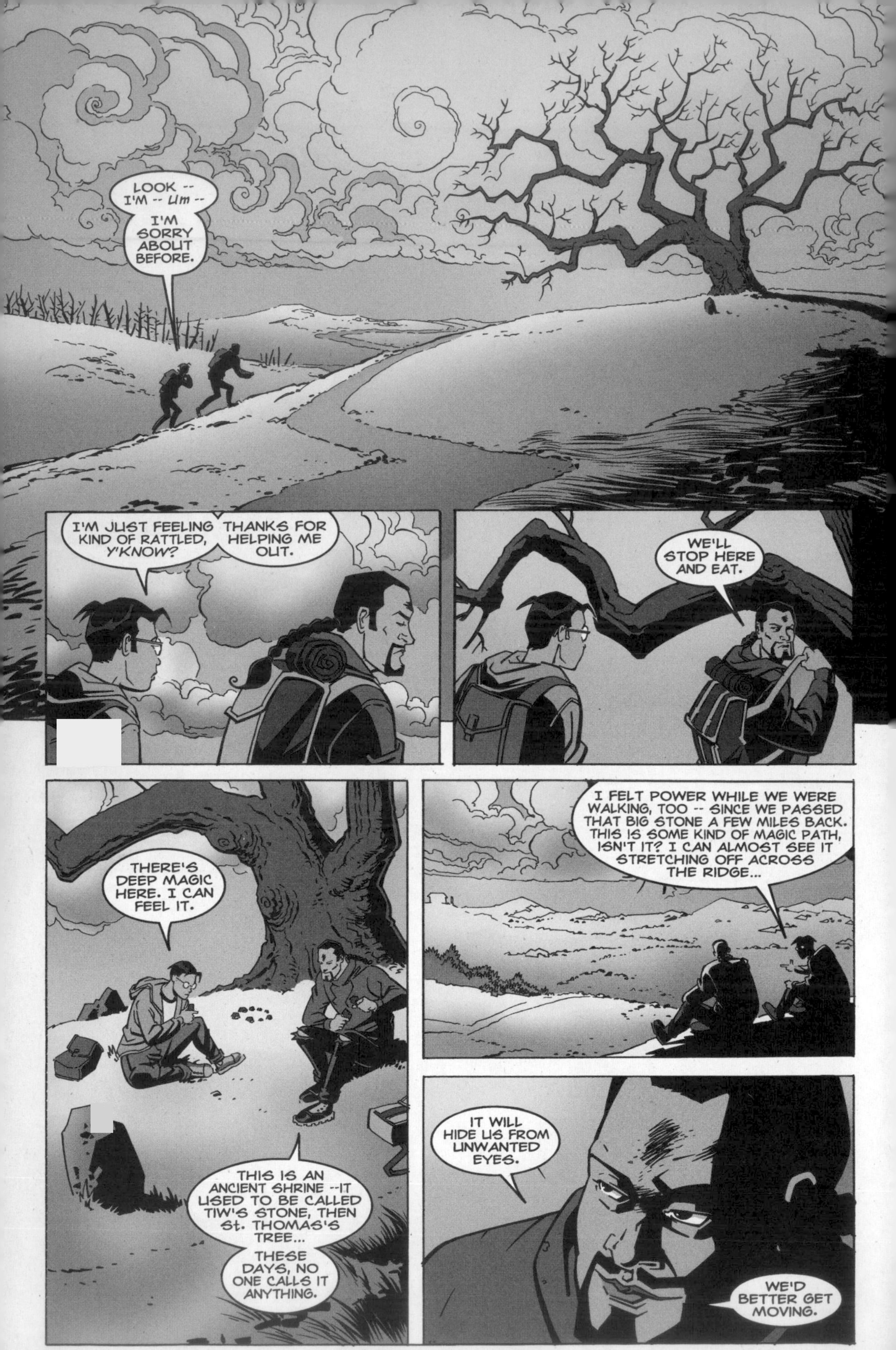
LOOK -- I'M -- Um --
I'M SORRY ABOUT BEFORE.
I'M JUST FEELING KIND OF RATTLED, Y'KNOW?
THANKS FOR HELPING ME OUT.
WE'LL STOP HERE AND EAT.
THERE'S DEEP MAGIC HERE. I CAN FEEL IT.
THIS IS AN ANCIENT SHRINE --IT USED TO BE CALLED TIW'S STONE, THEN St. THOMAS'S TREE...
THESE DAYS, NO ONE CALLS IT ANYTHING.
I FELT POWER WHILE WE WERE WALKING, TOO -- SINCE WE PASSED THAT BIG STONE A FEW MILES BACK. THIS IS SOME KIND OF MAGIC PATH, ISN'T IT? I CAN ALMOST SEE IT STRETCHING OFF ACROSS THE RIDGE...
IT WILL HIDE US FROM UNWANTED EYES.
WE'D BETTER GET MOVING.

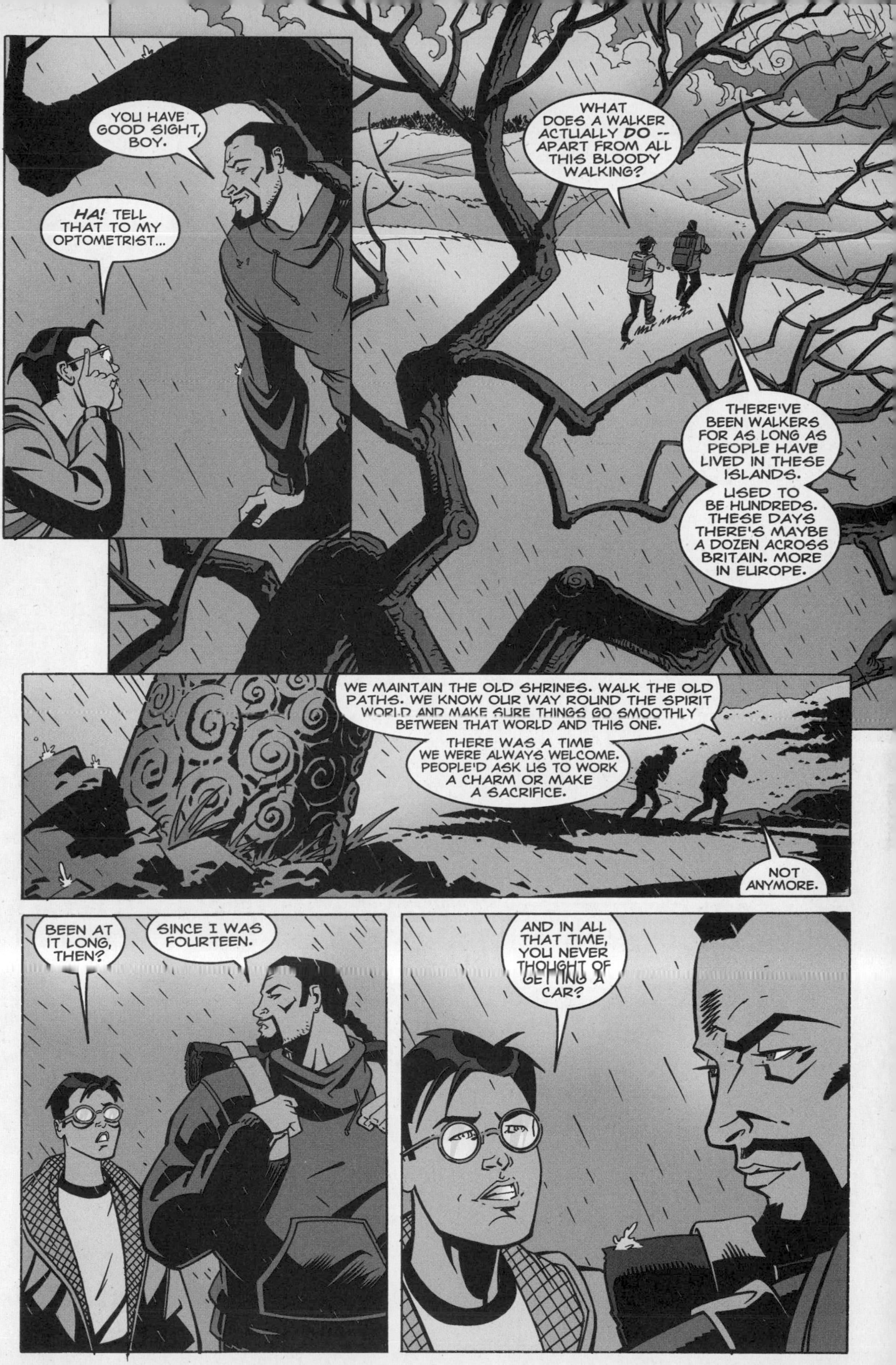
YOU HAVE GOOD SIGHT, BOY.
HA! TELL THAT TO MY OPTOMETRIST...
WHAT DOES A WALKER ACTUALLY DO -- APART FROM ALL THIS BLOODY WALKING?
THERE'VE BEEN WALKERS FOR AS LONG AS PEOPLE HAVE LIVED IN THESE ISLANDS.
USED TO BE HUNDREDS. THESE DAYS THERE'S MAYBE A DOZEN ACROSS BRITAIN. MORE IN EUROPE.
WE MAINTAIN THE OLD SHRINES. WALK THE OLD PATHS. WE KNOW OUR WAY ROUND THE SPIRIT WORLD AND MAKE SURE THINGS GO SMOOTHLY BETWEEN THAT WORLD AND THIS ONE.
THERE WAS A TIME WE WERE ALWAYS WELCOME. PEOPLE'D ASK US TO WORK A CHARM OR MAKE A SACRIFICE.
NOT ANYMORE.
BEEN AT IT LONG, THEN?
SINCE I WAS FOURTEEN.
AND IN ALL THAT TIME, YOU NEVER THOUGHT OF GETTING A CAR?

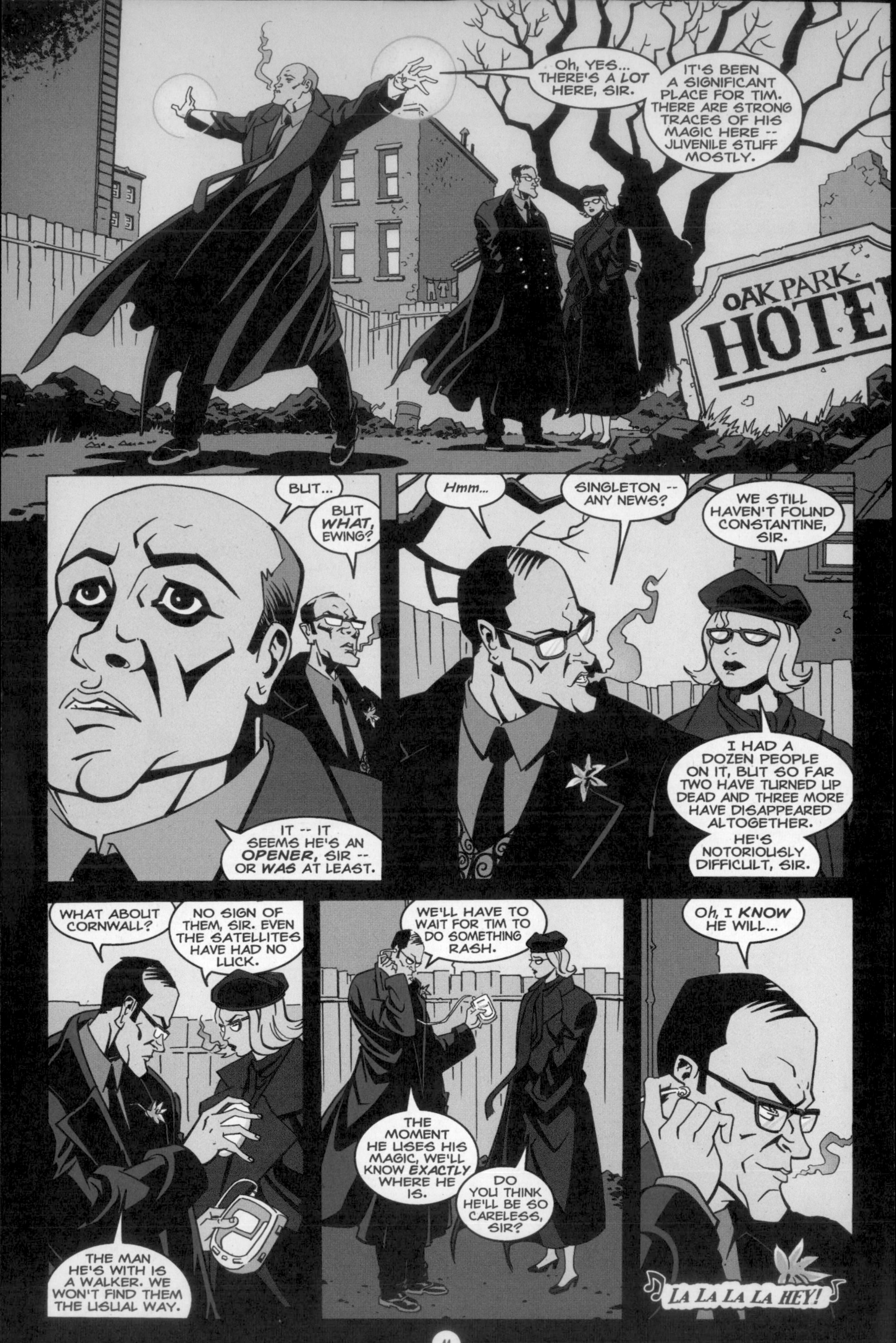
Oh, YES... THERE'S A LOT HERE, SIR.
IT'S BEEN A SIGNIFICANT PLACE FOR TIM. THERE ARE STRONG TRACES OF HIS MAGIC HERE -- JUVENILE STUFF MOSTLY.
OAK PARK HOTE
BUT...
BUT WHAT, EWING?
IT -- IT SEEMS HE'S AN OPENER, SIR -- OR WAS AT LEAST.
Hmm...
SINGLETON -- ANY NEWS?
WE STILL HAVEN'T FOUND CONSTANTINE, SIR.
I HAD A DOZEN PEOPLE ON IT, BUT SO FAR TWO HAVE TURNED UP DEAD AND THREE MORE HAVE DISAPPEARED ALTOGETHER.
HE'S NOTORIOUSLY DIFFICULT, SIR.
WHAT ABOUT CORNWALL?
NO SIGN OF THEM, SIR. EVEN THE SATELLITES HAVE HAD NO LUCK.
THE MAN HE'S WITH IS A WALKER. WE WON'T FIND THEM THE USUAL WAY.
WE'LL HAVE TO WAIT FOR TIM TO DO SOMETHING RASH.
THE MOMENT HE USES HIS MAGIC, WE'LL KNOW EXACTLY WHERE HE IS.
DO YOU THINK HE'LL BE SO CARELESS, SIR?
Oh, I KNOW HE WILL...
LA LA LA LA HEY!

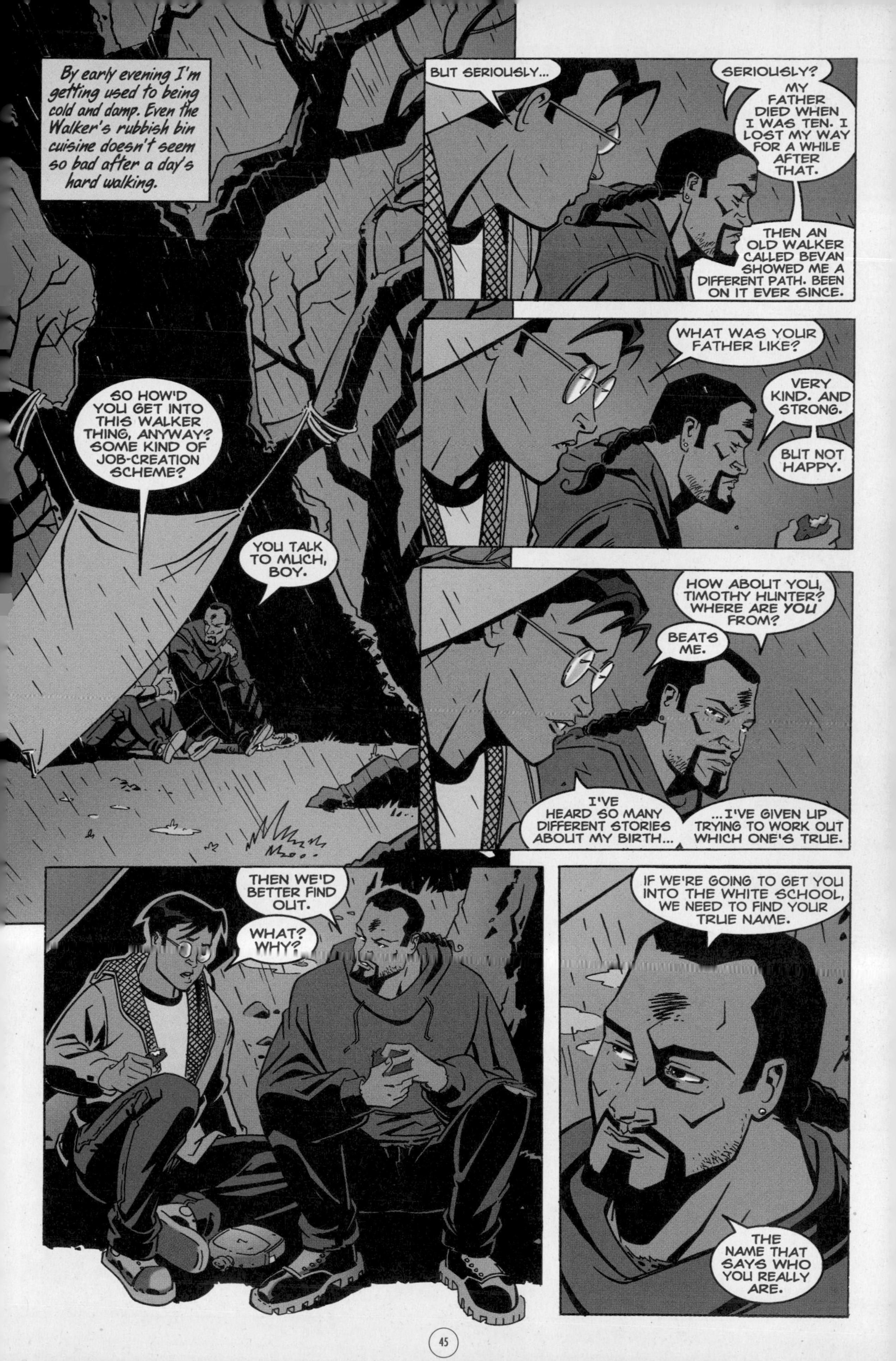
By early evening I'm getting used to being cold and damp. Even the Walker's rubbish bin cuisine doesn't seem so bad after a day's hard walking.
SO HOW'D YOU GET INTO THIS WALKER THING, ANYWAY? SOME KIND OF JOB-CREATION SCHEME?
YOU TALK TO MUCH, BOY.
BUT SERIOUSLY...
SERIOUSLY? MY FATHER DIED WHEN I WAS TEN. I LOST MY WAY FOR A WHILE AFTER THAT.
THEN AN OLD WALKER CALLED BEVAN SHOWED ME A DIFFERENT PATH. BEEN ON IT EVER SINCE.
WHAT WAS YOUR FATHER LIKE?
VERY KIND. AND STRONG.
BUT NOT HAPPY.
HOW ABOUT YOU, TIMOTHY HUNTER? WHERE ARE YOU FROM?
BEATS ME.
I'VE HEARD SO MANY DIFFERENT STORIES ABOUT MY BIRTH...
...I'VE GIVEN UP TRYING TO WORK OUT WHICH ONE'S TRUE.
THEN WE'D BETTER FIND OUT.
WHAT? WHY?
IF WE'RE GOING TO GET YOU INTO THE WHITE SCHOOL, WE NEED TO FIND YOUR TRUE NAME.
THE NAME THAT SAYS WHO YOU REALLY ARE.

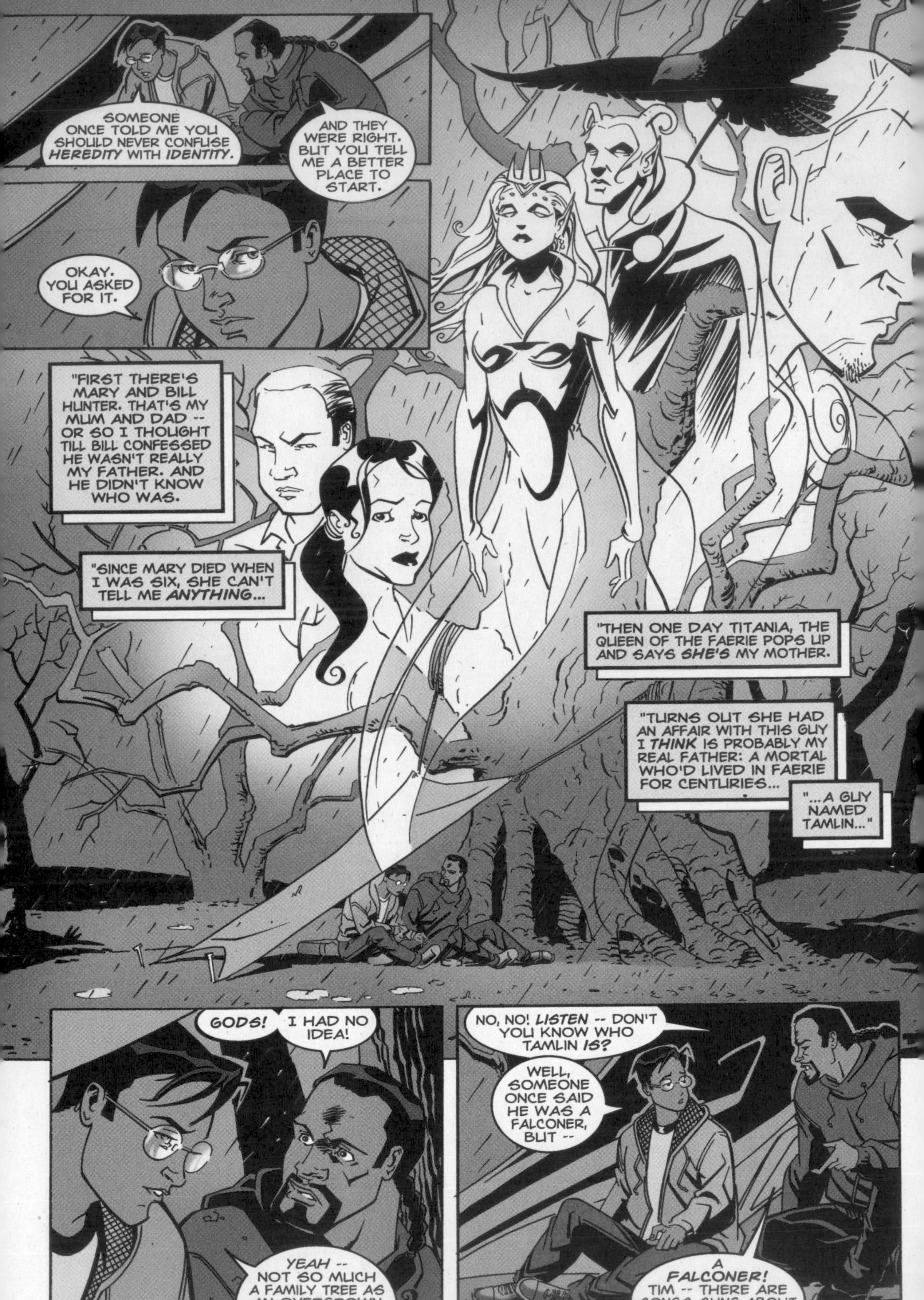
SOMEONE ONCE TOLD ME YOU SHOULD NEVER CONFUSE *HEREDITY* WITH *IDENTITY*.
AND THEY WERE RIGHT. BUT YOU TELL ME A BETTER PLACE TO START.
OKAY. YOU ASKED FOR IT.
"FIRST THERE'S MARY AND BILL HUNTER. THAT'S MY MUM AND DAD -- OR SO I THOUGHT TILL BILL CONFESSED HE WASN'T REALLY MY FATHER. AND HE DIDN'T KNOW WHO WAS.
"SINCE MARY DIED WHEN I WAS SIX, SHE CAN'T TELL ME *ANYTHING*...
"THEN ONE DAY TITANIA, THE QUEEN OF THE FAERIE POPS UP AND SAYS *SHE'S* MY MOTHER.
"TURNS OUT SHE HAD AN AFFAIR WITH THIS GUY I *THINK* IS PROBABLY MY REAL FATHER: A MORTAL WHO'D LIVED IN FAERIE FOR CENTURIES...
"...A GUY NAMED TAMLIN..."
GODS!
I HAD NO IDEA!
YEAH -- NOT SO MUCH A FAMILY TREE AS AN OVERGROWN BRAMBLE PATCH.
NO, NO! *LISTEN* -- DON'T YOU KNOW WHO TAMLIN *IS*?
WELL, SOMEONE ONCE SAID HE WAS A FALCONER, BUT --
A *FALCONER!* TIM -- THERE ARE SONGS SUNG ABOUT YOUR FATHER...

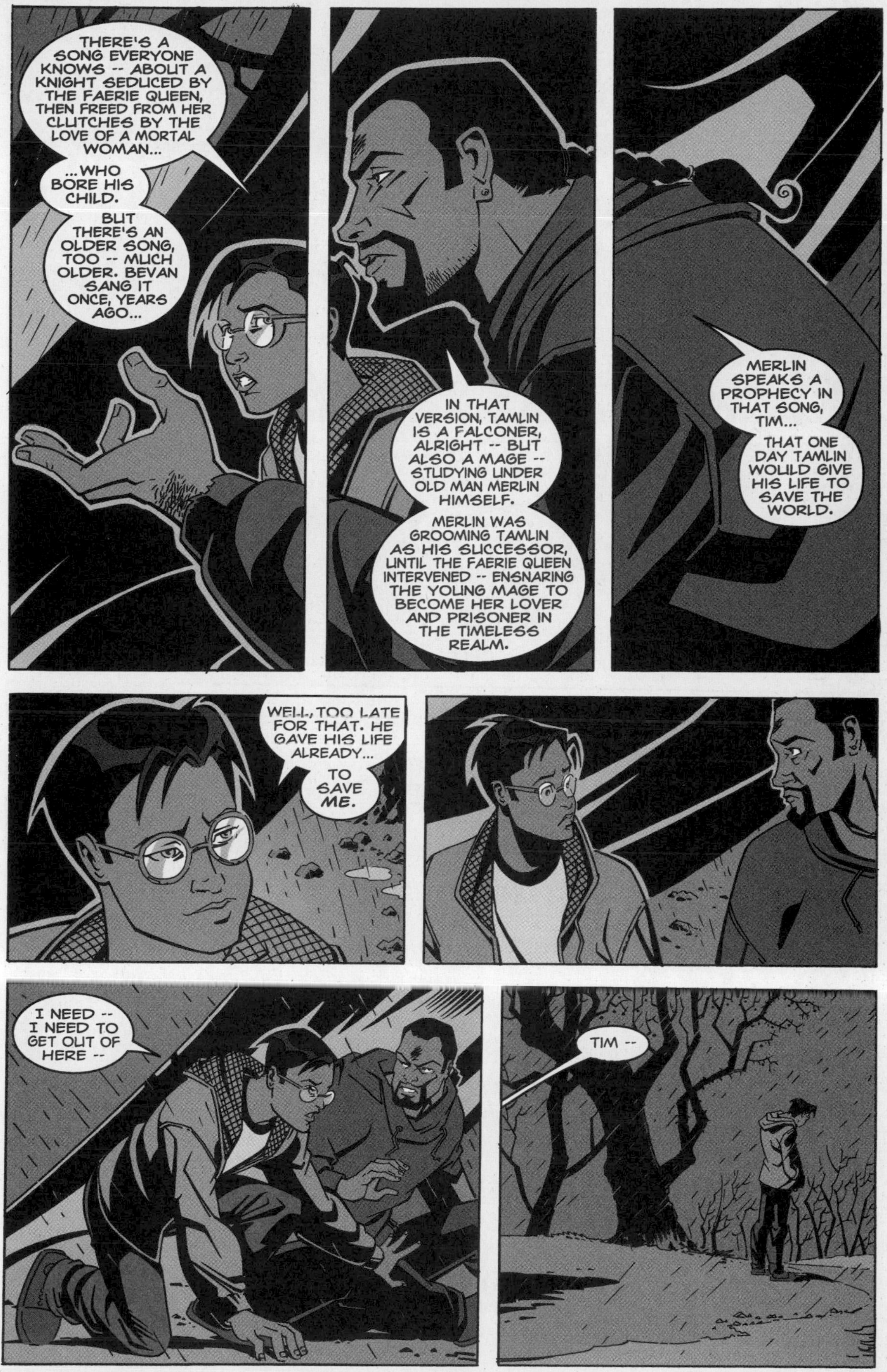
THERE'S A SONG EVERYONE KNOWS -- ABOUT A KNIGHT SEDUCED BY THE FAERIE QUEEN, THEN FREED FROM HER CLUTCHES BY THE LOVE OF A MORTAL WOMAN...
...WHO BORE HIS CHILD.
BUT THERE'S AN OLDER SONG, TOO -- MUCH OLDER. BEVAN SANG IT ONCE, YEARS AGO...
IN THAT VERSION, TAMLIN IS A FALCONER, ALRIGHT -- BUT ALSO A MAGE -- STUDYING UNDER OLD MAN MERLIN HIMSELF.
MERLIN WAS GROOMING TAMLIN AS HIS SUCCESSOR, UNTIL THE FAERIE QUEEN INTERVENED -- ENSNARING THE YOUNG MAGE TO BECOME HER LOVER AND PRISONER IN THE TIMELESS REALM.
MERLIN SPEAKS A PROPHECY IN THAT SONG, TIM...
THAT ONE DAY TAMLIN WOULD GIVE HIS LIFE TO SAVE THE WORLD.
WELL, TOO LATE FOR THAT. HE GAVE HIS LIFE ALREADY...
TO SAVE *ME.*
I NEED -- I NEED TO GET OUT OF HERE --
TIM --

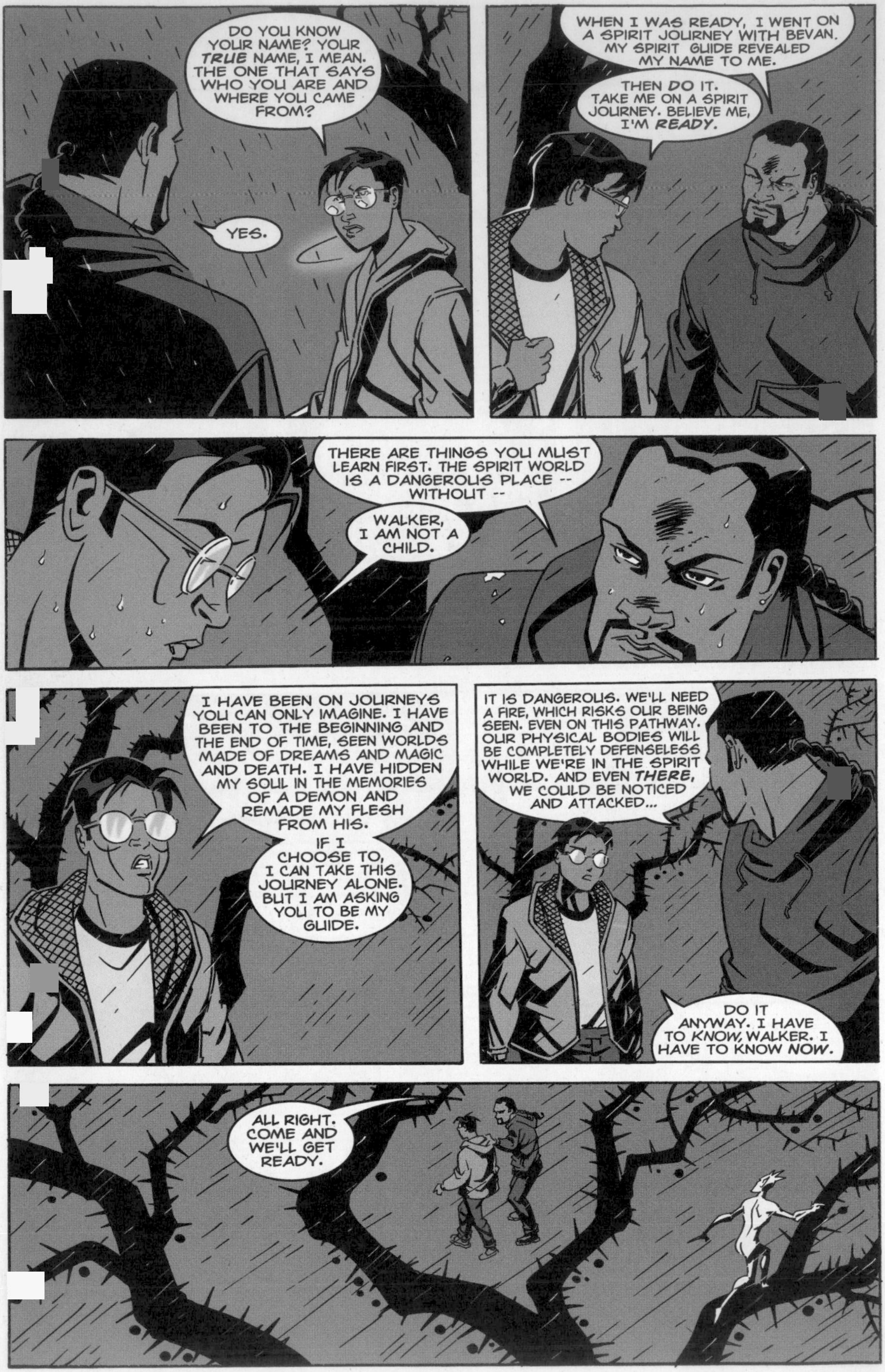
DO YOU KNOW YOUR NAME? YOUR TRUE NAME, I MEAN. THE ONE THAT SAYS WHO YOU ARE AND WHERE YOU CAME FROM?
YES.
WHEN I WAS READY, I WENT ON A SPIRIT JOURNEY WITH BEVAN. MY SPIRIT GUIDE REVEALED MY NAME TO ME.
THEN DO IT. TAKE ME ON A SPIRIT JOURNEY. BELIEVE ME, I'M READY.
THERE ARE THINGS YOU MUST LEARN FIRST. THE SPIRIT WORLD IS A DANGEROUS PLACE -- WITHOUT --
WALKER, I AM NOT A CHILD.
I HAVE BEEN ON JOURNEYS YOU CAN ONLY IMAGINE. I HAVE BEEN TO THE BEGINNING AND THE END OF TIME, SEEN WORLDS MADE OF DREAMS AND MAGIC AND DEATH. I HAVE HIDDEN MY SOUL IN THE MEMORIES OF A DEMON AND REMADE MY FLESH FROM HIS.
IF I CHOOSE TO, I CAN TAKE THIS JOURNEY ALONE. BUT I AM ASKING YOU TO BE MY GUIDE.
IT IS DANGEROUS. WE'LL NEED A FIRE, WHICH RISKS OUR BEING SEEN. EVEN ON THIS PATHWAY. OUR PHYSICAL BODIES WILL BE COMPLETELY DEFENSELESS WHILE WE'RE IN THE SPIRIT WORLD. AND EVEN THERE, WE COULD BE NOTICED AND ATTACKED...
DO IT ANYWAY. I HAVE TO KNOW, WALKER. I HAVE TO KNOW NOW.
ALL RIGHT. COME AND WE'LL GET READY.

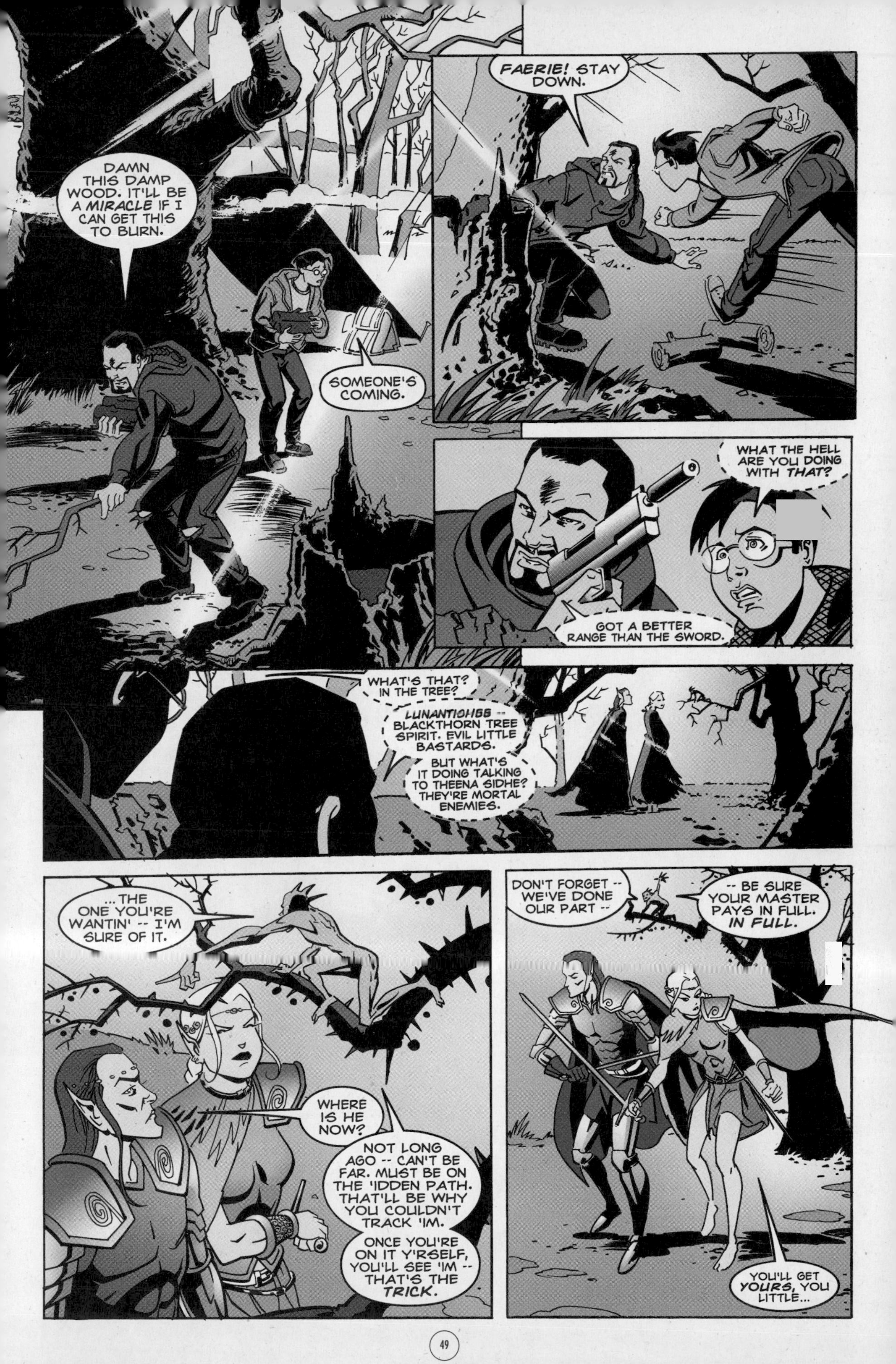
DAMN THIS DAMP WOOD. IT'LL BE A MIRACLE IF I CAN GET THIS TO BURN.
SOMEONE'S COMING.
FAERIE! STAY DOWN.
WHAT THE HELL ARE YOU DOING WITH THAT?
GOT A BETTER RANGE THAN THE SWORD.
WHAT'S THAT? IN THE TREE?
LUNANTISHEE -- BLACKTHORN TREE SPIRIT. EVIL LITTLE BASTARDS.
BUT WHAT'S IT DOING TALKING TO THEENA SIDHE? THEY'RE MORTAL ENEMIES.
...THE ONE YOU'RE WANTIN' -- I'M SURE OF IT.
WHERE IS HE NOW?
NOT LONG AGO -- CAN'T BE FAR. MUST BE ON THE 'IDDEN PATH. THAT'LL BE WHY YOU COULDN'T TRACK 'IM.
ONCE YOU'RE ON IT Y'RSELF, YOU'LL SEE 'IM -- THAT'S THE TRICK.
DON'T FORGET -- WE'VE DONE OUR PART --
-- BE SURE YOUR MASTER PAYS IN FULL. IN FULL.
YOU'LL GET YOURS, YOU LITTLE...

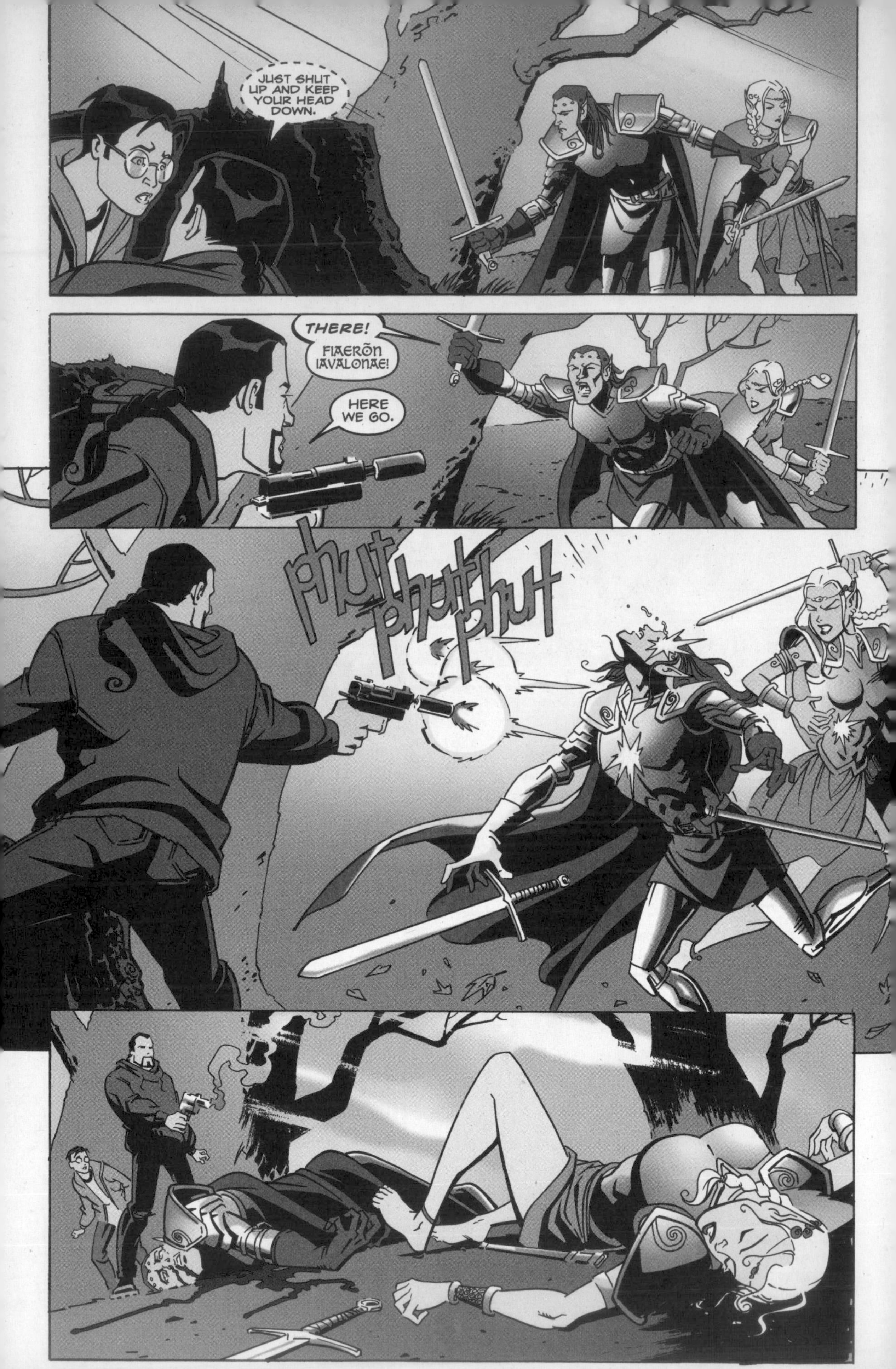
JUST SHUT UP AND KEEP YOUR HEAD DOWN.
THERE!
FIAERÕN IAVALONAE!
HERE WE GO.
phut phut phut

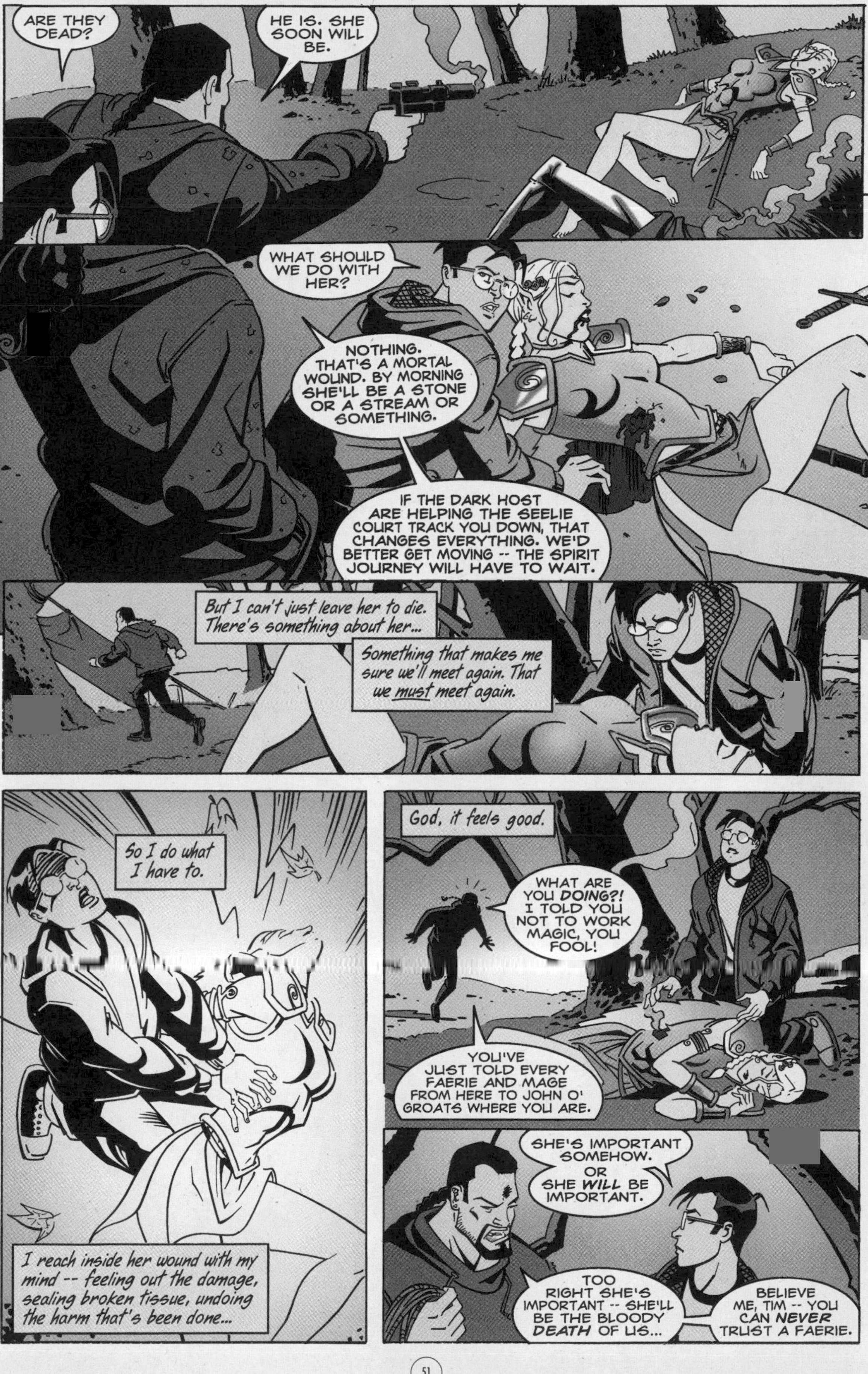

ARE THEY DEAD?
HE IS. SHE SOON WILL BE.
WHAT SHOULD WE DO WITH HER?
NOTHING. THAT'S A MORTAL WOUND. BY MORNING SHE'LL BE A STONE OR A STREAM OR SOMETHING.
IF THE DARK HOST ARE HELPING THE SEELIE COURT TRACK YOU DOWN, THAT CHANGES EVERYTHING. WE'D BETTER GET MOVING -- THE SPIRIT JOURNEY WILL HAVE TO WAIT.
But I can't just leave her to die. There's something about her...
Something that makes me sure we'll meet again. That we must meet again.
So I do what I have to.
I reach inside her wound with my mind -- feeling out the damage, sealing broken tissue, undoing the harm that's been done...
God, it feels good.
WHAT ARE YOU DOING?! I TOLD YOU NOT TO WORK MAGIC, YOU FOOL!
YOU'VE JUST TOLD EVERY FAERIE AND MAGE FROM HERE TO JOHN O' GROATS WHERE YOU ARE.
SHE'S IMPORTANT SOMEHOW. OR SHE WILL BE IMPORTANT.
TOO RIGHT SHE'S IMPORTANT -- SHE'LL BE THE BLOODY DEATH OF US...
BELIEVE ME, TIM -- YOU CAN NEVER TRUST A FAERIE.

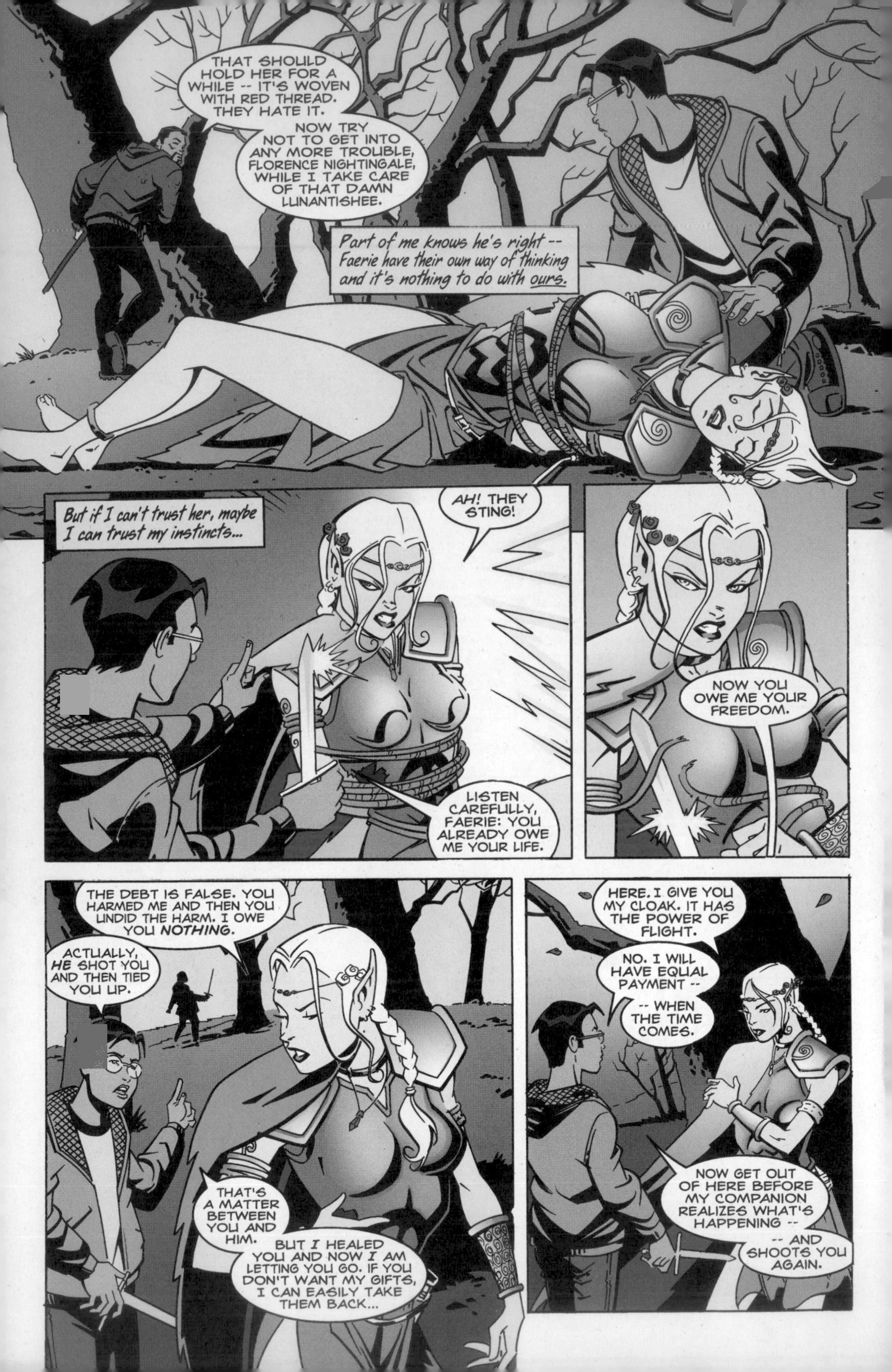
THAT SHOULD HOLD HER FOR A WHILE -- IT'S WOVEN WITH RED THREAD. THEY HATE IT.
NOW TRY NOT TO GET INTO ANY MORE TROUBLE, FLORENCE NIGHTINGALE, WHILE I TAKE CARE OF THAT DAMN LUNANTISHEE.
Part of me knows he's right -- Faerie have their own way of thinking and it's nothing to do with ours.
But if I can't trust her, maybe I can trust my instincts...
AH! THEY STING!
LISTEN CAREFULLY, FAERIE: YOU ALREADY OWE ME YOUR LIFE.
NOW YOU OWE ME YOUR FREEDOM.
THE DEBT IS FALSE. YOU HARMED ME AND THEN YOU UNDID THE HARM. I OWE YOU NOTHING.
ACTUALLY, HE SHOT YOU AND THEN TIED YOU UP.
THAT'S A MATTER BETWEEN YOU AND HIM.
BUT I HEALED YOU AND NOW I AM LETTING YOU GO. IF YOU DON'T WANT MY GIFTS, I CAN EASILY TAKE THEM BACK...
HERE. I GIVE YOU MY CLOAK. IT HAS THE POWER OF FLIGHT.
NO. I WILL HAVE EQUAL PAYMENT --
-- WHEN THE TIME COMES.
NOW GET OUT OF HERE BEFORE MY COMPANION REALIZES WHAT'S HAPPENING --
-- AND SHOOTS YOU AGAIN.

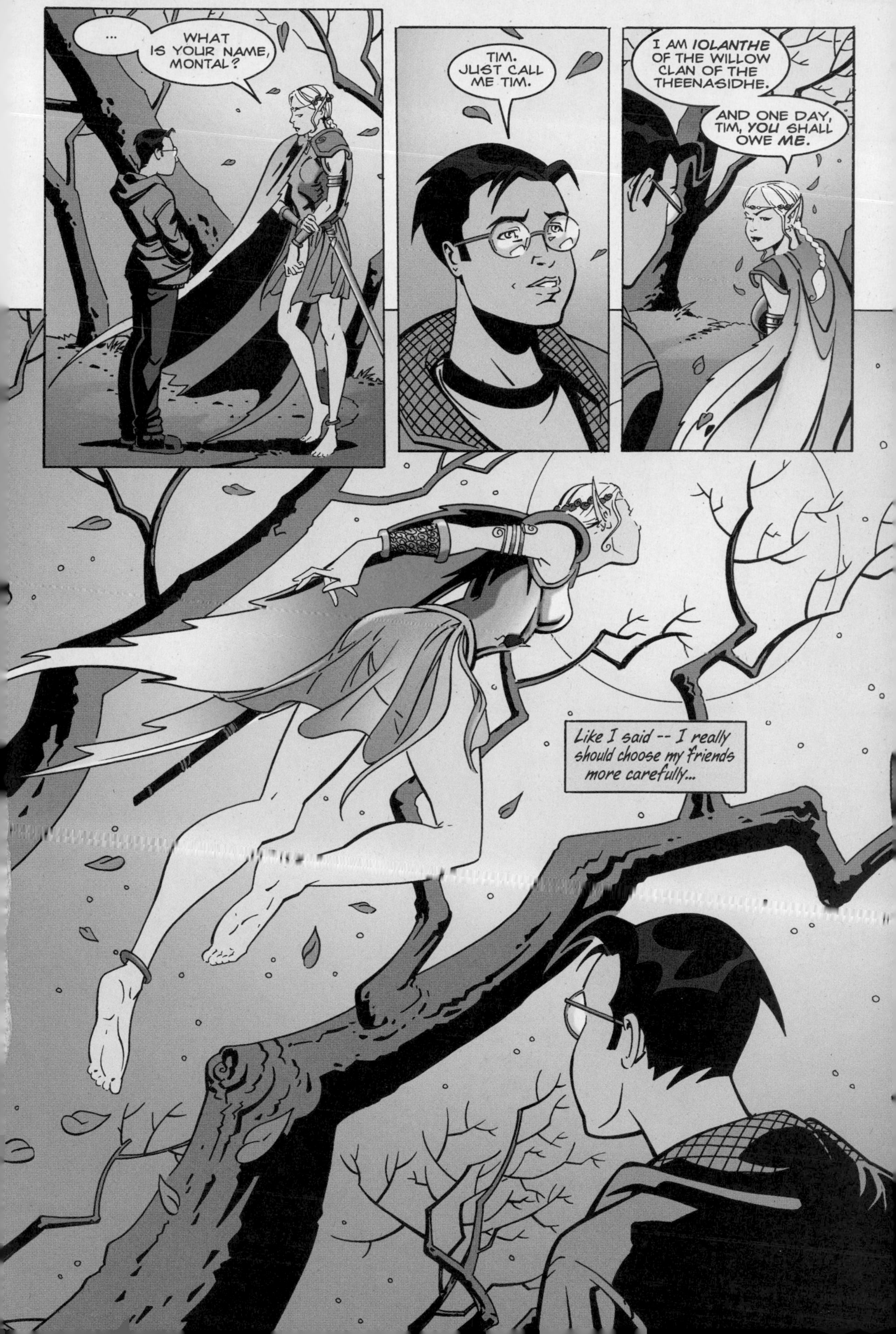
...
WHAT IS YOUR NAME, MONTAL?
TIM. JUST CALL ME TIM.
I AM IOLANTHE OF THE WILLOW CLAN OF THE THEENASIDHE.
AND ONE DAY, TIM, YOU SHALL OWE ME.
Like I said -- I really should choose my friends more carefully...

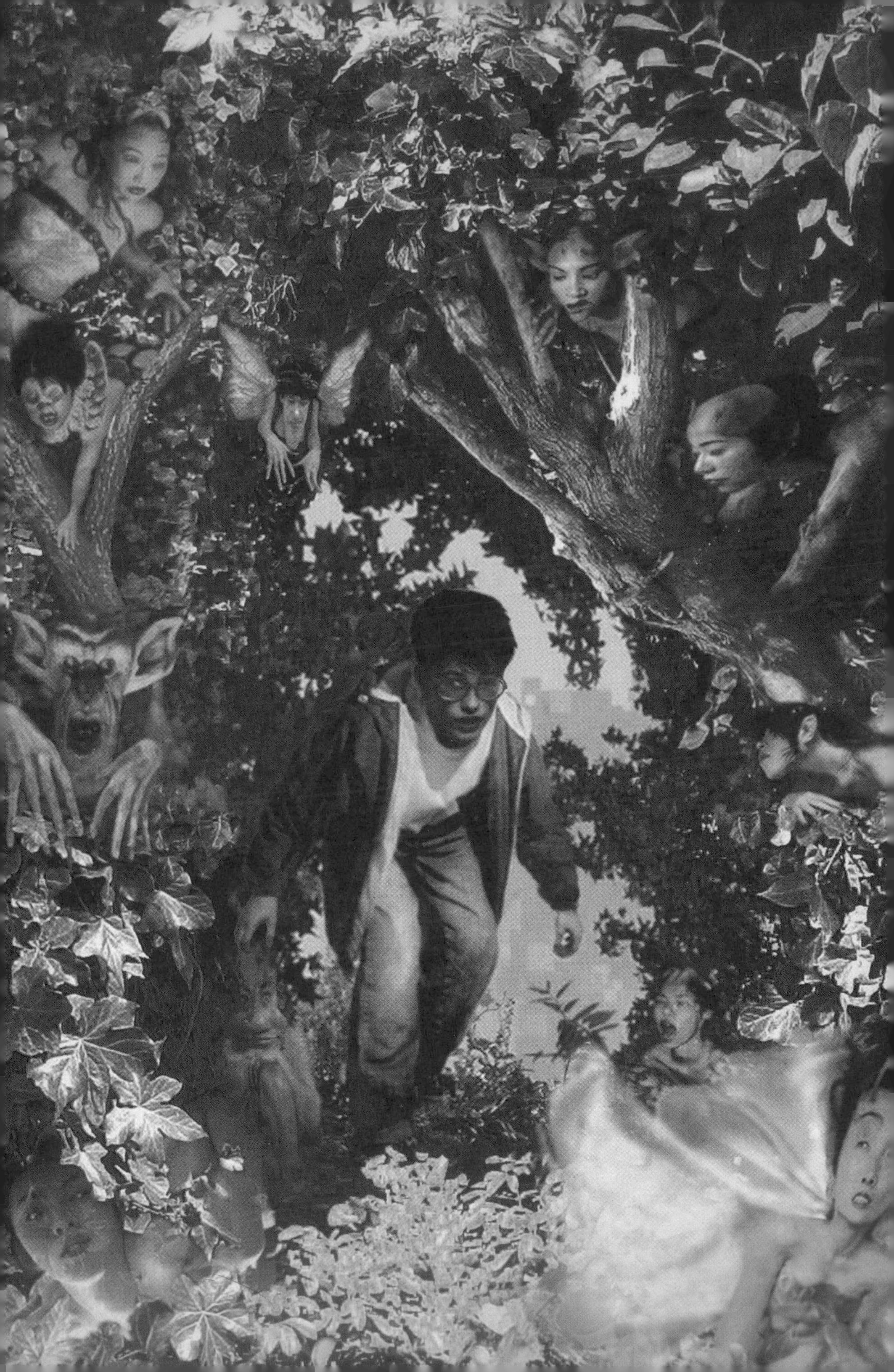

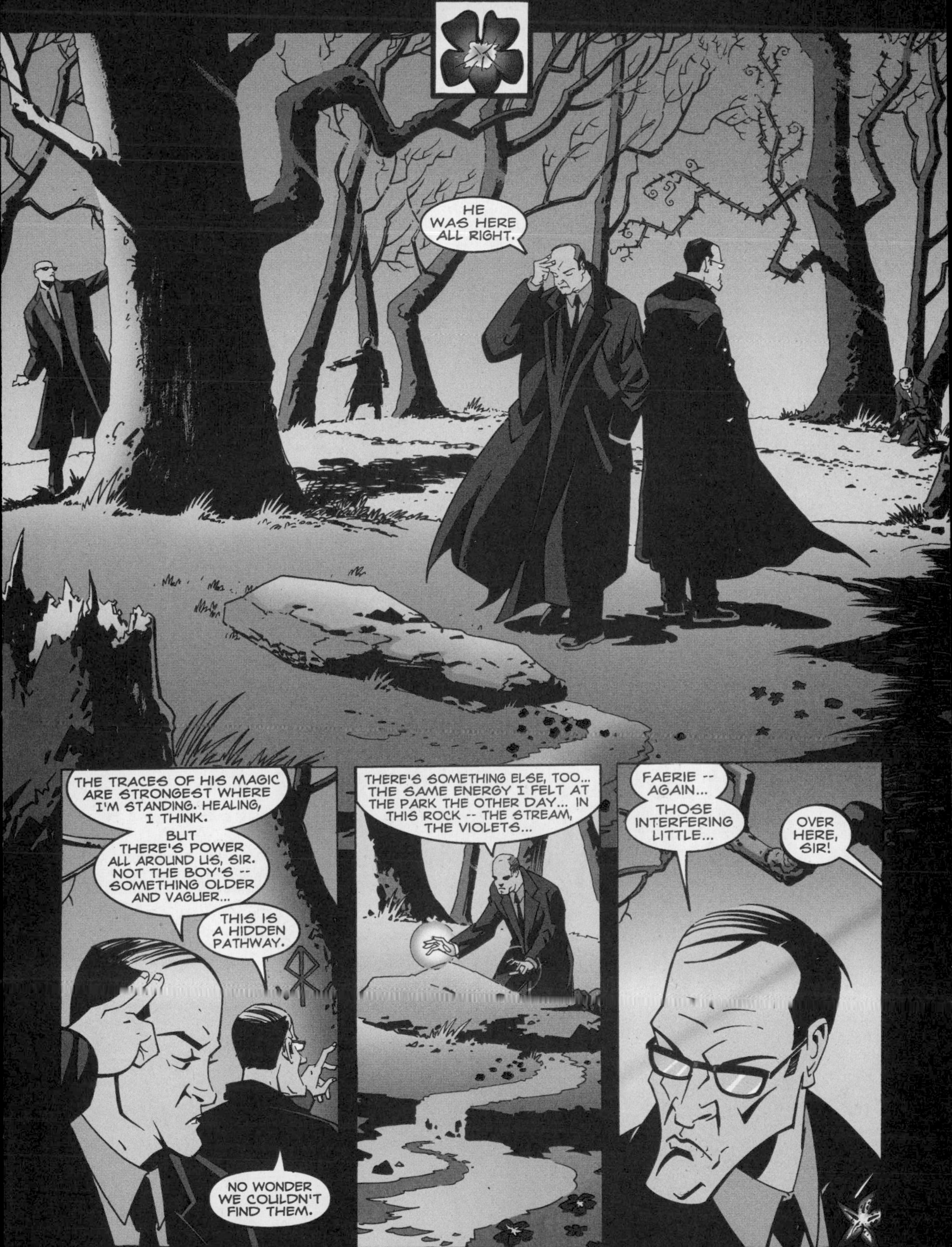
HE WAS HERE ALL RIGHT.
THE TRACES OF HIS MAGIC ARE STRONGEST WHERE I'M STANDING. HEALING, I THINK.
BUT THERE'S POWER ALL AROUND US, SIR. NOT THE BOY'S -- SOMETHING OLDER AND VAGUER...
THIS IS A HIDDEN PATHWAY.
NO WONDER WE COULDN'T FIND THEM.
THERE'S SOMETHING ELSE, TOO... THE SAME ENERGY I FELT AT THE PARK THE OTHER DAY... IN THIS ROCK -- THE STREAM, THE VIOLETS...
FAERIE -- AGAIN...
THOSE INTERFERING LITTLE...
OVER HERE, SIR!

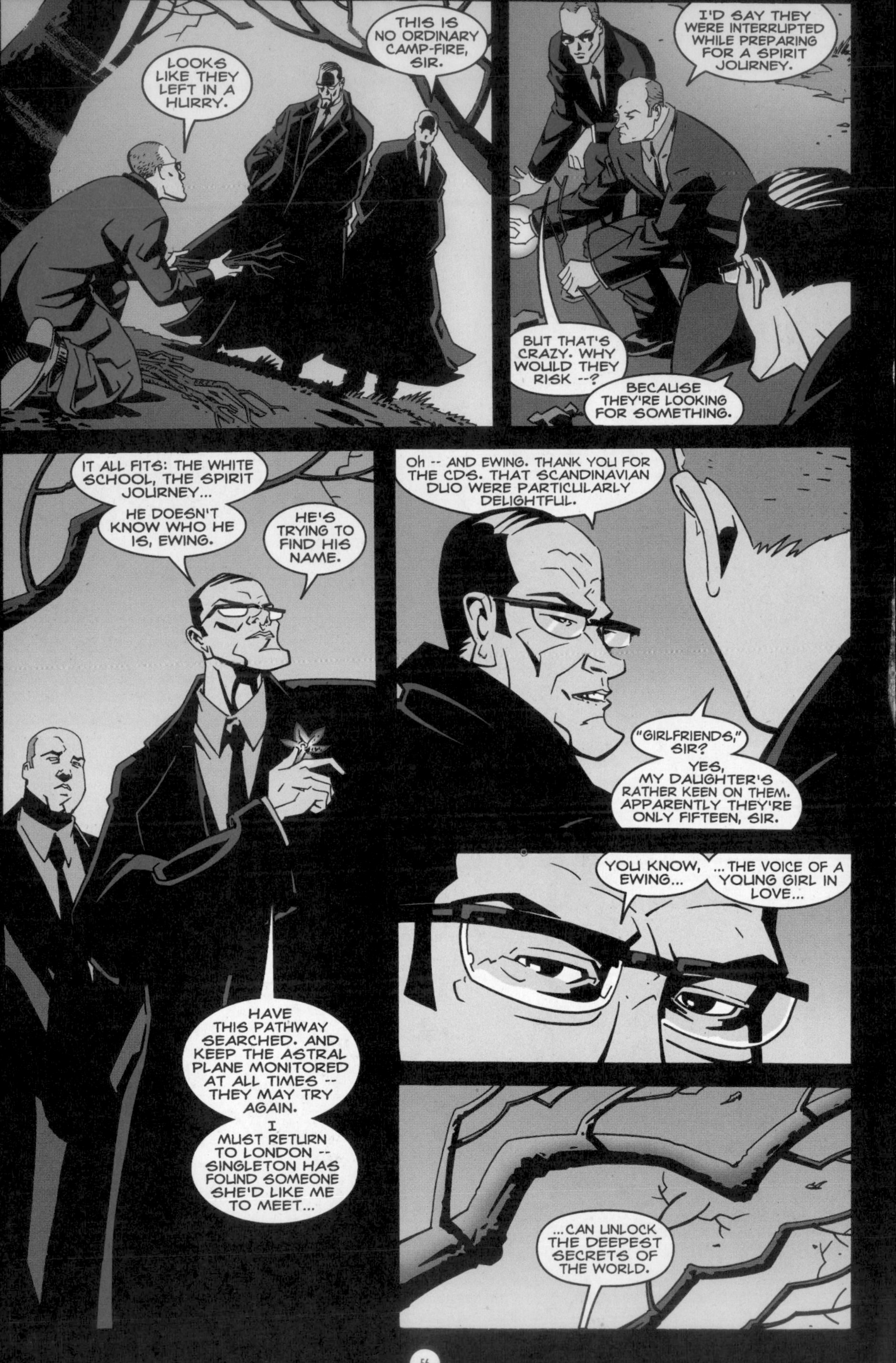
LOOKS LIKE THEY LEFT IN A HURRY.
THIS IS NO ORDINARY CAMP-FIRE, SIR.
I'D SAY THEY WERE INTERRUPTED WHILE PREPARING FOR A SPIRIT JOURNEY.
BUT THAT'S CRAZY. WHY WOULD THEY RISK --?
BECAUSE THEY'RE LOOKING FOR SOMETHING.
IT ALL FITS: THE WHITE SCHOOL, THE SPIRIT JOURNEY...
HE DOESN'T KNOW WHO HE IS, EWING.
HE'S TRYING TO FIND HIS NAME.
HAVE THIS PATHWAY SEARCHED. AND KEEP THE ASTRAL PLANE MONITORED AT ALL TIMES -- THEY MAY TRY AGAIN.
I MUST RETURN TO LONDON -- SINGLETON HAS FOUND SOMEONE SHE'D LIKE ME TO MEET...
Oh -- AND EWING. THANK YOU FOR THE CDS. THAT SCANDINAVIAN DUO WERE PARTICULARLY DELIGHTFUL.
"GIRLFRIENDS," SIR?
YES, MY DAUGHTER'S RATHER KEEN ON THEM. APPARENTLY THEY'RE ONLY FIFTEEN, SIR.
YOU KNOW, EWING...
...THE VOICE OF A YOUNG GIRL IN LOVE...
...CAN UNLOCK THE DEEPEST SECRETS OF THE WORLD.

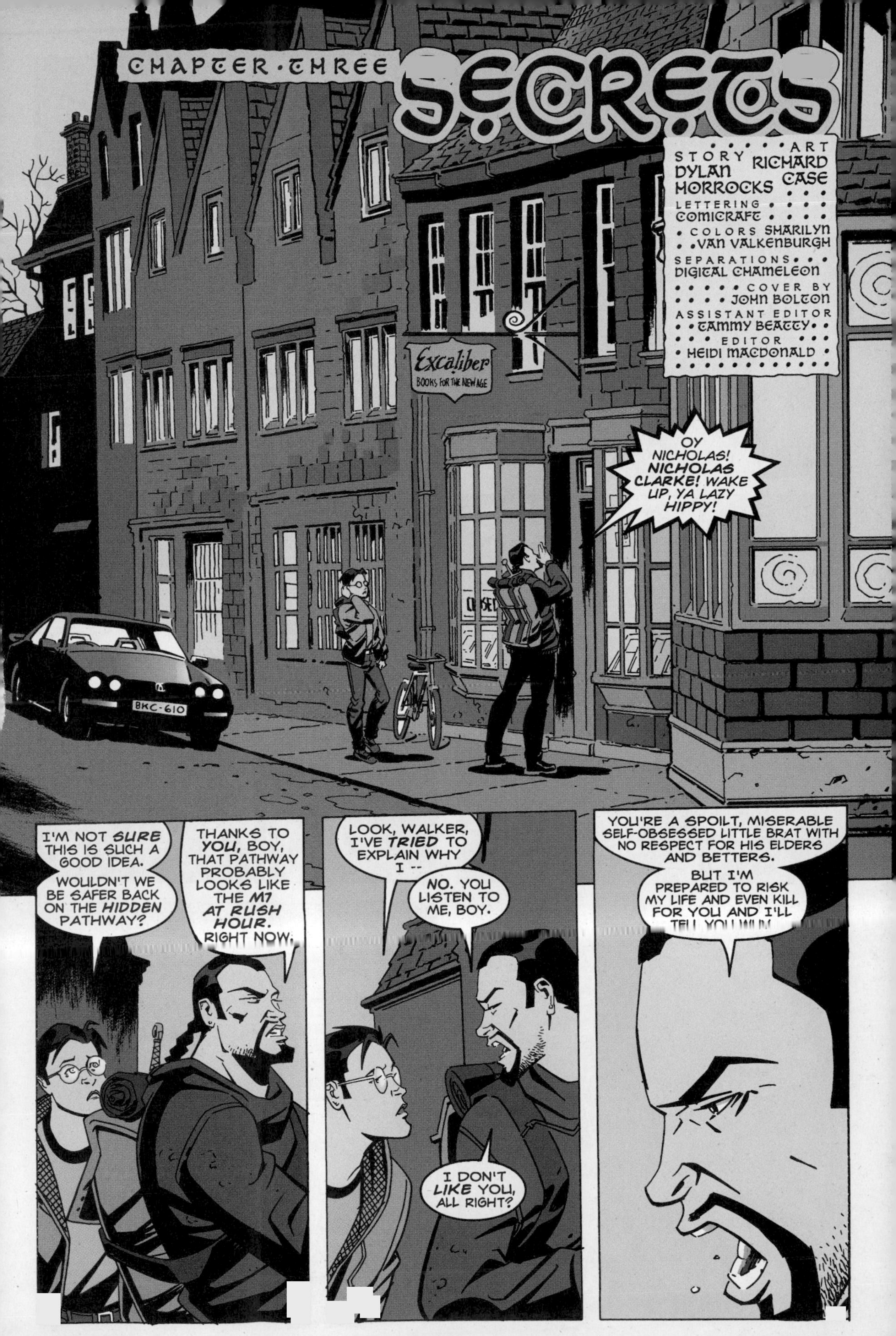
CHAPTER • THREE
SECRETS
STORY DYLAN HORROCKS
ART RICHARD CASE
LETTERING COMICRAFT
COLORS SHARILYN VAN VALKENBURGH
SEPARATIONS DIGITAL CHAMELEON
COVER BY JOHN BOLTON
ASSISTANT EDITOR TAMMY BEATTY
EDITOR HEIDI MACDONALD
Excaliber
BOOKS FOR THE NEW AGE
OY NICHOLAS! NICHOLAS CLARKE! WAKE UP, YA LAZY HIPPY!
BKC-610
I'M NOT SURE THIS IS SUCH A GOOD IDEA.
WOULDN'T WE BE SAFER BACK ON THE HIDDEN PATHWAY?
THANKS TO YOU, BOY, THAT PATHWAY PROBABLY LOOKS LIKE THE M7 AT RUSH HOUR. RIGHT NOW.
LOOK, WALKER, I'VE TRIED TO EXPLAIN WHY I --
NO. YOU LISTEN TO ME, BOY.
I DON'T LIKE YOU, ALL RIGHT?
YOU'RE A SPOILT, MISERABLE SELF-OBSESSED LITTLE BRAT WITH NO RESPECT FOR HIS ELDERS AND BETTERS.
BUT I'M PREPARED TO RISK MY LIFE AND EVEN KILL FOR YOU AND I'LL

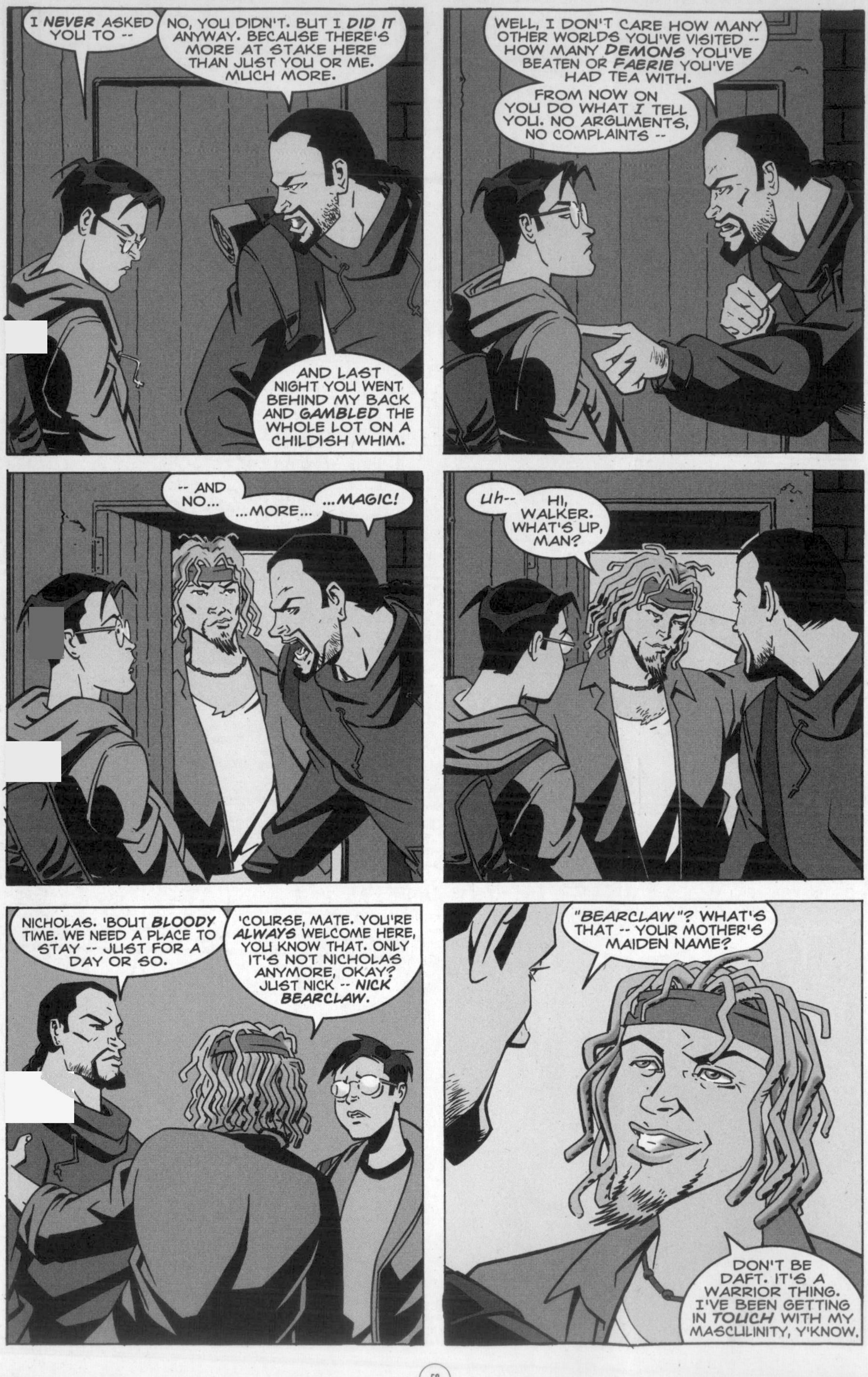
I NEVER ASKED YOU TO --
NO, YOU DIDN'T. BUT I DID IT ANYWAY. BECAUSE THERE'S MORE AT STAKE HERE THAN JUST YOU OR ME. MUCH MORE.
AND LAST NIGHT YOU WENT BEHIND MY BACK AND GAMBLED THE WHOLE LOT ON A CHILDISH WHIM.
WELL, I DON'T CARE HOW MANY OTHER WORLDS YOU'VE VISITED -- HOW MANY DEMONS YOU'VE BEATEN OR FAERIE YOU'VE HAD TEA WITH.
FROM NOW ON YOU DO WHAT I TELL YOU. NO ARGUMENTS, NO COMPLAINTS --
-- AND NO...
...MORE...
...MAGIC!
Uh--
HI, WALKER. WHAT'S UP, MAN?
NICHOLAS. 'BOUT BLOODY TIME. WE NEED A PLACE TO STAY -- JUST FOR A DAY OR SO.
'COURSE, MATE. YOU'RE ALWAYS WELCOME HERE, YOU KNOW THAT. ONLY IT'S NOT NICHOLAS ANYMORE, OKAY? JUST NICK -- NICK BEARCLAW.
"BEARCLAW"? WHAT'S THAT -- YOUR MOTHER'S MAIDEN NAME?
DON'T BE DAFT. IT'S A WARRIOR THING. I'VE BEEN GETTING IN TOUCH WITH MY MASCULINITY, Y'KNOW.

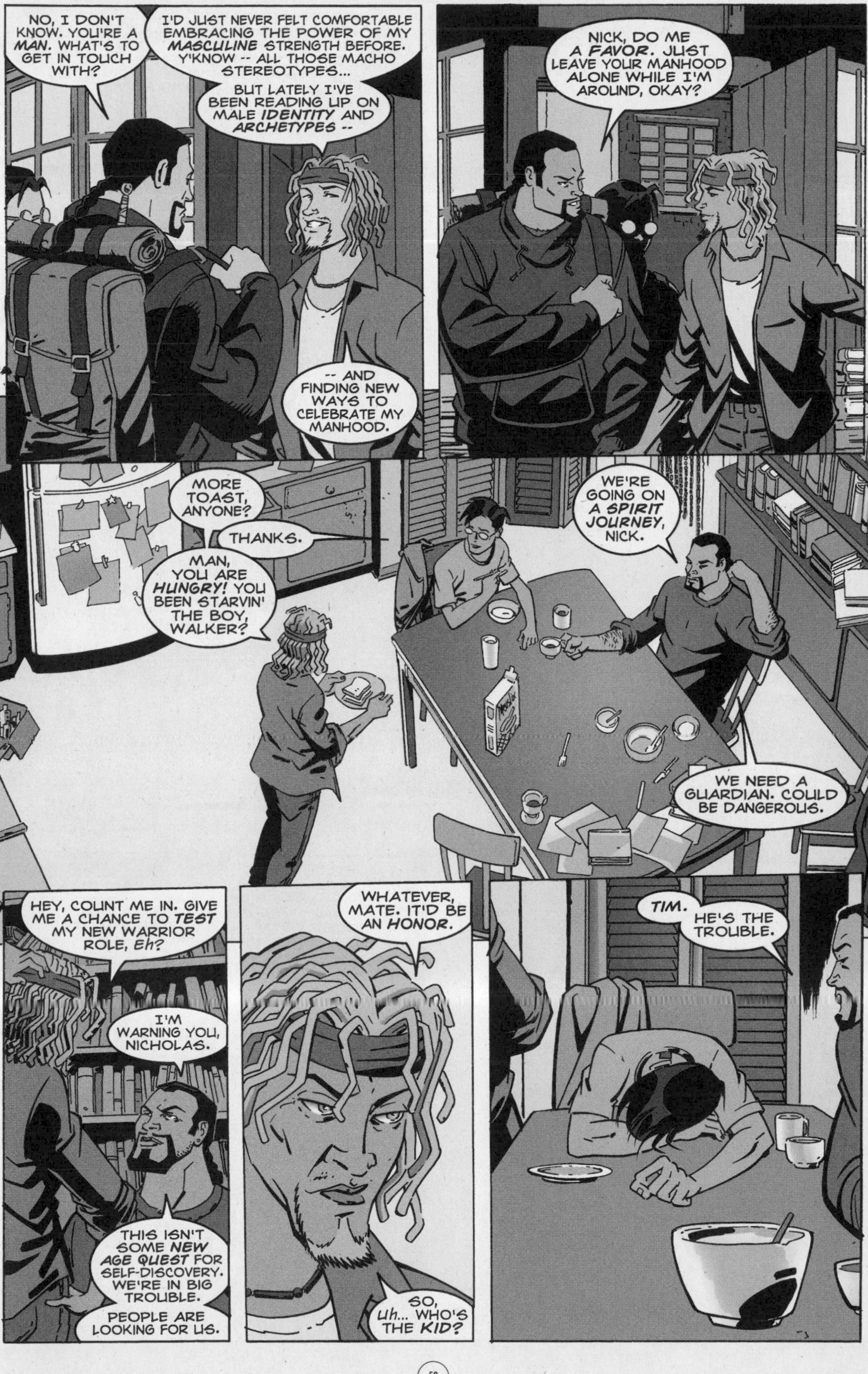
NO, I DON'T KNOW. YOU'RE A MAN. WHAT'S TO GET IN TOUCH WITH?
I'D JUST NEVER FELT COMFORTABLE EMBRACING THE POWER OF MY MASCULINE STRENGTH BEFORE. Y'KNOW -- ALL THOSE MACHO STEREOTYPES...
BUT LATELY I'VE BEEN READING UP ON MALE IDENTITY AND ARCHETYPES --
-- AND FINDING NEW WAYS TO CELEBRATE MY MANHOOD.
NICK, DO ME A FAVOR. JUST LEAVE YOUR MANHOOD ALONE WHILE I'M AROUND, OKAY?
MORE TOAST, ANYONE?
THANKS.
MAN, YOU ARE HUNGRY! YOU BEEN STARVIN' THE BOY, WALKER?
WE'RE GOING ON A SPIRIT JOURNEY, NICK.
WE NEED A GUARDIAN. COULD BE DANGEROUS.
HEY, COUNT ME IN. GIVE ME A CHANCE TO TEST MY NEW WARRIOR ROLE, Eh?
I'M WARNING YOU, NICHOLAS.
THIS ISN'T SOME NEW AGE QUEST FOR SELF-DISCOVERY. WE'RE IN BIG TROUBLE.
PEOPLE ARE LOOKING FOR US.
WHATEVER, MATE. IT'D BE AN HONOR.
SO, Uh... WHO'S THE KID?
TIM.
HE'S THE TROUBLE.

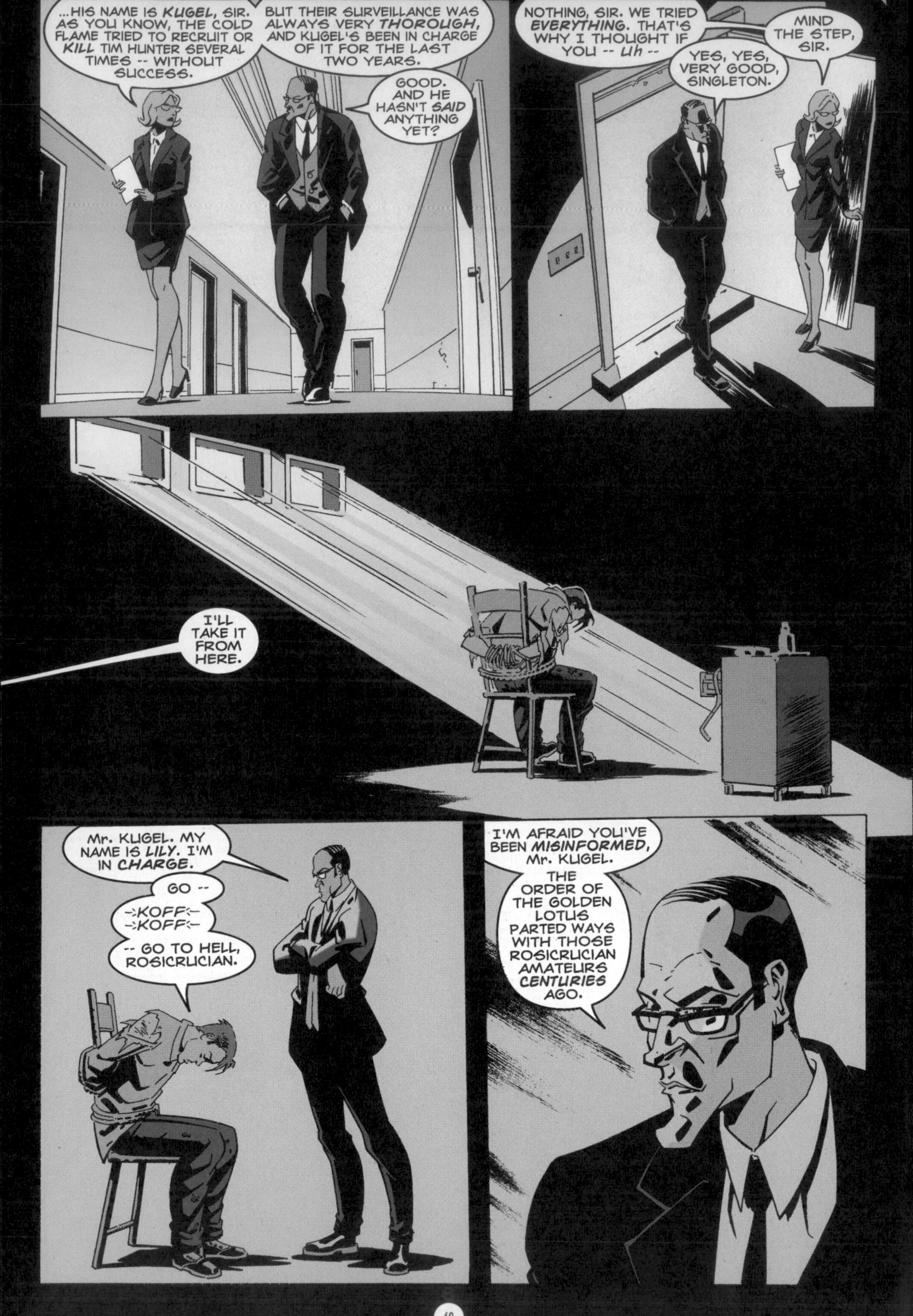
...HIS NAME IS KUGEL, SIR. AS YOU KNOW, THE COLD FLAME TRIED TO RECRUIT OR KILL TIM HUNTER SEVERAL TIMES -- WITHOUT SUCCESS.
BUT THEIR SURVEILLANCE WAS ALWAYS VERY THOROUGH, AND KUGEL'S BEEN IN CHARGE OF IT FOR THE LAST TWO YEARS.
GOOD. AND HE HASN'T SAID ANYTHING YET?
NOTHING, SIR. WE TRIED EVERYTHING. THAT'S WHY I THOUGHT IF YOU -- UH --
YES, YES, VERY GOOD, SINGLETON.
MIND THE STEP, SIR.
I'LL TAKE IT FROM HERE.
Mr. KUGEL. MY NAME IS LILY. I'M IN CHARGE.
GO --
KOFF
KOFF
-- GO TO HELL, ROSICRUCIAN.
I'M AFRAID YOU'VE BEEN MISINFORMED, Mr. KUGEL.
THE ORDER OF THE GOLDEN LOTUS PARTED WAYS WITH THOSE ROSICRUCIAN AMATEURS CENTURIES AGO.

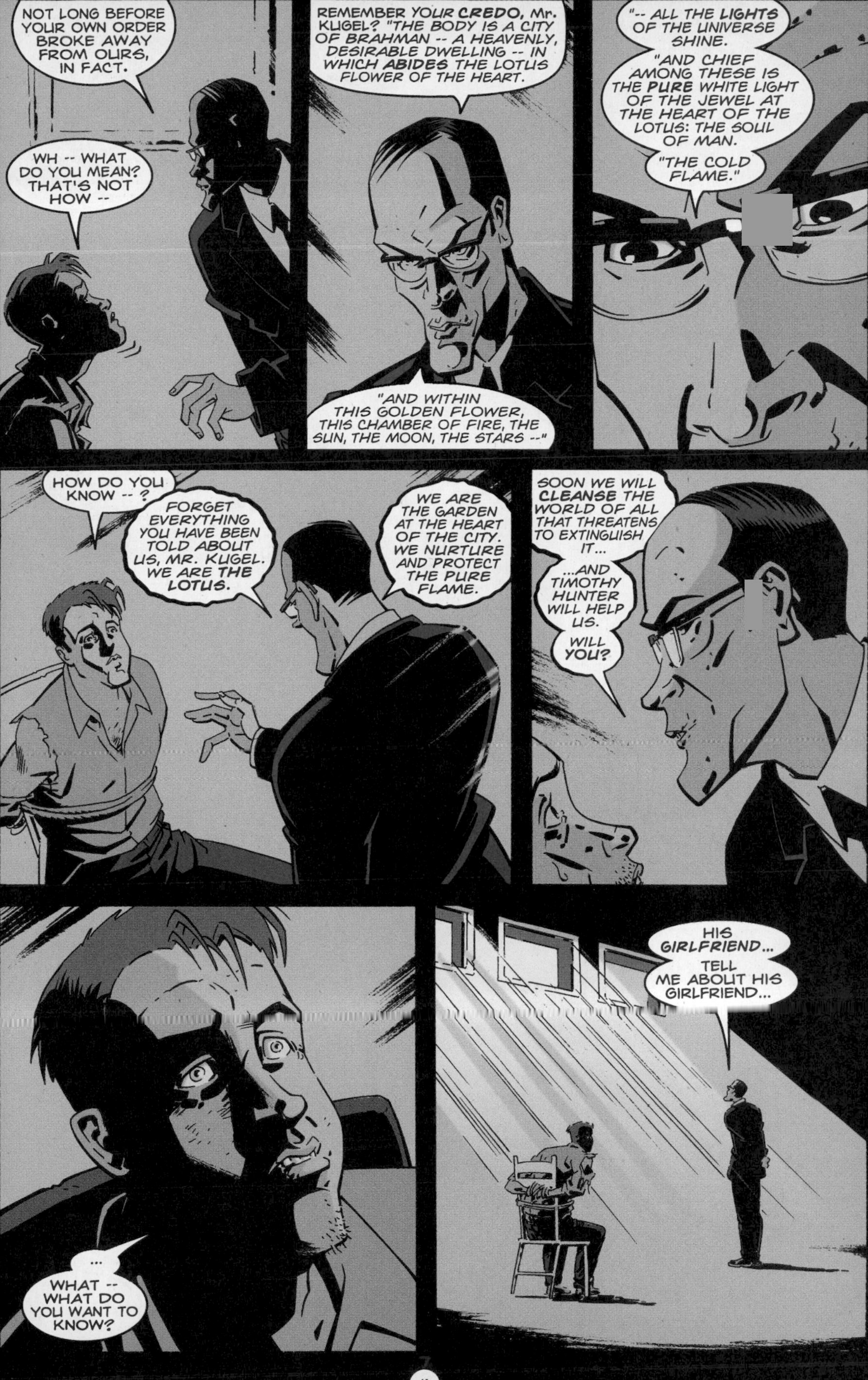
NOT LONG BEFORE YOUR OWN ORDER BROKE AWAY FROM OURS, IN FACT.
WH -- WHAT DO YOU MEAN? THAT'S NOT HOW --
REMEMBER YOUR CREDO, Mr. KUGEL? "THE BODY IS A CITY OF BRAHMAN -- A HEAVENLY, DESIRABLE DWELLING -- IN WHICH ABIDES THE LOTUS FLOWER OF THE HEART.
"AND WITHIN THIS GOLDEN FLOWER, THIS CHAMBER OF FIRE, THE SUN, THE MOON, THE STARS --"
"-- ALL THE LIGHTS OF THE UNIVERSE SHINE.
"AND CHIEF AMONG THESE IS THE PURE WHITE LIGHT OF THE JEWEL AT THE HEART OF THE LOTUS: THE SOUL OF MAN.
"THE COLD FLAME."
HOW DO YOU KNOW -- ?
FORGET EVERYTHING YOU HAVE BEEN TOLD ABOUT US, MR. KUGEL. WE ARE THE LOTUS.
WE ARE THE GARDEN AT THE HEART OF THE CITY. WE NURTURE AND PROTECT THE PURE FLAME.
SOON WE WILL CLEANSE THE WORLD OF ALL THAT THREATENS TO EXTINGUISH IT...
...AND TIMOTHY HUNTER WILL HELP US.
WILL YOU?
...
WHAT -- WHAT DO YOU WANT TO KNOW?
HIS GIRLFRIEND...
TELL ME ABOUT HIS GIRLFRIEND...

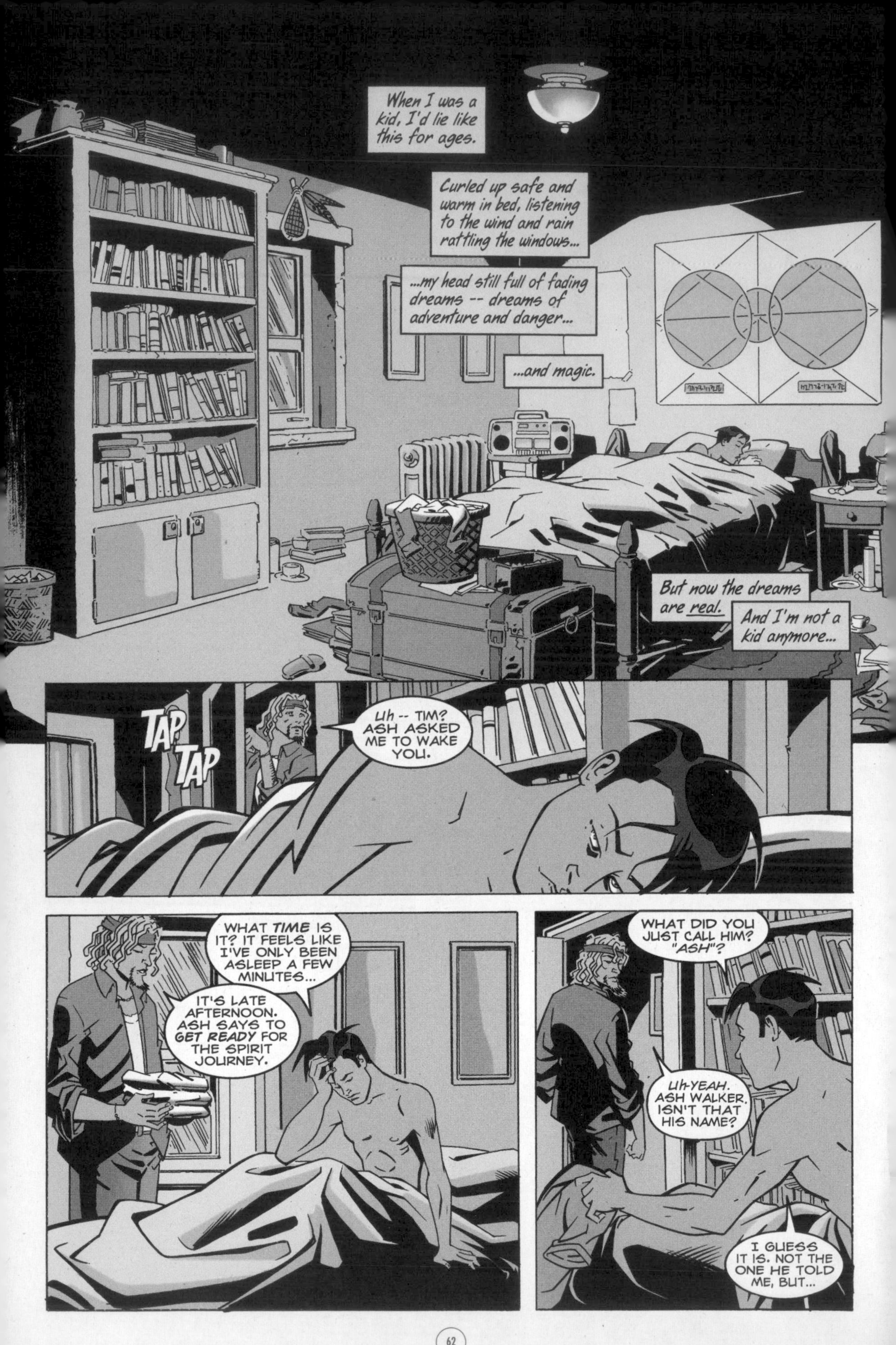

When I was a kid, I'd lie like this for ages.
Curled up safe and warm in bed, listening to the wind and rain rattling the windows...
...my head still full of fading dreams -- dreams of adventure and danger...
...and magic.
But now the dreams are real.
And I'm not a kid anymore...
TAP TAP
Uh -- TIM? ASH ASKED ME TO WAKE YOU.
WHAT TIME IS IT? IT FEELS LIKE I'VE ONLY BEEN ASLEEP A FEW MINUTES...
IT'S LATE AFTERNOON. ASH SAYS TO GET READY FOR THE SPIRIT JOURNEY.
WHAT DID YOU JUST CALL HIM? "ASH"?
Uh-YEAH. ASH WALKER. ISN'T THAT HIS NAME?
I GUESS IT IS. NOT THE ONE HE TOLD ME, BUT...

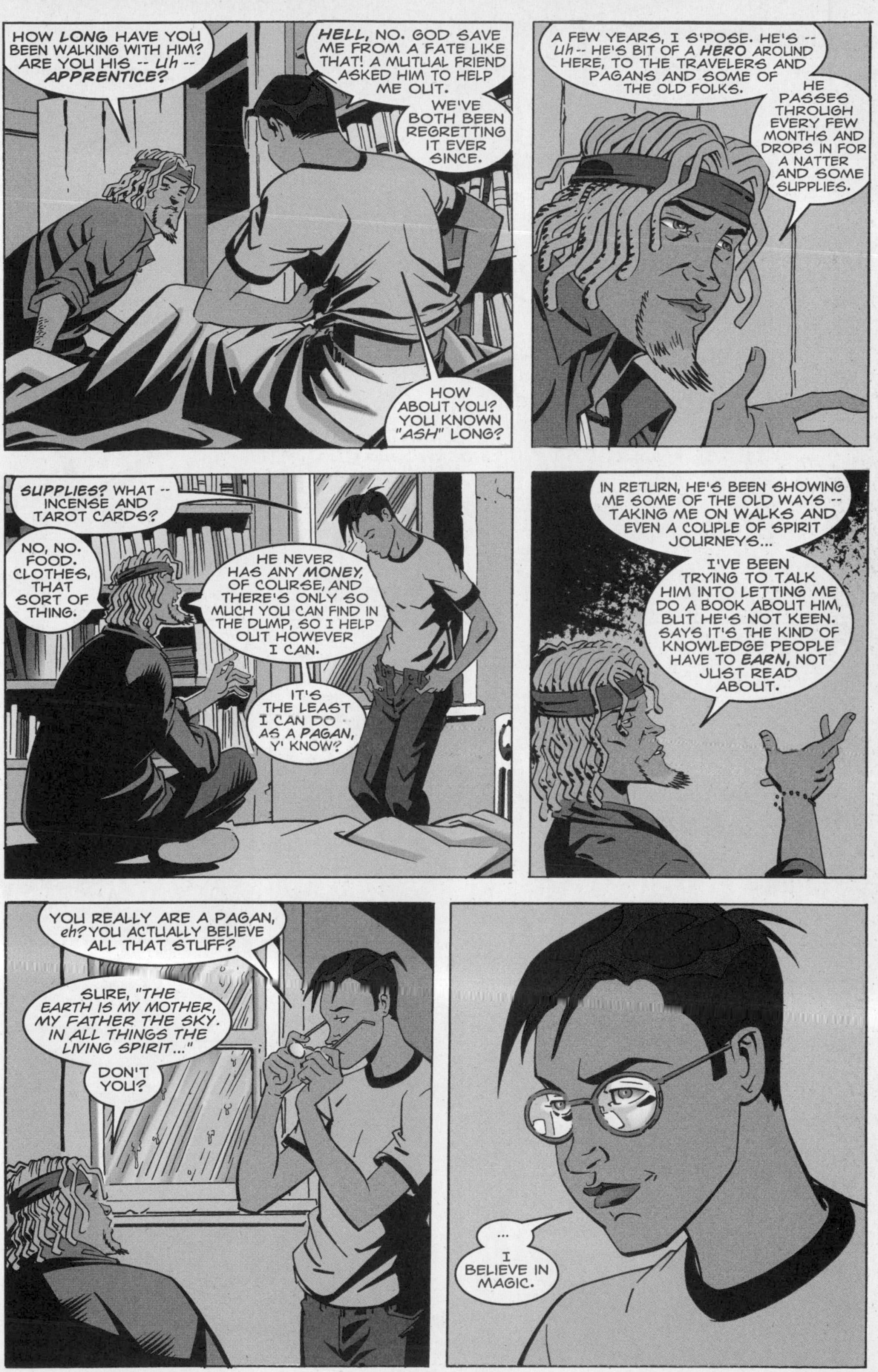
HOW LONG HAVE YOU BEEN WALKING WITH HIM? ARE YOU HIS -- Uh -- APPRENTICE?
HELL, NO. GOD SAVE ME FROM A FATE LIKE THAT! A MUTUAL FRIEND ASKED HIM TO HELP ME OUT.
WE'VE BOTH BEEN REGRETTING IT EVER SINCE.
HOW ABOUT YOU? YOU KNOWN "ASH" LONG?
A FEW YEARS, I S'POSE. HE'S -- Uh -- HE'S BIT OF A HERO AROUND HERE, TO THE TRAVELERS AND PAGANS AND SOME OF THE OLD FOLKS.
HE PASSES THROUGH EVERY FEW MONTHS AND DROPS IN FOR A NATTER AND SOME SUPPLIES.
SUPPLIES? WHAT -- INCENSE AND TAROT CARDS?
NO, NO. FOOD. CLOTHES, THAT SORT OF THING.
HE NEVER HAS ANY MONEY, OF COURSE, AND THERE'S ONLY SO MUCH YOU CAN FIND IN THE DUMP, SO I HELP OUT HOWEVER I CAN.
IT'S THE LEAST I CAN DO AS A PAGAN, Y' KNOW?
IN RETURN, HE'S BEEN SHOWING ME SOME OF THE OLD WAYS -- TAKING ME ON WALKS AND EVEN A COUPLE OF SPIRIT JOURNEYS...
I'VE BEEN TRYING TO TALK HIM INTO LETTING ME DO A BOOK ABOUT HIM, BUT HE'S NOT KEEN. SAYS IT'S THE KIND OF KNOWLEDGE PEOPLE HAVE TO EARN, NOT JUST READ ABOUT.
YOU REALLY ARE A PAGAN, eh? YOU ACTUALLY BELIEVE ALL THAT STUFF?
SURE, "THE EARTH IS MY MOTHER, MY FATHER THE SKY. IN ALL THINGS THE LIVING SPIRIT..."
DON'T YOU?
... I BELIEVE IN MAGIC.

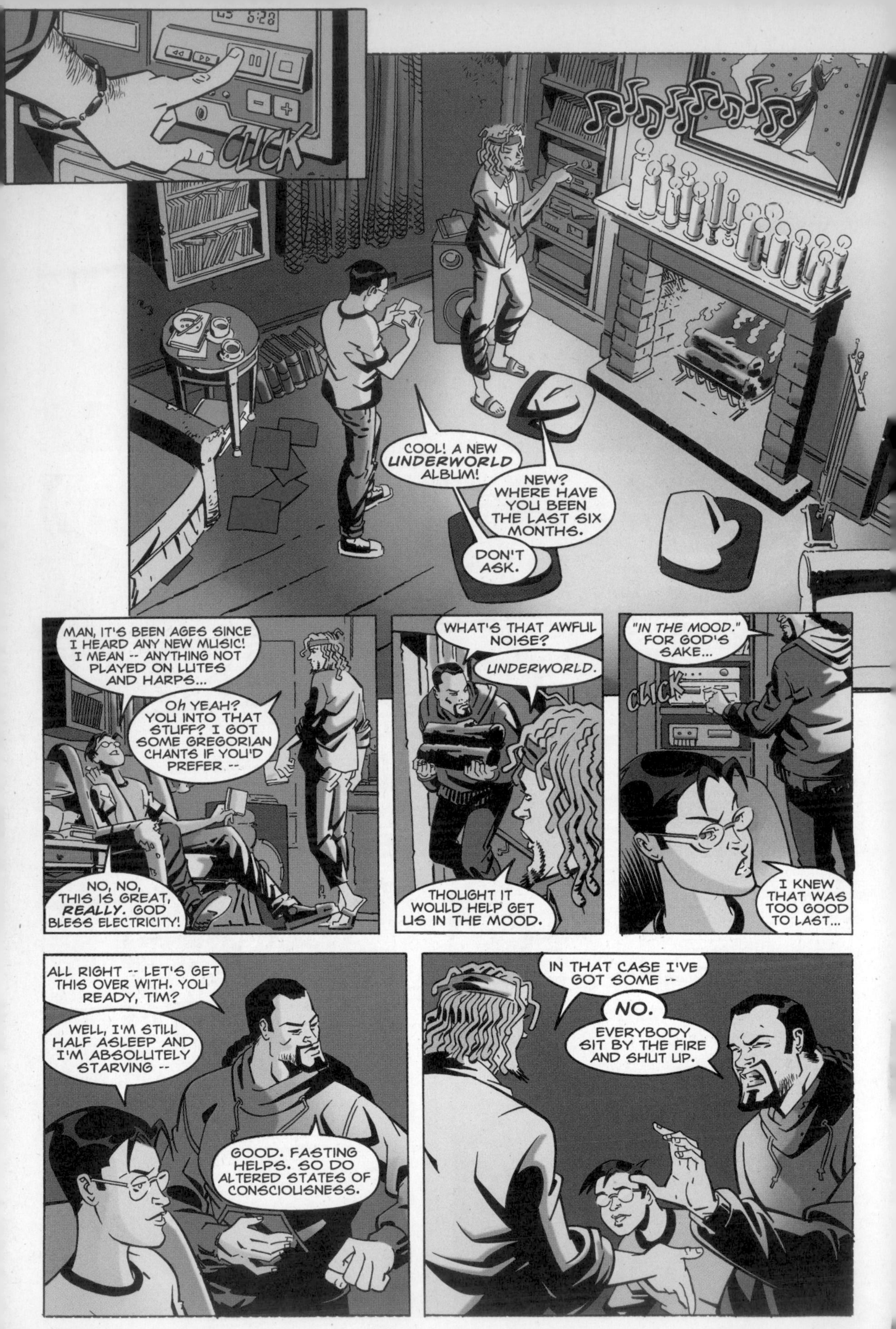

CLICK
COOL! A NEW UNDERWORLD ALBUM!
NEW? WHERE HAVE YOU BEEN THE LAST SIX MONTHS.
DON'T ASK.
MAN, IT'S BEEN AGES SINCE I HEARD ANY NEW MUSIC! I MEAN -- ANYTHING NOT PLAYED ON LUTES AND HARPS...
Oh YEAH? YOU INTO THAT STUFF? I GOT SOME GREGORIAN CHANTS IF YOU'D PREFER --
NO, NO, THIS IS GREAT, REALLY. GOD BLESS ELECTRICITY!
WHAT'S THAT AWFUL NOISE?
UNDERWORLD.
THOUGHT IT WOULD HELP GET US IN THE MOOD.
"IN THE MOOD." FOR GOD'S SAKE...
CLICK
I KNEW THAT WAS TOO GOOD TO LAST...
ALL RIGHT -- LET'S GET THIS OVER WITH. YOU READY, TIM?
WELL, I'M STILL HALF ASLEEP AND I'M ABSOLUTELY STARVING --
GOOD. FASTING HELPS. SO DO ALTERED STATES OF CONSCIOUSNESS.
IN THAT CASE I'VE GOT SOME --
NO.
EVERYBODY SIT BY THE FIRE AND SHUT UP.

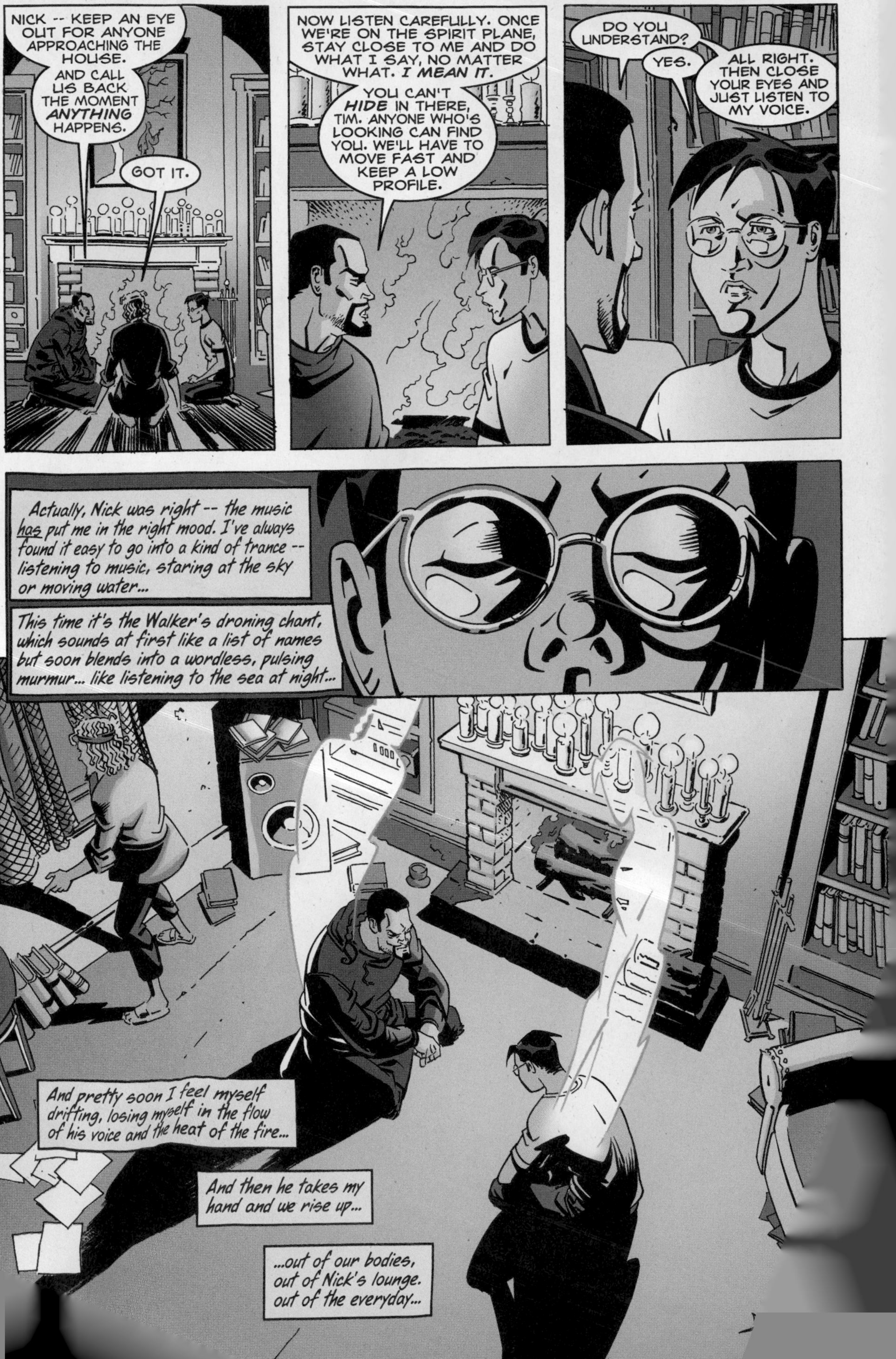
NICK -- KEEP AN EYE OUT FOR ANYONE APPROACHING THE HOUSE.
AND CALL US BACK THE MOMENT **ANYTHING** HAPPENS.
GOT IT.
NOW LISTEN CAREFULLY. ONCE WE'RE ON THE SPIRIT PLANE, STAY CLOSE TO ME AND DO WHAT I SAY, NO MATTER WHAT. ***I MEAN IT.***
YOU CAN'T **HIDE** IN THERE, TIM. ANYONE WHO'S LOOKING CAN FIND YOU. WE'LL HAVE TO MOVE FAST AND KEEP A LOW PROFILE.
DO YOU UNDERSTAND?
YES.
ALL RIGHT. THEN CLOSE YOUR EYES AND JUST LISTEN TO MY VOICE.
Actually, Nick was right -- the music has put me in the right mood. I've always found it easy to go into a kind of trance -- listening to music, staring at the sky or moving water...
This time it's the Walker's droning chant, which sounds at first like a list of names but soon blends into a wordless, pulsing murmur... like listening to the sea at night...
And pretty soon I feel myself drifting, losing myself in the flow of his voice and the heat of the fire...
And then he takes my hand and we rise up...
...out of our bodies, out of Nick's lounge. out of the everyday...

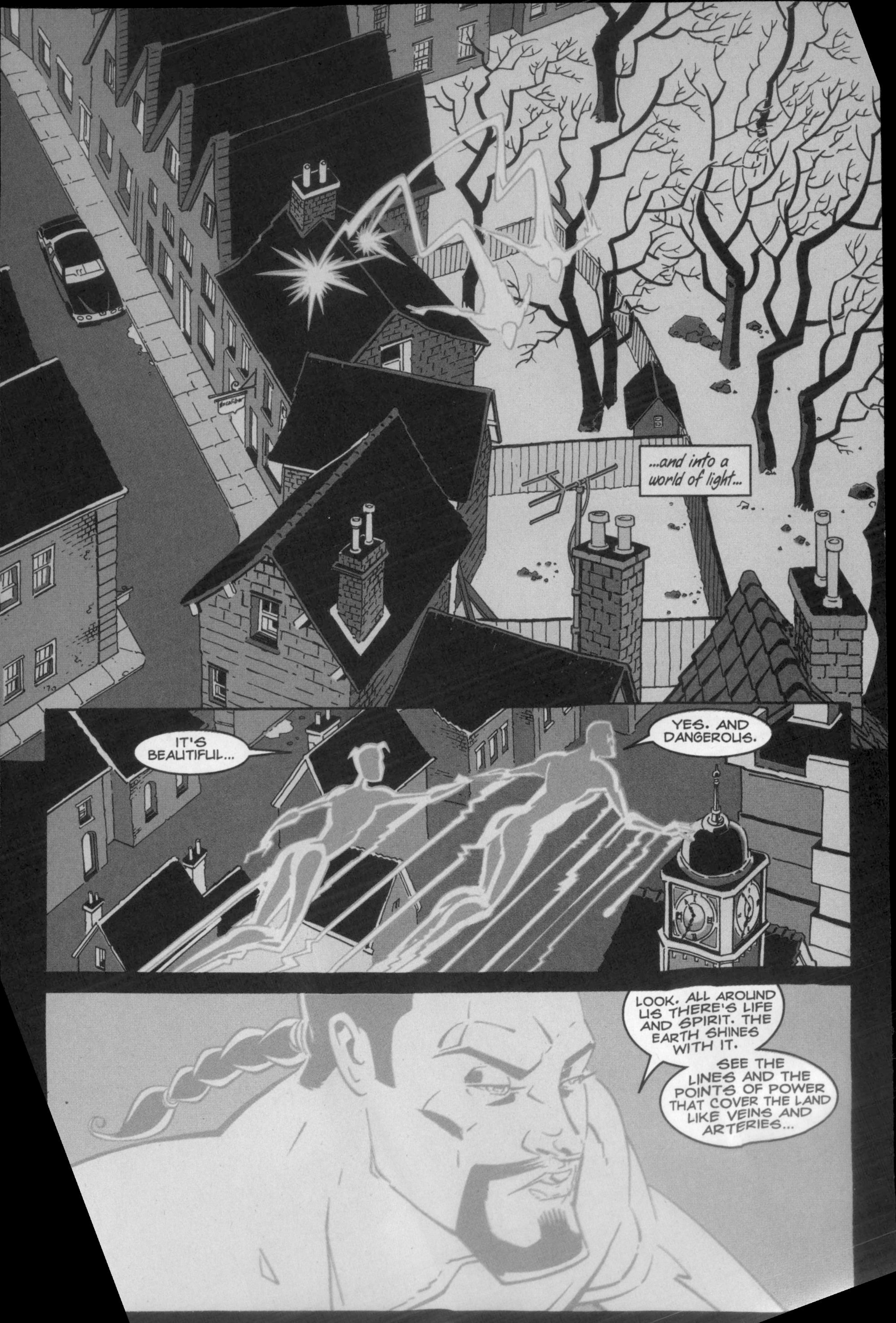

...and into a world of light...
IT'S BEAUTIFUL...
YES. AND DANGEROUS.
LOOK. ALL AROUND US THERE'S LIFE AND SPIRIT. THE EARTH SHINES WITH IT.
SEE THE LINES AND THE POINTS OF POWER THAT COVER THE LAND LIKE VEINS AND ARTERIES...

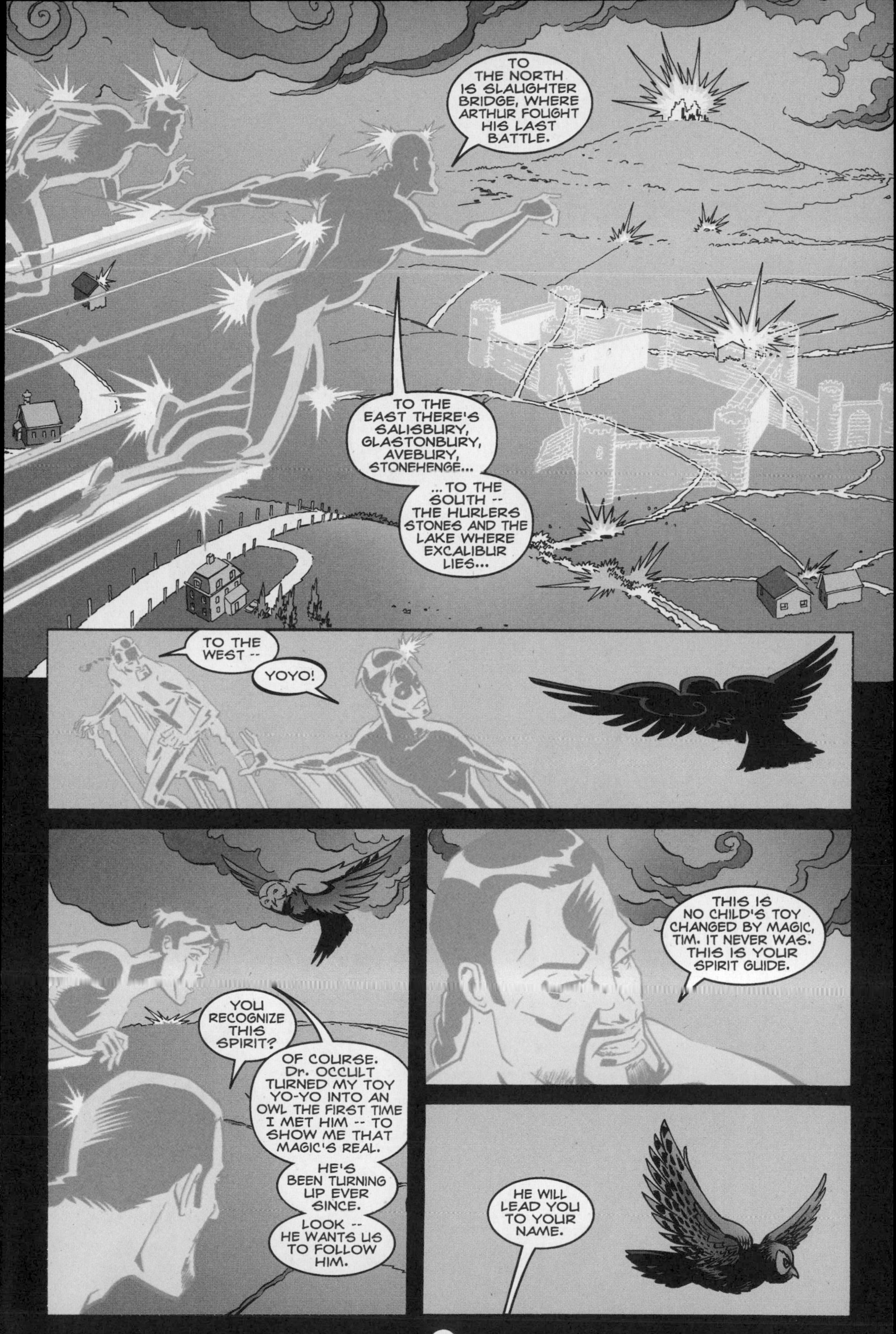
TO THE NORTH IS SLAUGHTER BRIDGE, WHERE ARTHUR FOUGHT HIS LAST BATTLE.
TO THE EAST THERE'S SALISBURY, GLASTONBURY, AVEBURY, STONEHENGE...
...TO THE SOUTH -- THE HURLERS STONES AND THE LAKE WHERE EXCALIBUR LIES...
TO THE WEST --
YOYO!
YOU RECOGNIZE THIS SPIRIT?
OF COURSE. Dr. OCCULT TURNED MY TOY YO-YO INTO AN OWL THE FIRST TIME I MET HIM -- TO SHOW ME THAT MAGIC'S REAL.
HE'S BEEN TURNING UP EVER SINCE.
LOOK -- HE WANTS US TO FOLLOW HIM.
THIS IS NO CHILD'S TOY CHANGED BY MAGIC, TIM. IT NEVER WAS. THIS IS YOUR SPIRIT GUIDE.
HE WILL LEAD YOU TO YOUR NAME.

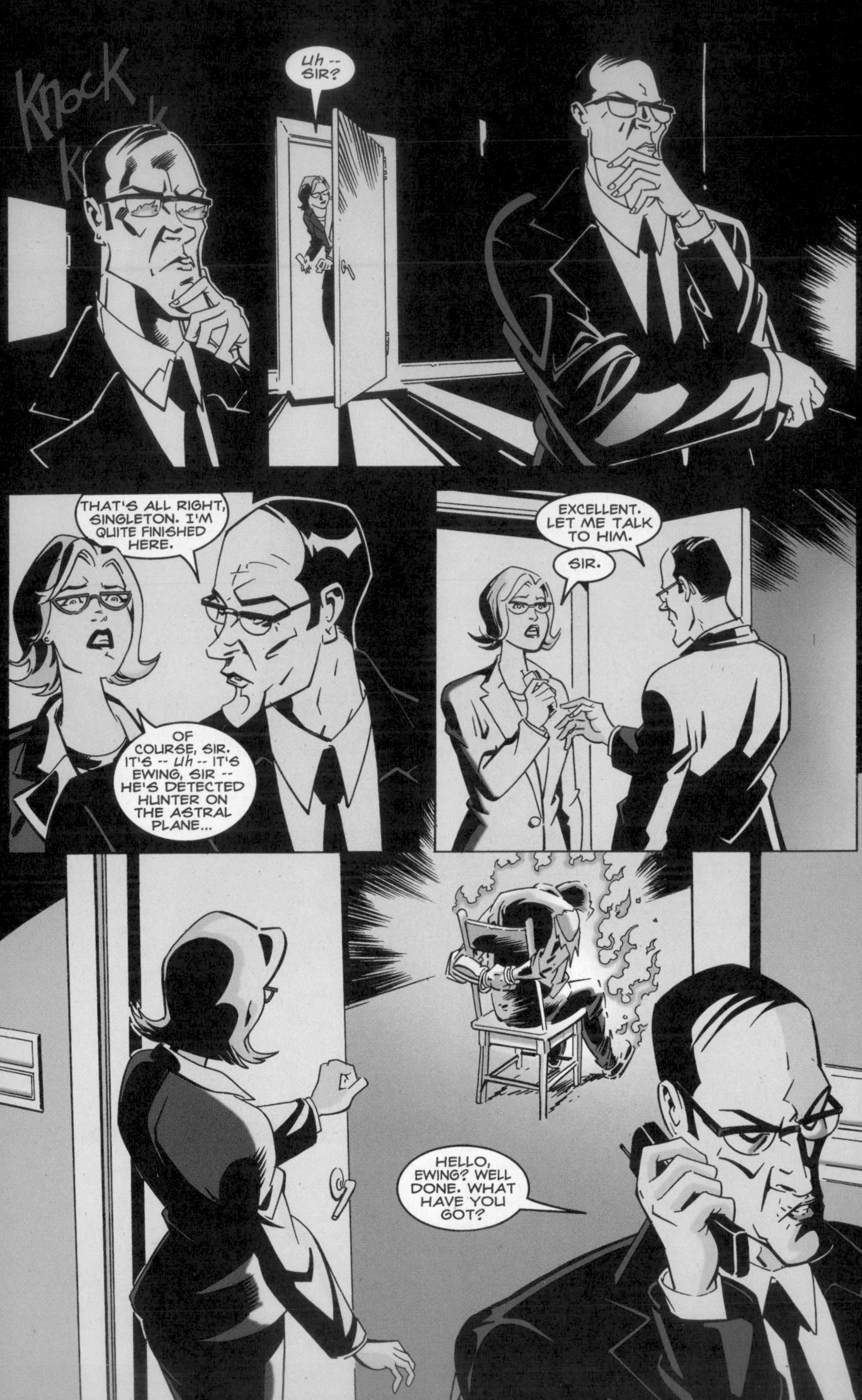
KNOCK KNOCK
UH -- SIR?
THAT'S ALL RIGHT, SINGLETON. I'M QUITE FINISHED HERE.
OF COURSE, SIR. IT'S -- UH -- IT'S EWING, SIR -- HE'S DETECTED HUNTER ON THE ASTRAL PLANE...
SIR.
EXCELLENT. LET ME TALK TO HIM.
HELLO, EWING? WELL DONE. WHAT HAVE YOU GOT?

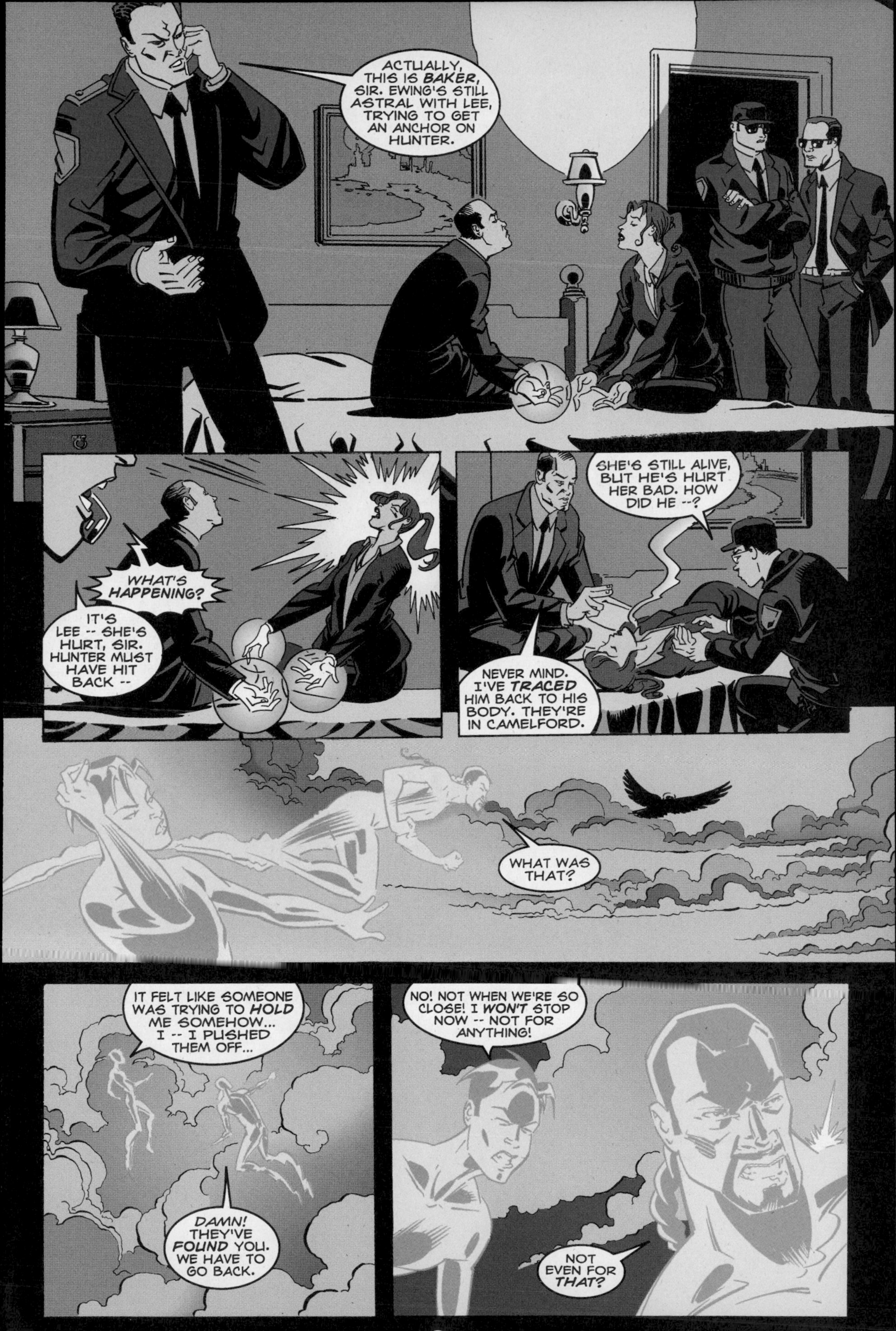
ACTUALLY, THIS IS BAKER, SIR. EWING'S STILL ASTRAL WITH LEE, TRYING TO GET AN ANCHOR ON HUNTER.
WHAT'S HAPPENING?
IT'S LEE -- SHE'S HURT, SIR. HUNTER MUST HAVE HIT BACK --
SHE'S STILL ALIVE, BUT HE'S HURT HER BAD. HOW DID HE --?
NEVER MIND. I'VE TRACED HIM BACK TO HIS BODY. THEY'RE IN CAMELFORD.
WHAT WAS THAT?
IT FELT LIKE SOMEONE WAS TRYING TO HOLD ME SOMEHOW... I -- I PUSHED THEM OFF...
DAMN! THEY'VE FOUND YOU. WE HAVE TO GO BACK.
NO! NOT WHEN WE'RE SO CLOSE! I WON'T STOP NOW -- NOT FOR ANYTHING!
NOT EVEN FOR THAT?

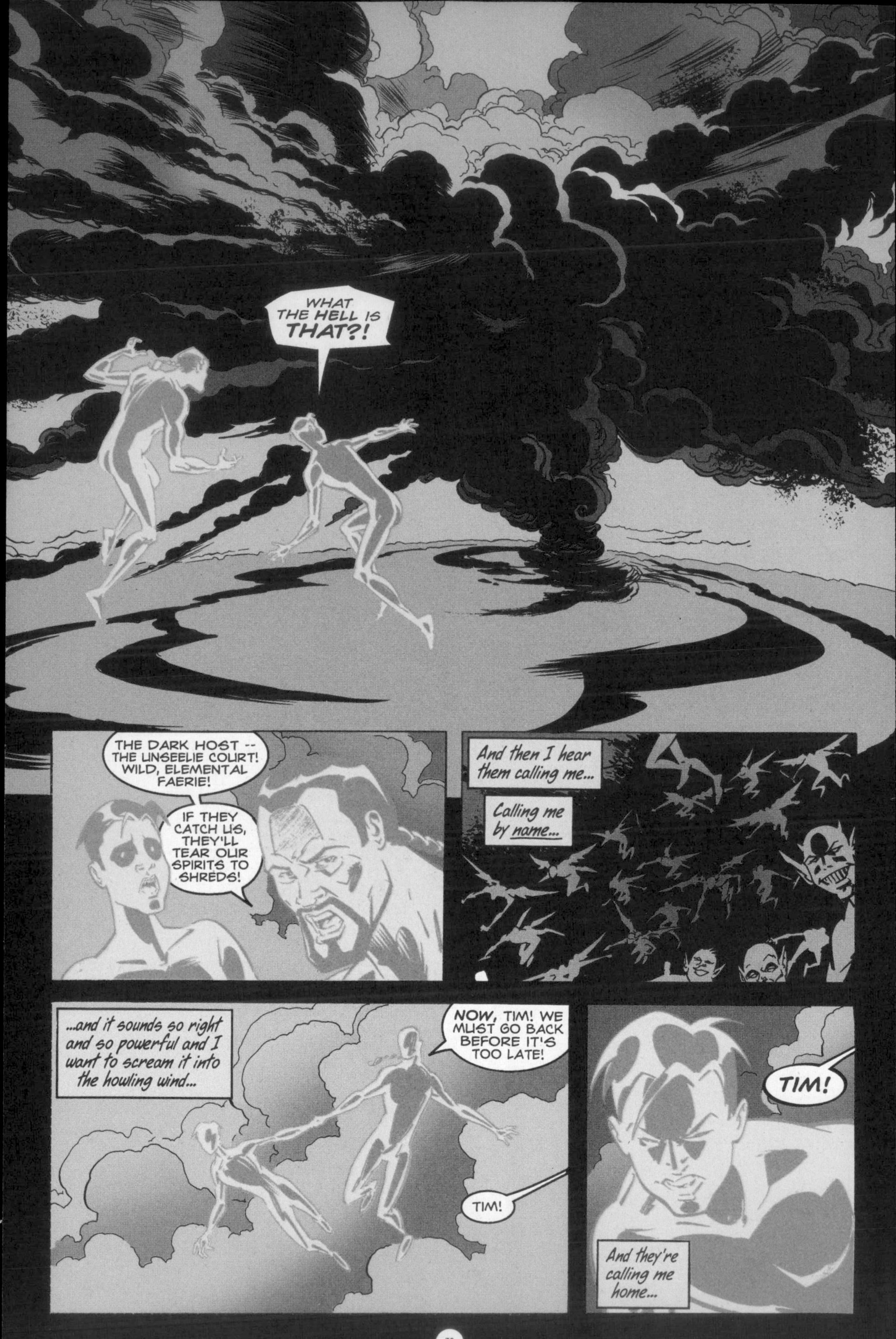
WHAT THE HELL IS THAT?!
THE DARK HOST -- THE UNSEELIE COURT! WILD, ELEMENTAL FAERIE!
IF THEY CATCH US, THEY'LL TEAR OUR SPIRITS TO SHREDS!
And then I hear them calling me...
Calling me by name...
...and it sounds so right and so powerful and I want to scream it into the howling wind...
NOW, TIM! WE MUST GO BACK BEFORE IT'S TOO LATE!
TIM!
TIM!
And they're calling me home...

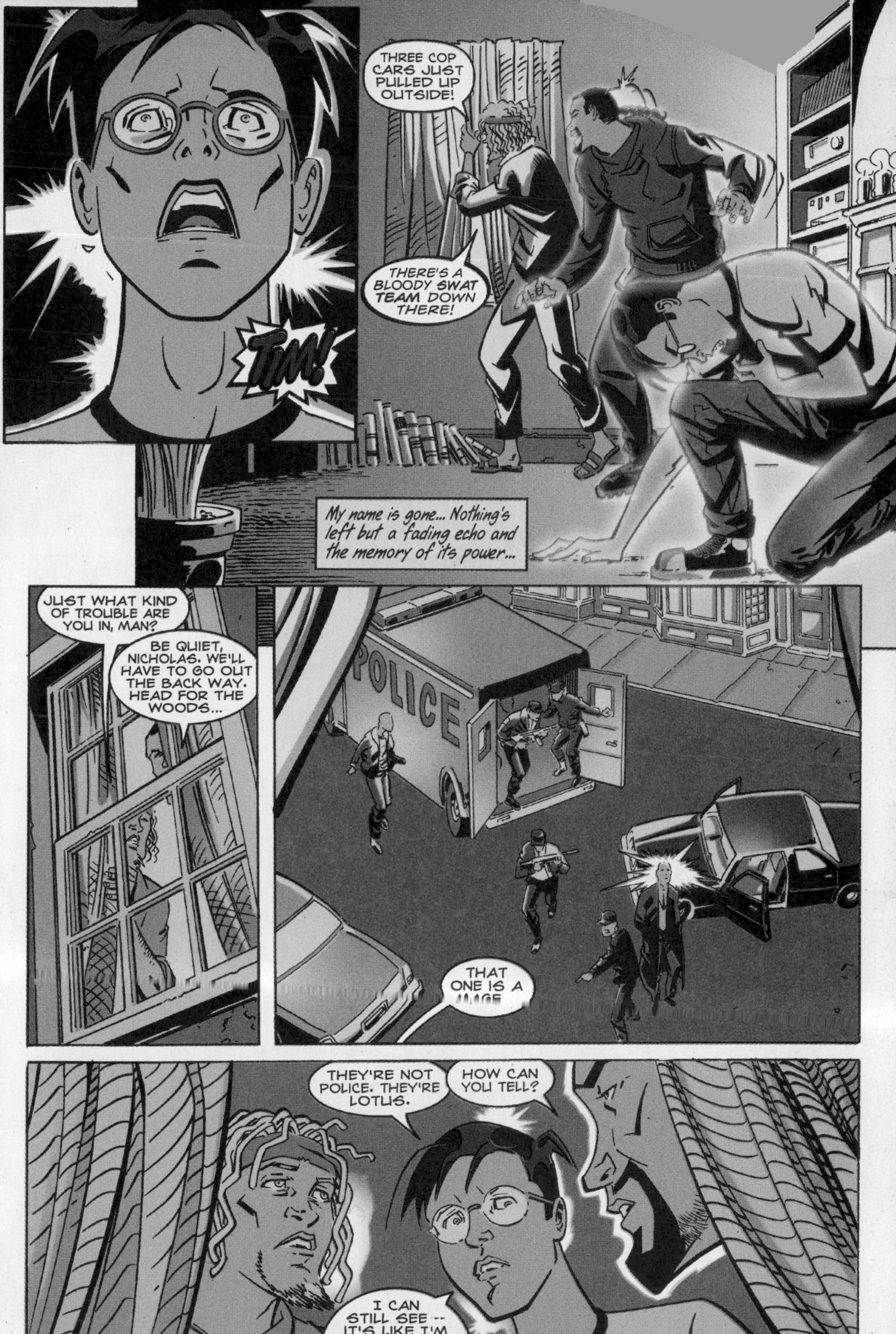
TIM!
THREE COP CARS JUST PULLED UP OUTSIDE!
THERE'S A BLOODY SWAT TEAM DOWN THERE!
My name is gone... Nothing's left but a fading echo and the memory of its power...
JUST WHAT KIND OF TROUBLE ARE YOU IN, MAN?
BE QUIET, NICHOLAS. WE'LL HAVE TO GO OUT THE BACK WAY. HEAD FOR THE WOODS...
POLICE
THAT ONE IS A
THEY'RE NOT POLICE. THEY'RE LOTUS.
HOW CAN YOU TELL?
I CAN STILL SEE -- IT'S LIKE I'M STILL SEEING THE SPIRIT WORLD...

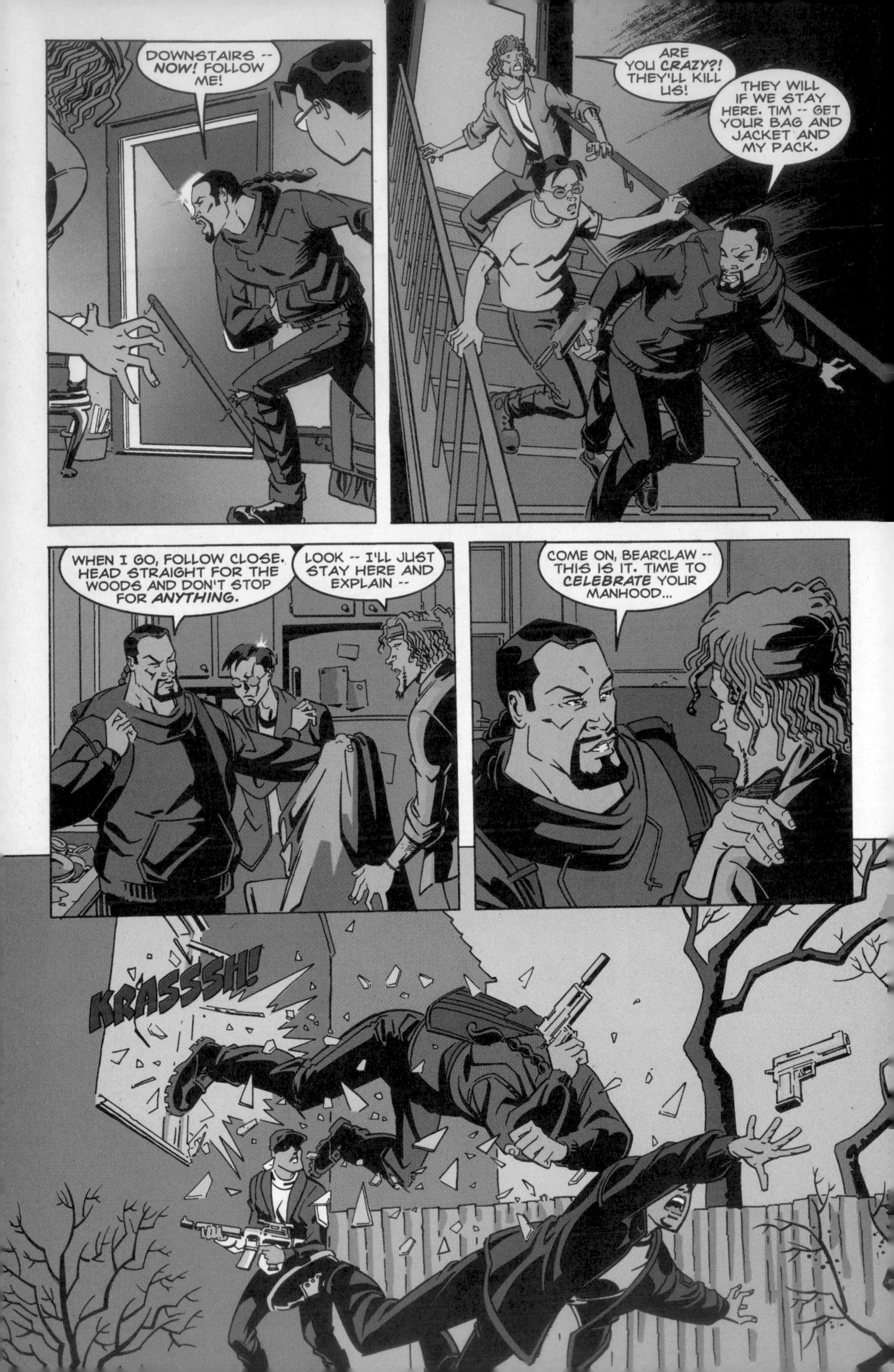
DOWNSTAIRS -- NOW! FOLLOW ME!
ARE YOU CRAZY?! THEY'LL KILL US!
THEY WILL IF WE STAY HERE. TIM -- GET YOUR BAG AND JACKET AND MY PACK.
WHEN I GO, FOLLOW CLOSE. HEAD STRAIGHT FOR THE WOODS AND DON'T STOP FOR ANYTHING.
LOOK -- I'LL JUST STAY HERE AND EXPLAIN --
COME ON, BEARCLAW -- THIS IS IT. TIME TO CELEBRATE YOUR MANHOOD...
KRASSSSH!

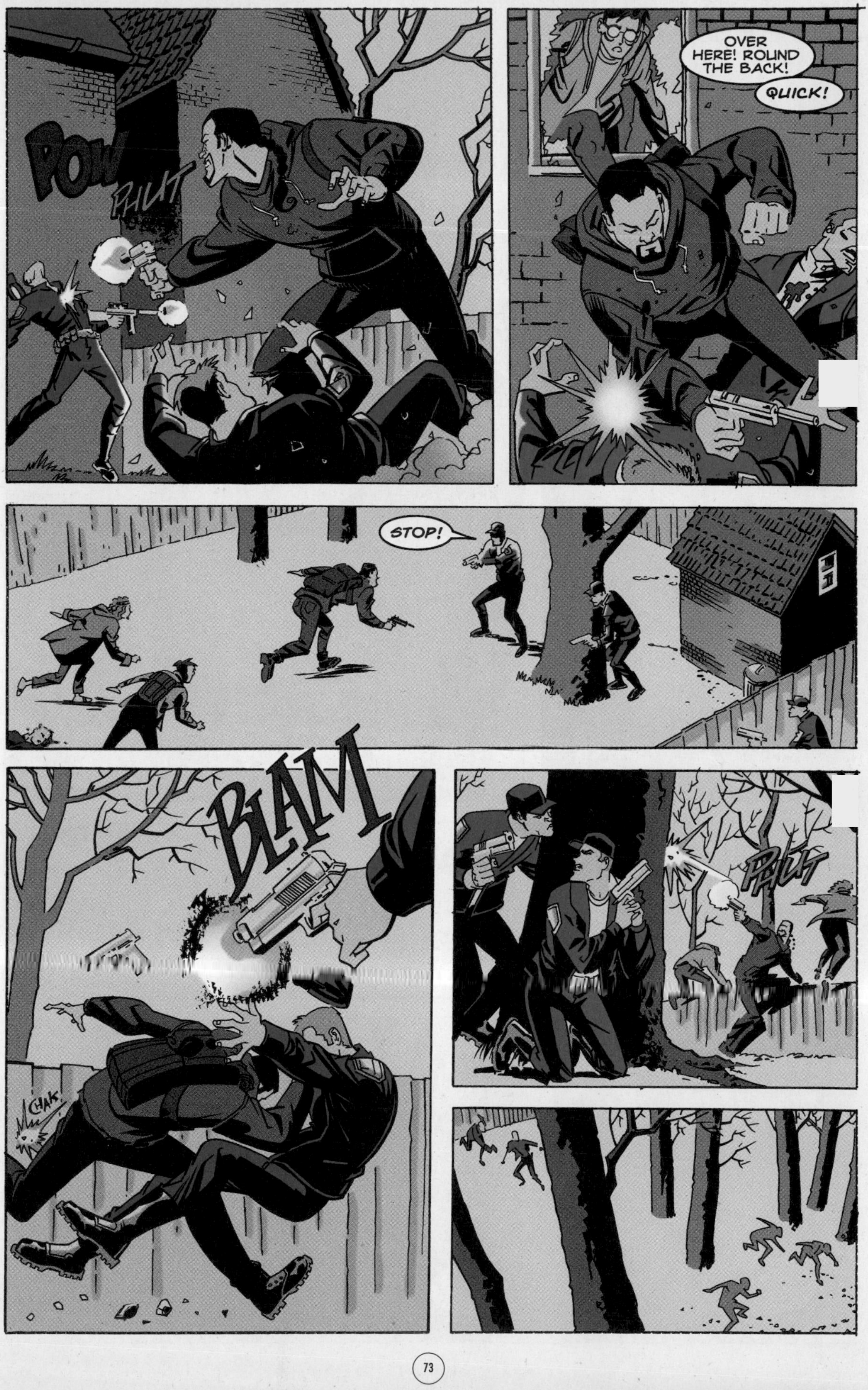
POW
PHUT
OVER HERE! ROUND THE BACK!
QUICK!
STOP!
BLAM
CHAK
PHUT

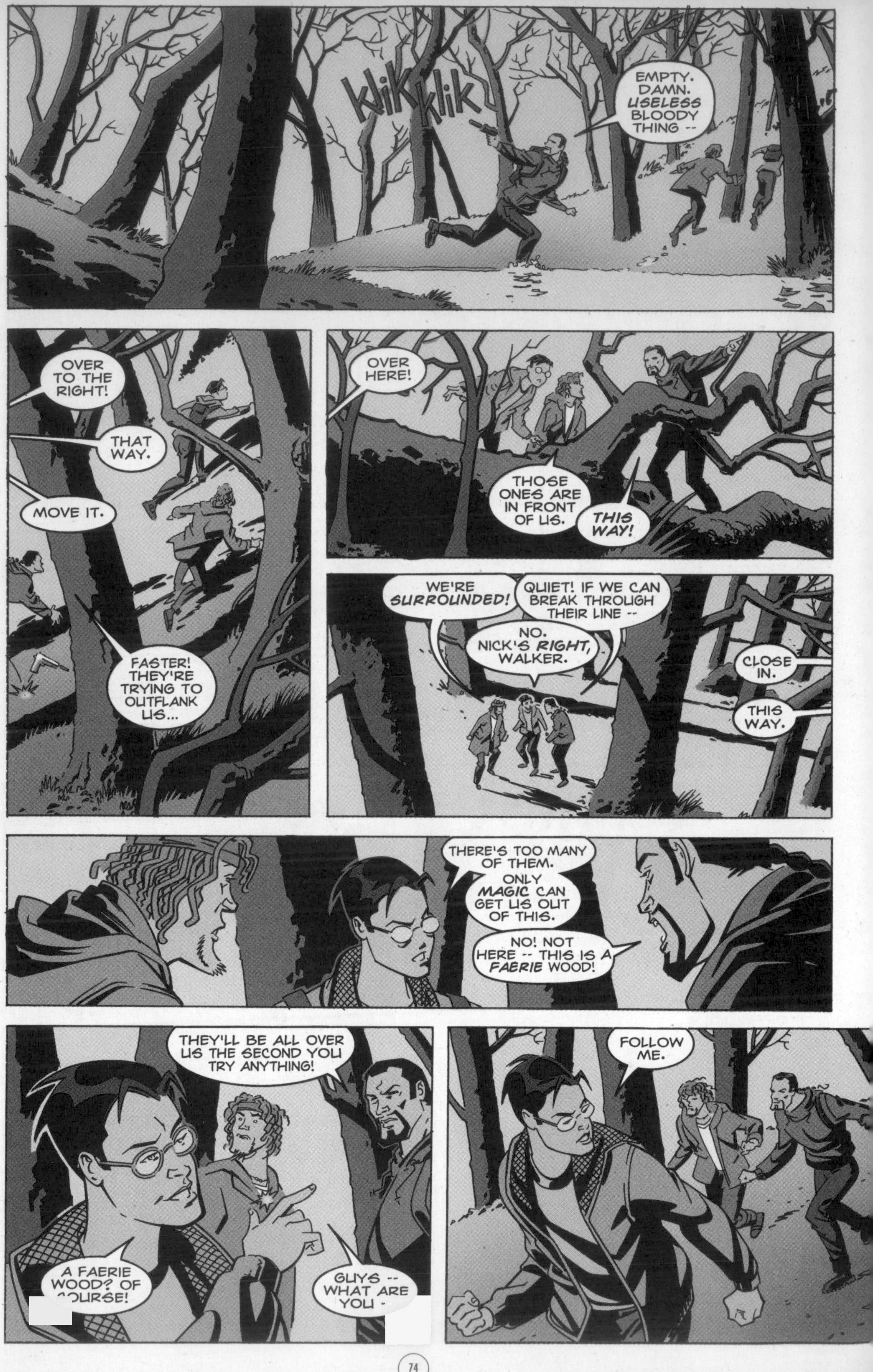
KLIK KLIK
EMPTY. DAMN. USELESS BLOODY THING --
OVER TO THE RIGHT!
THAT WAY.
MOVE IT.
FASTER! THEY'RE TRYING TO OUTFLANK US...
OVER HERE!
THOSE ONES ARE IN FRONT OF US.
THIS WAY!
WE'RE SURROUNDED!
QUIET! IF WE CAN BREAK THROUGH THEIR LINE --
NO. NICK'S RIGHT, WALKER.
CLOSE IN.
THIS WAY.
THERE'S TOO MANY OF THEM. ONLY MAGIC CAN GET US OUT OF THIS.
NO! NOT HERE -- THIS IS A FAERIE WOOD!
THEY'LL BE ALL OVER US THE SECOND YOU TRY ANYTHING!
A FAERIE WOOD? OF COURSE!
GUYS -- WHAT ARE YOU --
FOLLOW ME.

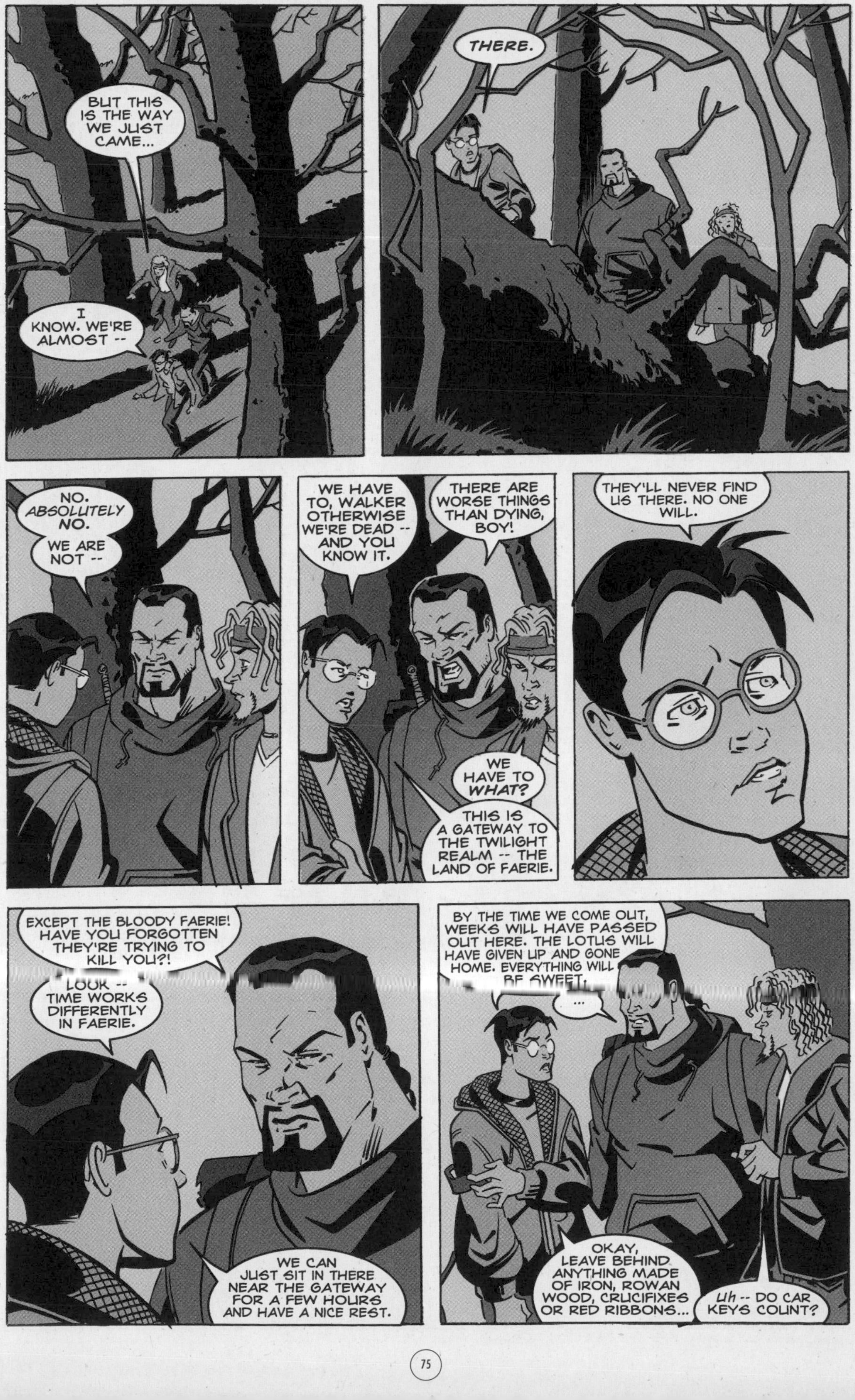
BUT THIS IS THE WAY WE JUST CAME...
I KNOW. WE'RE ALMOST --
THERE.
NO. *ABSOLUTELY* NO.
WE ARE NOT --
WE HAVE TO, WALKER OTHERWISE WE'RE DEAD -- AND YOU KNOW IT.
THERE ARE WORSE THINGS THAN DYING, BOY!
WE HAVE TO *WHAT?*
THIS IS A GATEWAY TO THE TWILIGHT REALM -- THE LAND OF FAERIE.
THEY'LL NEVER FIND US THERE. NO ONE WILL.
EXCEPT THE BLOODY FAERIE! HAVE YOU FORGOTTEN THEY'RE TRYING TO KILL YOU?!
LOOK -- TIME WORKS DIFFERENTLY IN FAERIE.
WE CAN JUST SIT IN THERE NEAR THE GATEWAY FOR A FEW HOURS AND HAVE A NICE REST.
BY THE TIME WE COME OUT, WEEKS WILL HAVE PASSED OUT HERE. THE LOTUS WILL HAVE GIVEN UP AND GONE HOME. EVERYTHING WILL BE SWEET.
...
OKAY, LEAVE BEHIND ANYTHING MADE OF IRON, ROWAN WOOD, CRUCIFIXES OR RED RIBBONS...
UH -- DO CAR KEYS COUNT?

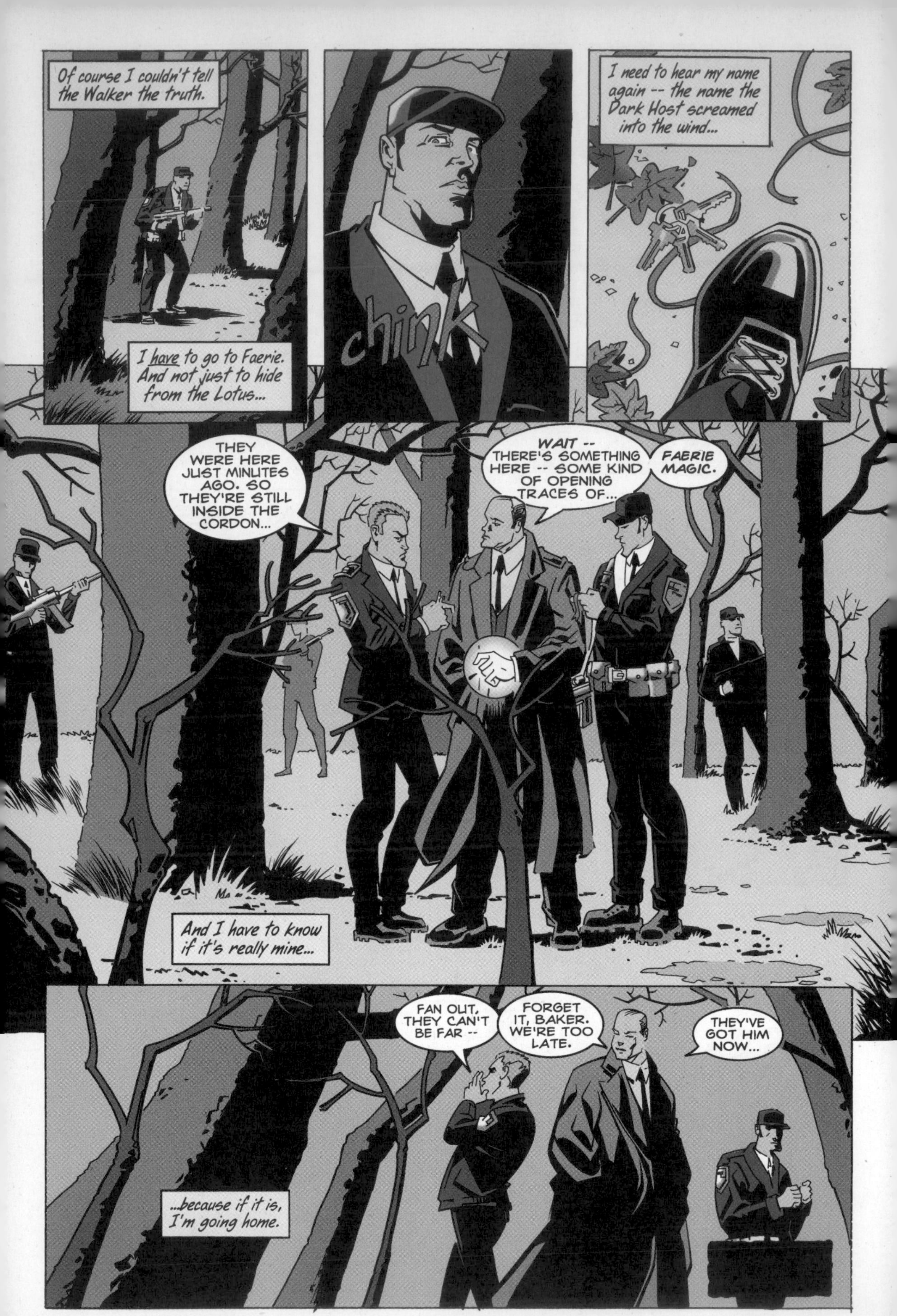
Of course I couldn't tell the Walker the truth.
I have to go to Faerie. And not just to hide from the Lotus...
chink
I need to hear my name again -- the name the Dark Host screamed into the wind...
THEY WERE HERE JUST MINUTES AGO. SO THEY'RE STILL INSIDE THE CORDON...
WAIT -- THERE'S SOMETHING HERE -- SOME KIND OF OPENING TRACES OF...
FAERIE MAGIC.
And I have to know if it's really mine...
FAN OUT, THEY CAN'T BE FAR --
FORGET IT, BAKER. WE'RE TOO LATE.
THEY'VE GOT HIM NOW...
...because if it is, I'm going home.

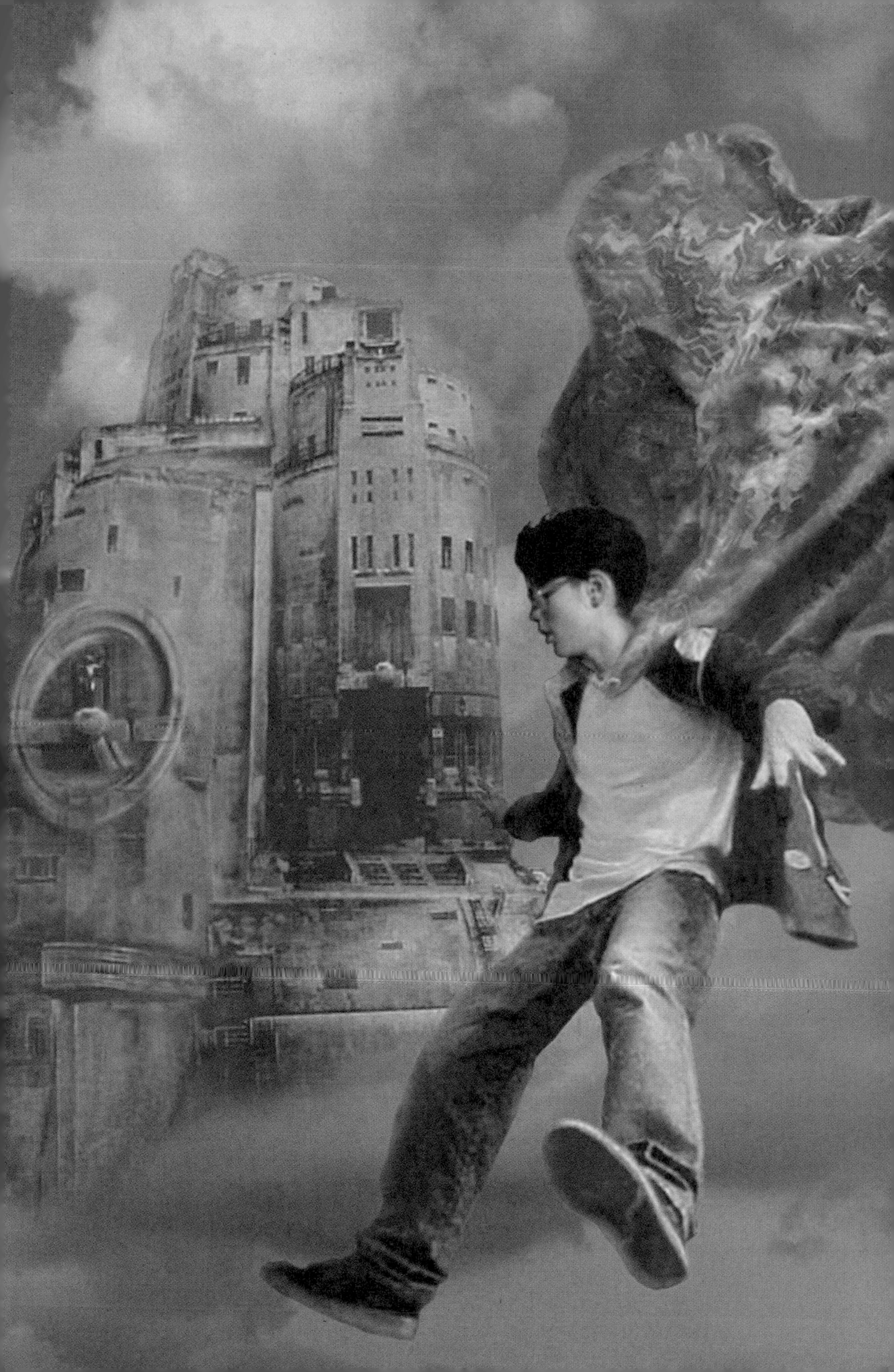

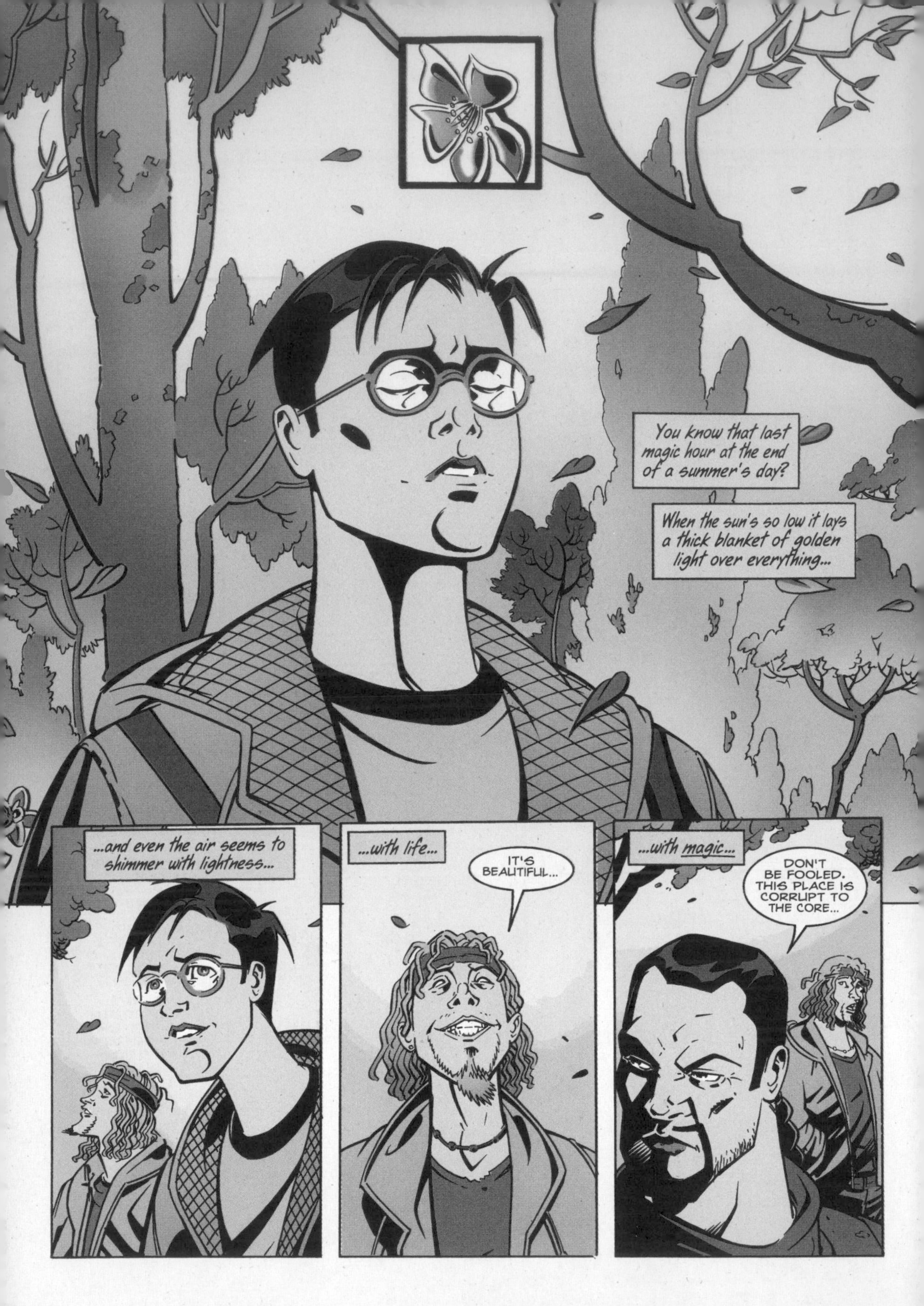

You know that last magic hour at the end of a summer's day?
When the sun's so low it lays a thick blanket of golden light over everything...
...and even the air seems to shimmer with lightness...
...with life...
IT'S BEAUTIFUL...
...with magic...
DON'T BE FOOLED. THIS PLACE IS CORRUPT TO THE CORE...

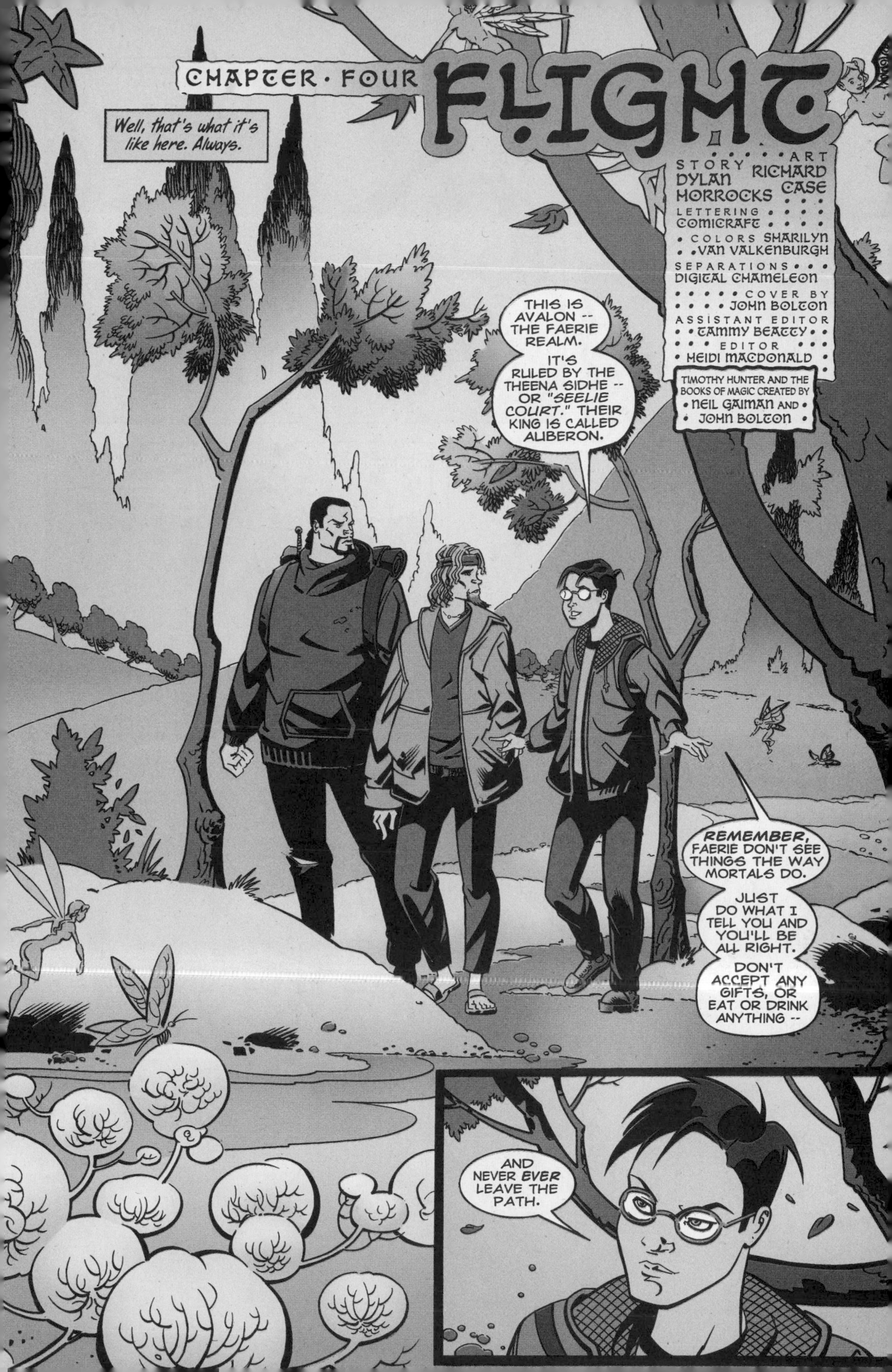
CHAPTER · FOUR FLIGHT
Well, that's what it's like here. Always.
STORY DYLAN HORROCKS ART RICHARD CASE
LETTERING COMICRAFT
COLORS SHARILYN VAN VALKENBURGH
SEPARATIONS DIGITAL CHAMELEON
COVER BY JOHN BOLTON
ASSISTANT EDITOR TAMMY BEATTY
EDITOR HEIDI MACDONALD
TIMOTHY HUNTER AND THE BOOKS OF MAGIC CREATED BY NEIL GAIMAN AND JOHN BOLTON
THIS IS AVALON -- THE FAERIE REALM.
IT'S RULED BY THE THEENA SIDHE -- OR "SEELIE COURT." THEIR KING IS CALLED AUBERON.
REMEMBER, FAERIE DON'T SEE THINGS THE WAY MORTALS DO.
JUST DO WHAT I TELL YOU AND YOU'LL BE ALL RIGHT.
DON'T ACCEPT ANY GIFTS, OR EAT OR DRINK ANYTHING --
AND NEVER EVER LEAVE THE PATH.

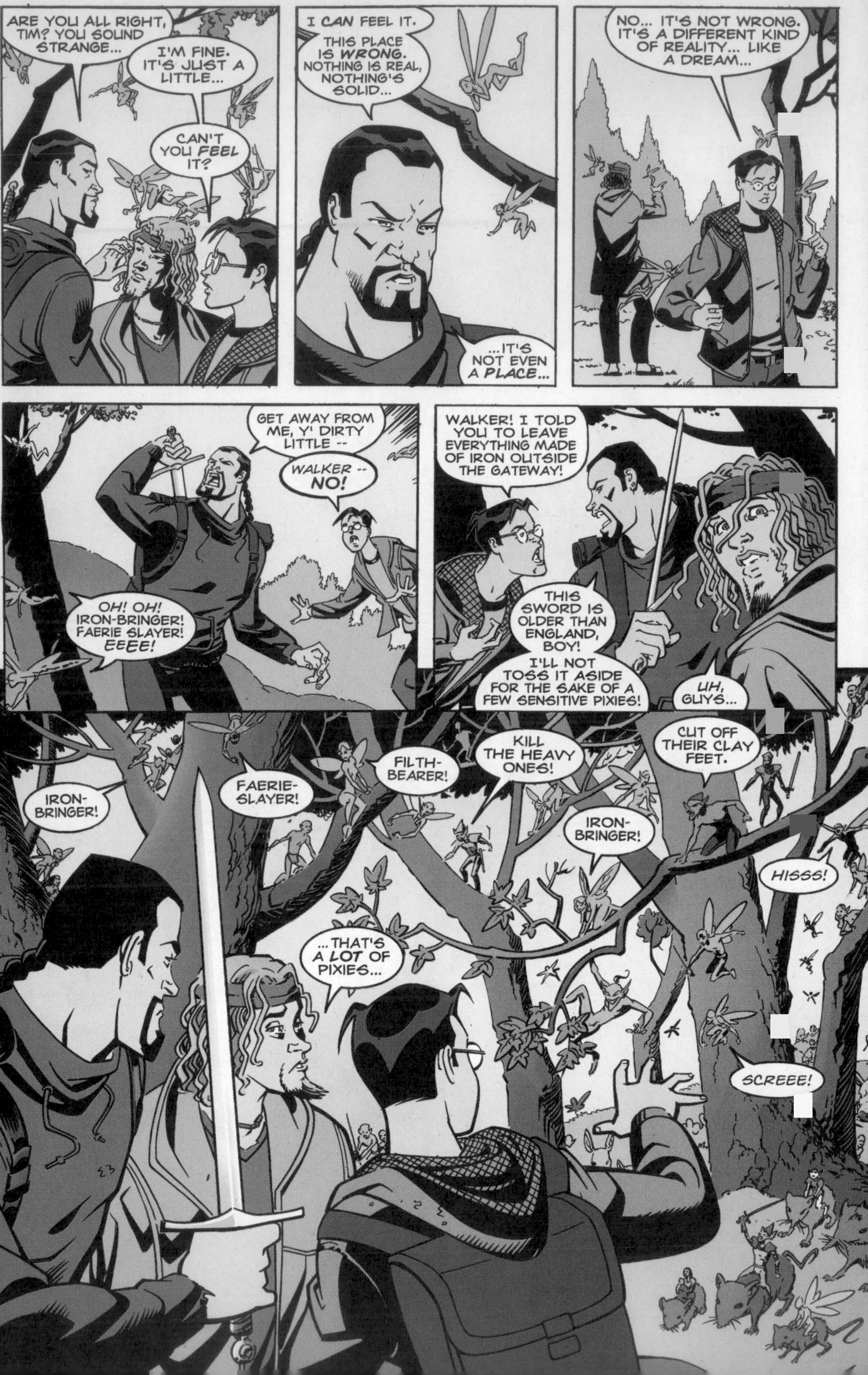
ARE YOU ALL RIGHT, TIM? YOU SOUND STRANGE...
I'M FINE. IT'S JUST A LITTLE...
CAN'T YOU FEEL IT?
I CAN FEEL IT.
THIS PLACE IS WRONG. NOTHING IS REAL, NOTHING'S SOLID...
...IT'S NOT EVEN A PLACE...
NO... IT'S NOT WRONG. IT'S A DIFFERENT KIND OF REALITY... LIKE A DREAM...
GET AWAY FROM ME, Y' DIRTY LITTLE --
WALKER -- NO!
OH! OH! IRON-BRINGER! FAERIE SLAYER! EEEE!
WALKER! I TOLD YOU TO LEAVE EVERYTHING MADE OF IRON OUTSIDE THE GATEWAY!
THIS SWORD IS OLDER THAN ENGLAND, BOY!
I'LL NOT TOSS IT ASIDE FOR THE SAKE OF A FEW SENSITIVE PIXIES!
UH, GUYS...
IRON-BRINGER!
FAERIE-SLAYER!
FILTH-BEARER!
KILL THE HEAVY ONES!
CUT OFF THEIR CLAY FEET.
IRON-BRINGER!
HISSS!
...THAT'S A LOT OF PIXIES...
SCREEE!

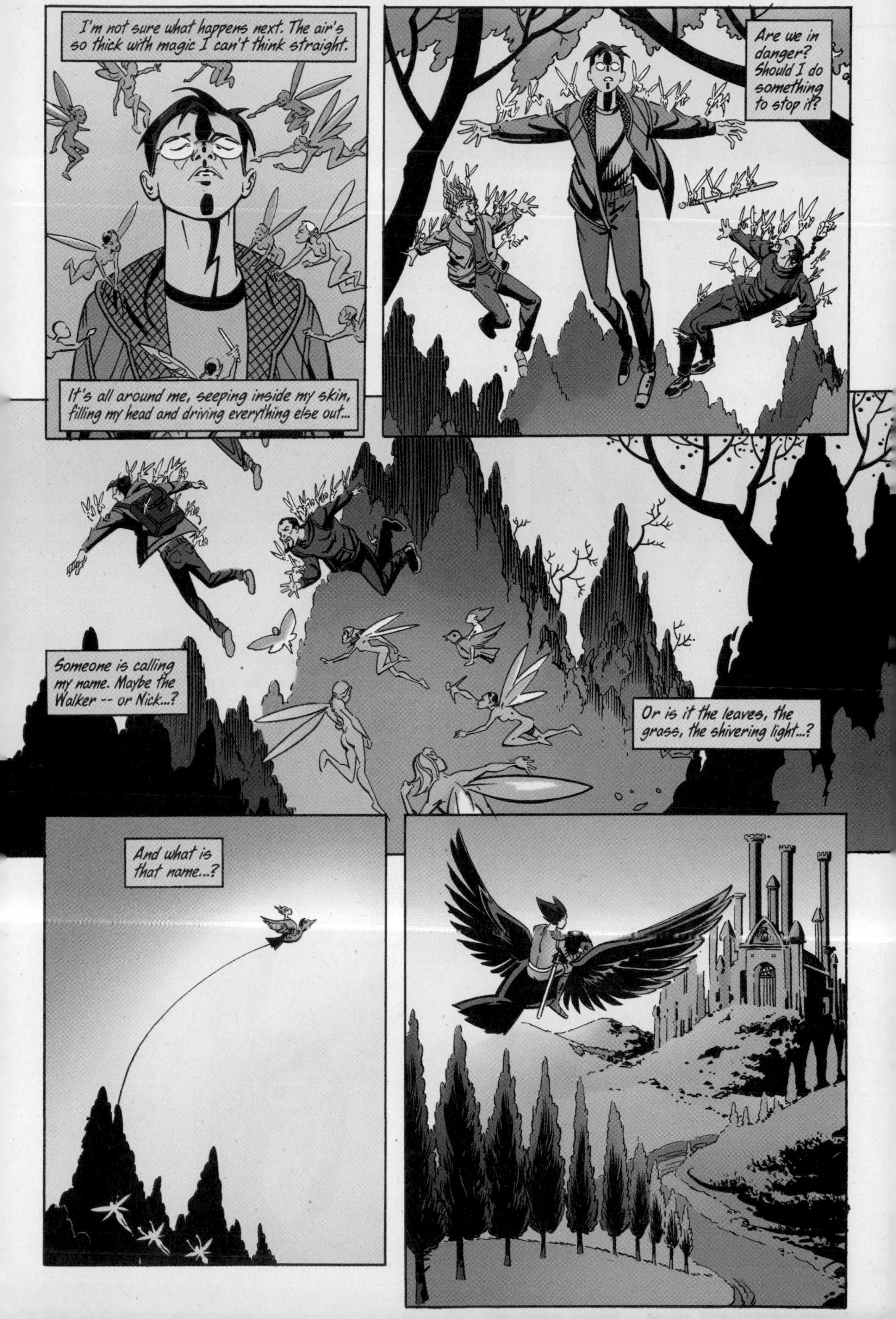
I'm not sure what happens next. The air's so thick with magic I can't think straight.
It's all around me, seeping inside my skin, filling my head and driving everything else out...
Are we in danger? Should I do something to stop it?
Someone is calling my name. Maybe the Walker -- or Nick...?
Or is it the leaves, the grass, the shivering light...?
And what is that name...?

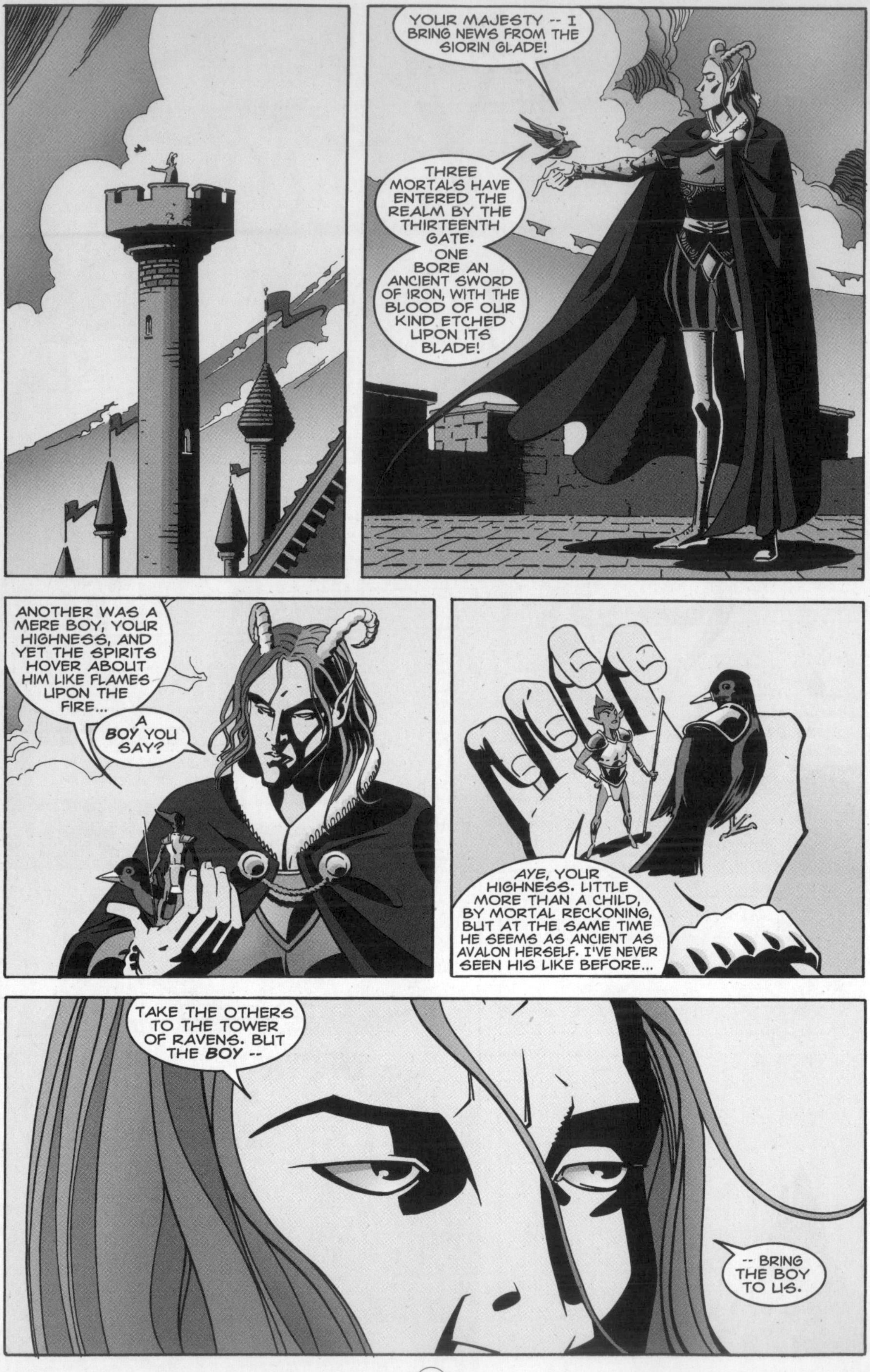
YOUR MAJESTY -- I BRING NEWS FROM THE SIORIN GLADE!
THREE MORTALS HAVE ENTERED THE REALM BY THE THIRTEENTH GATE. ONE BORE AN ANCIENT SWORD OF IRON, WITH THE BLOOD OF OUR KIND ETCHED UPON ITS BLADE!
ANOTHER WAS A MERE BOY, YOUR HIGHNESS, AND YET THE SPIRITS HOVER ABOUT HIM LIKE FLAMES UPON THE FIRE...
A *BOY* YOU SAY?
AYE, YOUR HIGHNESS. LITTLE MORE THAN A CHILD, BY MORTAL RECKONING, BUT AT THE SAME TIME HE SEEMS AS ANCIENT AS AVALON HERSELF. I'VE NEVER SEEN HIS LIKE BEFORE...
TAKE THE OTHERS TO THE TOWER OF RAVENS. BUT THE *BOY* --
-- BRING THE BOY TO US.

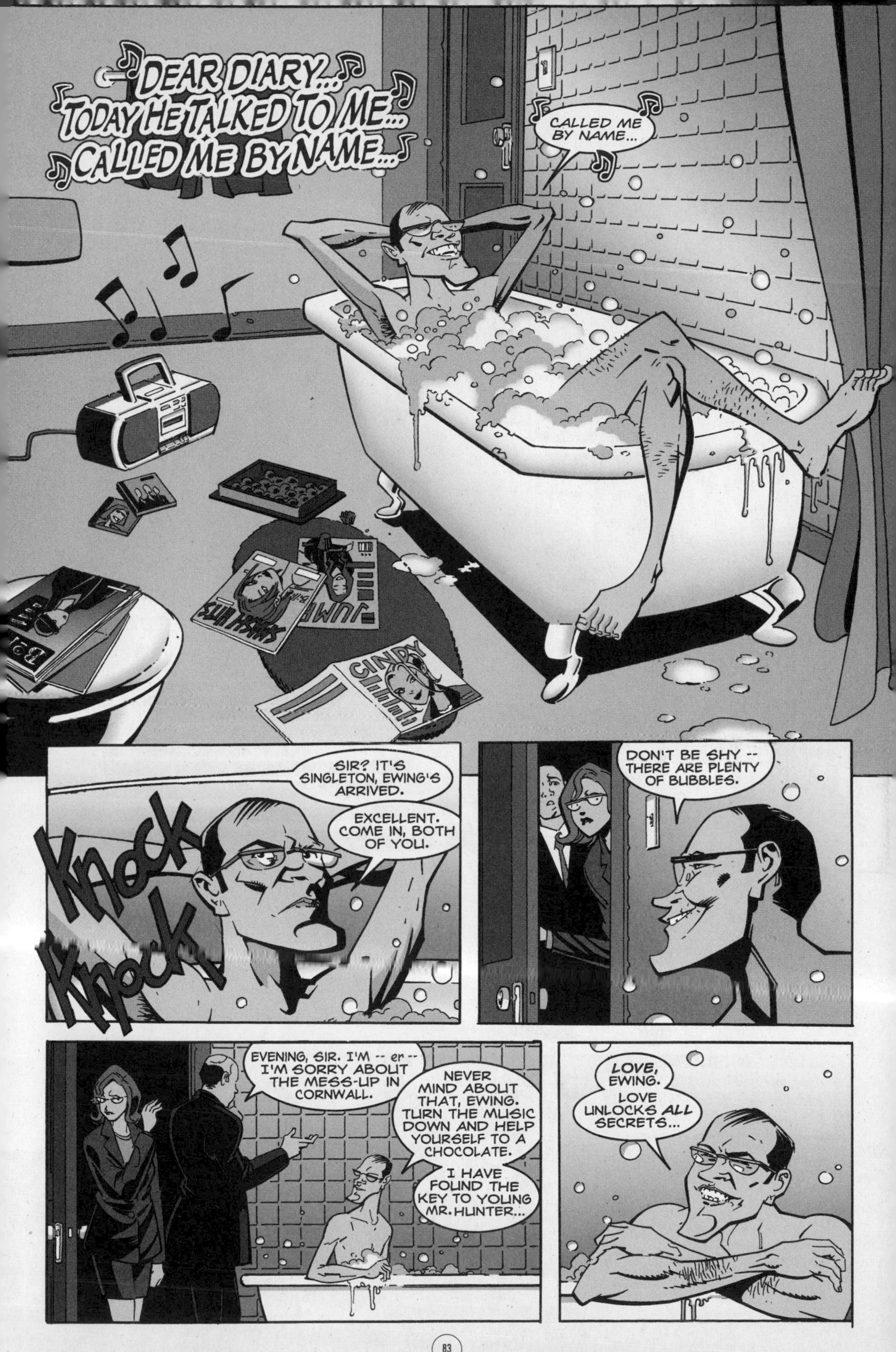
DEAR DIARY... TODAY HE TALKED TO ME... CALLED ME BY NAME...
CALLED ME BY NAME...
SMASH HITS
JUMP
CINDY
SIR? IT'S SINGLETON. EWING'S ARRIVED.
EXCELLENT. COME IN, BOTH OF YOU.
KNOCK KNOCK
DON'T BE SHY -- THERE ARE PLENTY OF BUBBLES.
EVENING, SIR. I'M -- er -- I'M SORRY ABOUT THE MESS-UP IN CORNWALL.
NEVER MIND ABOUT THAT, EWING. TURN THE MUSIC DOWN AND HELP YOURSELF TO A CHOCOLATE.
I HAVE FOUND THE KEY TO YOUNG MR. HUNTER...
LOVE, EWING. LOVE UNLOCKS ALL SECRETS...

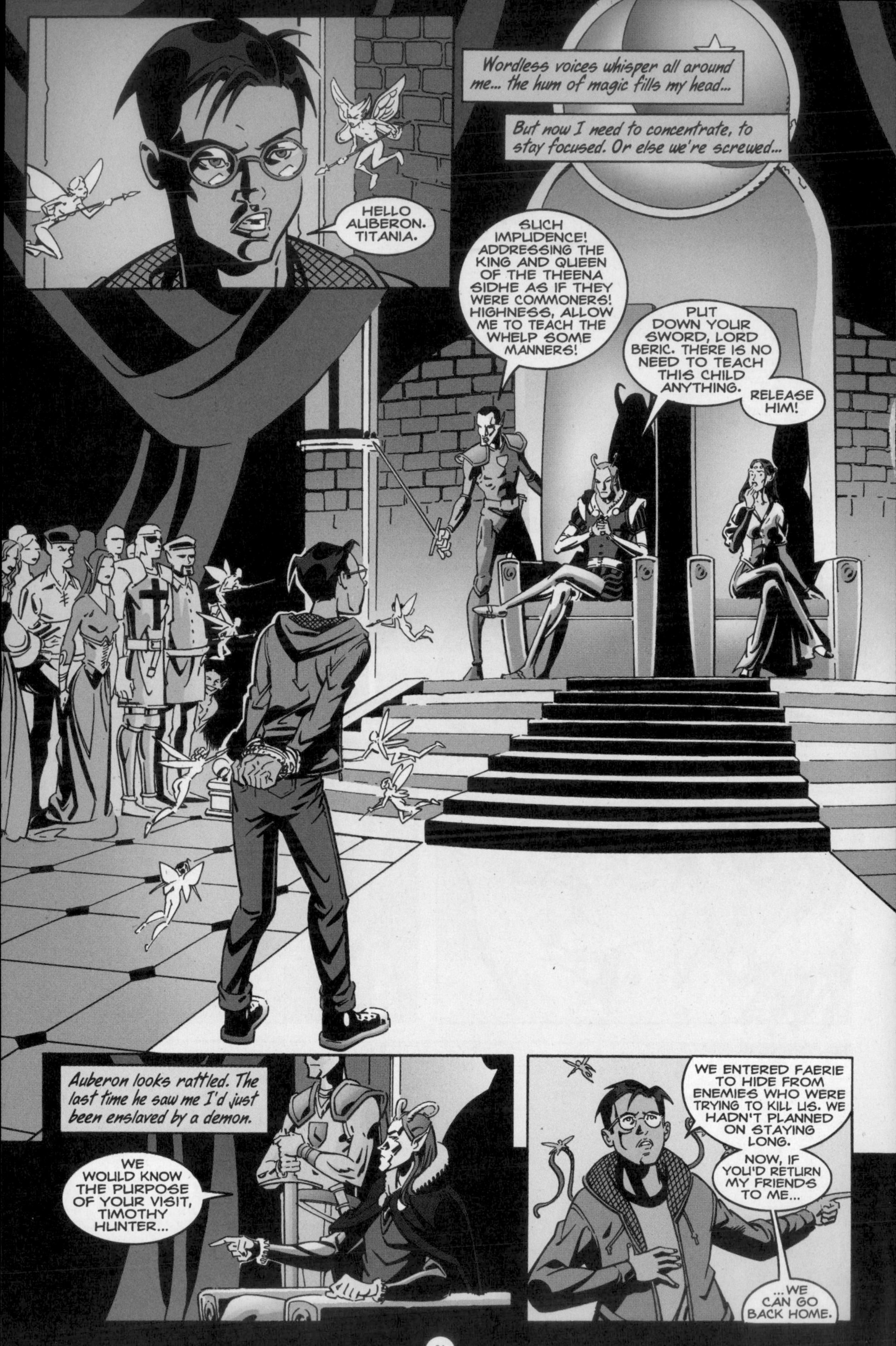

HELLO AUBERON. TITANIA.
Wordless voices whisper all around me... the hum of magic fills my head...
But now I need to concentrate, to stay focused. Or else we're screwed...
SUCH IMPUDENCE! ADDRESSING THE KING AND QUEEN OF THE THEENA SIDHE AS IF THEY WERE COMMONERS! HIGHNESS, ALLOW ME TO TEACH THE WHELP SOME MANNERS!
PUT DOWN YOUR SWORD, LORD BERIC. THERE IS NO NEED TO TEACH THIS CHILD ANYTHING.
RELEASE HIM!
Auberon looks rattled. The last time he saw me I'd just been enslaved by a demon.
WE WOULD KNOW THE PURPOSE OF YOUR VISIT, TIMOTHY HUNTER...
WE ENTERED FAERIE TO HIDE FROM ENEMIES WHO WERE TRYING TO KILL US. WE HADN'T PLANNED ON STAYING LONG.
NOW, IF YOU'D RETURN MY FRIENDS TO ME...
...WE CAN GO BACK HOME.

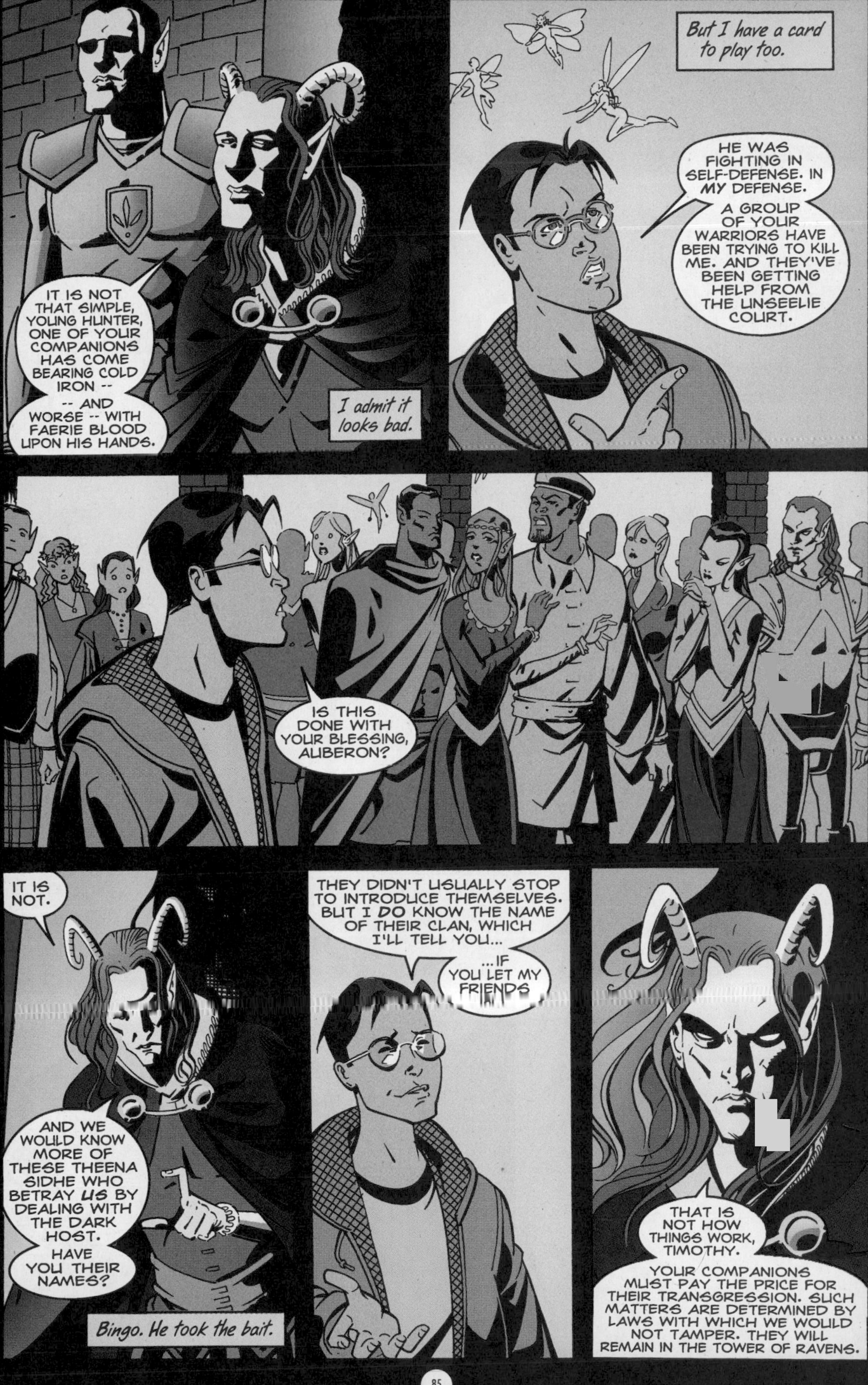

IT IS NOT THAT SIMPLE, YOUNG HUNTER, ONE OF YOUR COMPANIONS HAS COME BEARING COLD IRON --
-- AND WORSE -- WITH FAERIE BLOOD UPON HIS HANDS.
I admit it looks bad.
But I have a card to play too.
HE WAS FIGHTING IN SELF-DEFENSE. IN MY DEFENSE.
A GROUP OF YOUR WARRIORS HAVE BEEN TRYING TO KILL ME. AND THEY'VE BEEN GETTING HELP FROM THE UNSEELIE COURT.
IS THIS DONE WITH YOUR BLESSING, AUBERON?
IT IS NOT.
AND WE WOULD KNOW MORE OF THESE THEENA SIDHE WHO BETRAY US BY DEALING WITH THE DARK HOST.
HAVE YOU THEIR NAMES?
Bingo. He took the bait.
THEY DIDN'T USUALLY STOP TO INTRODUCE THEMSELVES. BUT I DO KNOW THE NAME OF THEIR CLAN, WHICH I'LL TELL YOU...
...IF YOU LET MY FRIENDS GO.
THAT IS NOT HOW THINGS WORK, TIMOTHY.
YOUR COMPANIONS MUST PAY THE PRICE FOR THEIR TRANSGRESSION. SUCH MATTERS ARE DETERMINED BY LAWS WITH WHICH WE WOULD NOT TAMPER. THEY WILL REMAIN IN THE TOWER OF RAVENS.

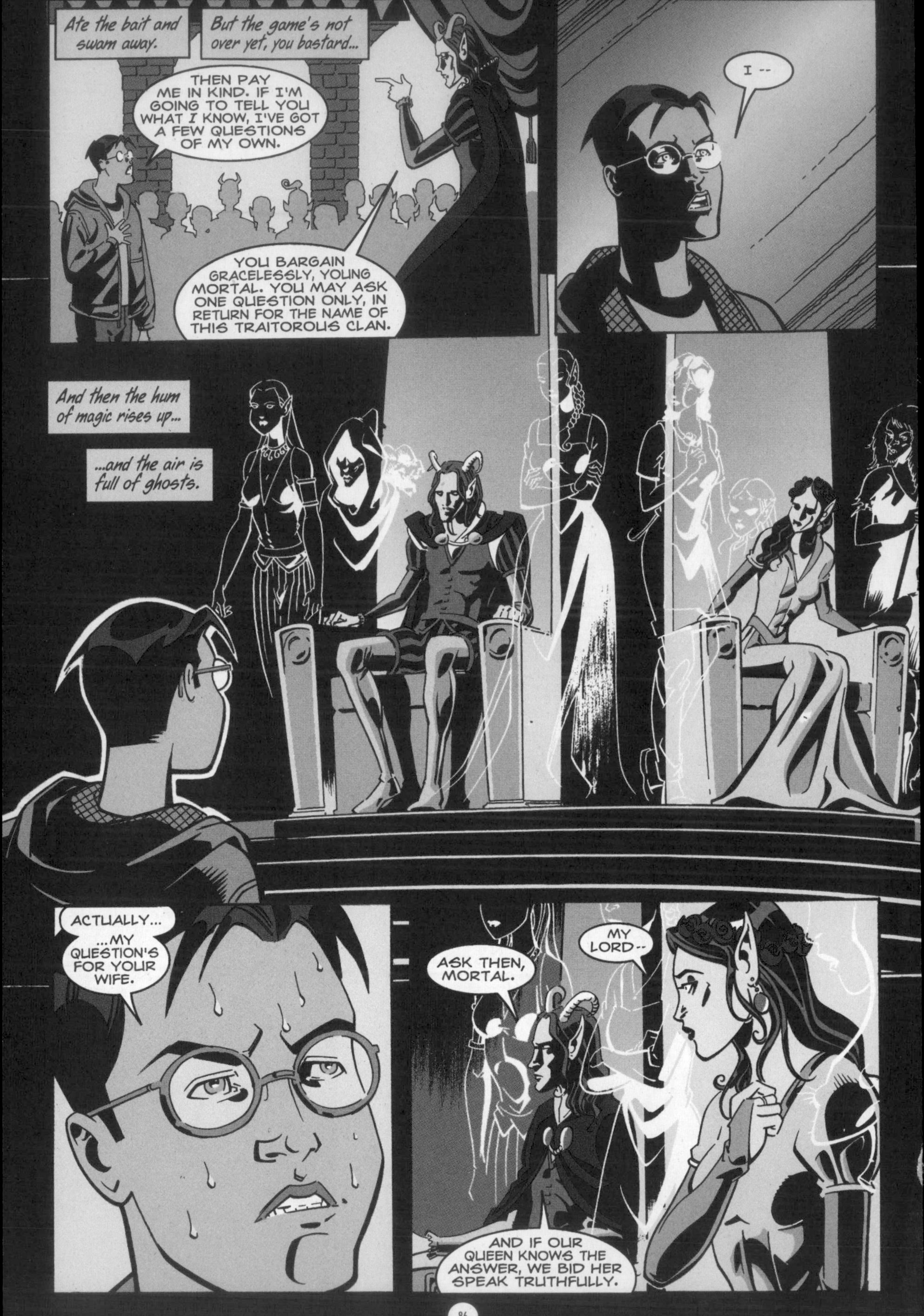

Ate the bait and swam away.
But the game's not over yet, you bastard...
THEN PAY ME IN KIND. IF I'M GOING TO TELL YOU WHAT I KNOW, I'VE GOT A FEW QUESTIONS OF MY OWN.
YOU BARGAIN GRACELESSLY, YOUNG MORTAL. YOU MAY ASK ONE QUESTION ONLY, IN RETURN FOR THE NAME OF THIS TRAITOROUS CLAN.
I --
And then the hum of magic rises up...
...and the air is full of ghosts.
ACTUALLY...
...MY QUESTION'S FOR YOUR WIFE.
ASK THEN, MORTAL.
MY LORD --
AND IF OUR QUEEN KNOWS THE ANSWER, WE BID HER SPEAK TRUTHFULLY.

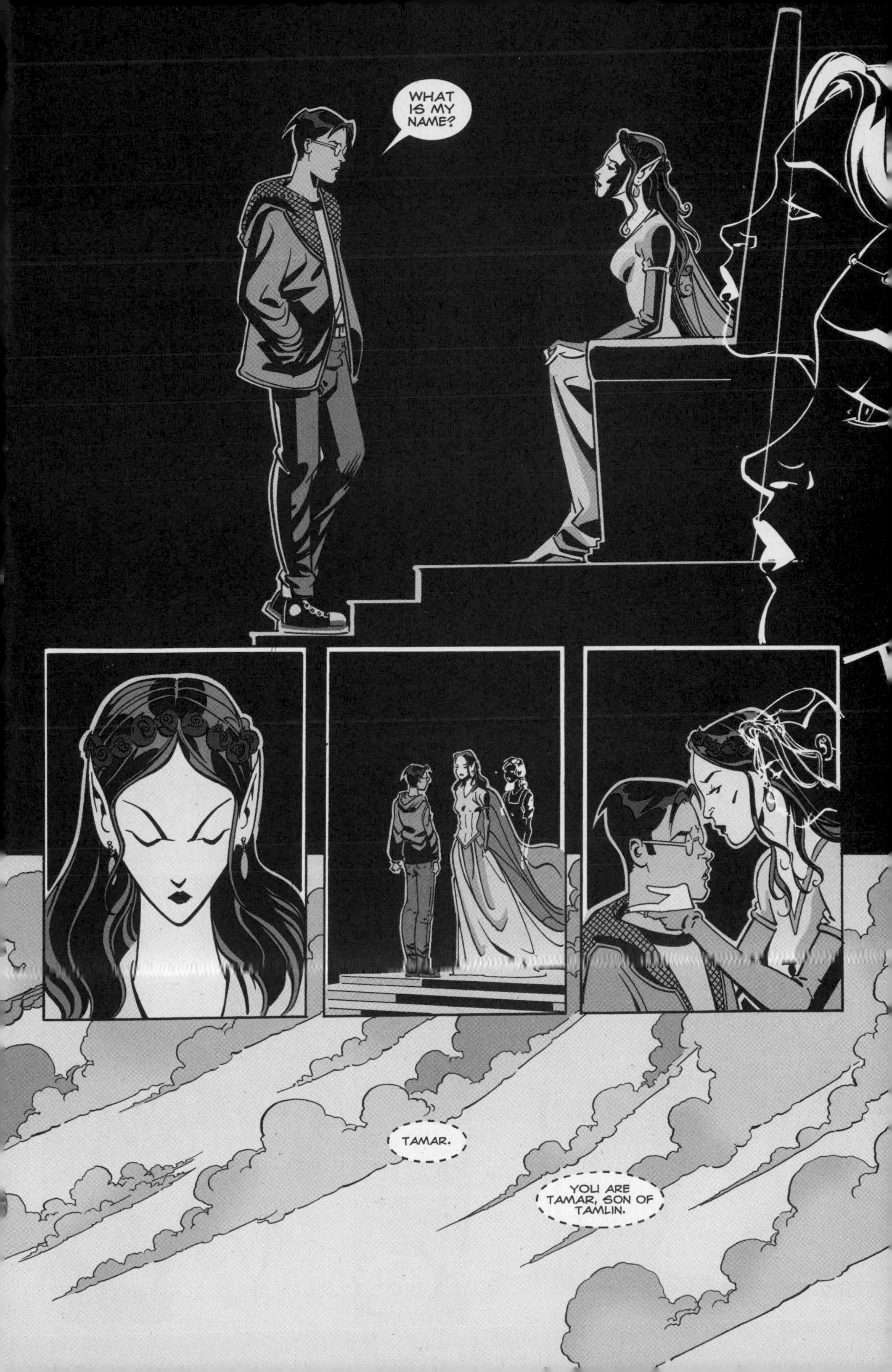
WHAT IS MY NAME?
TAMAR.
YOU ARE TAMAR, SON OF TAMLIN.

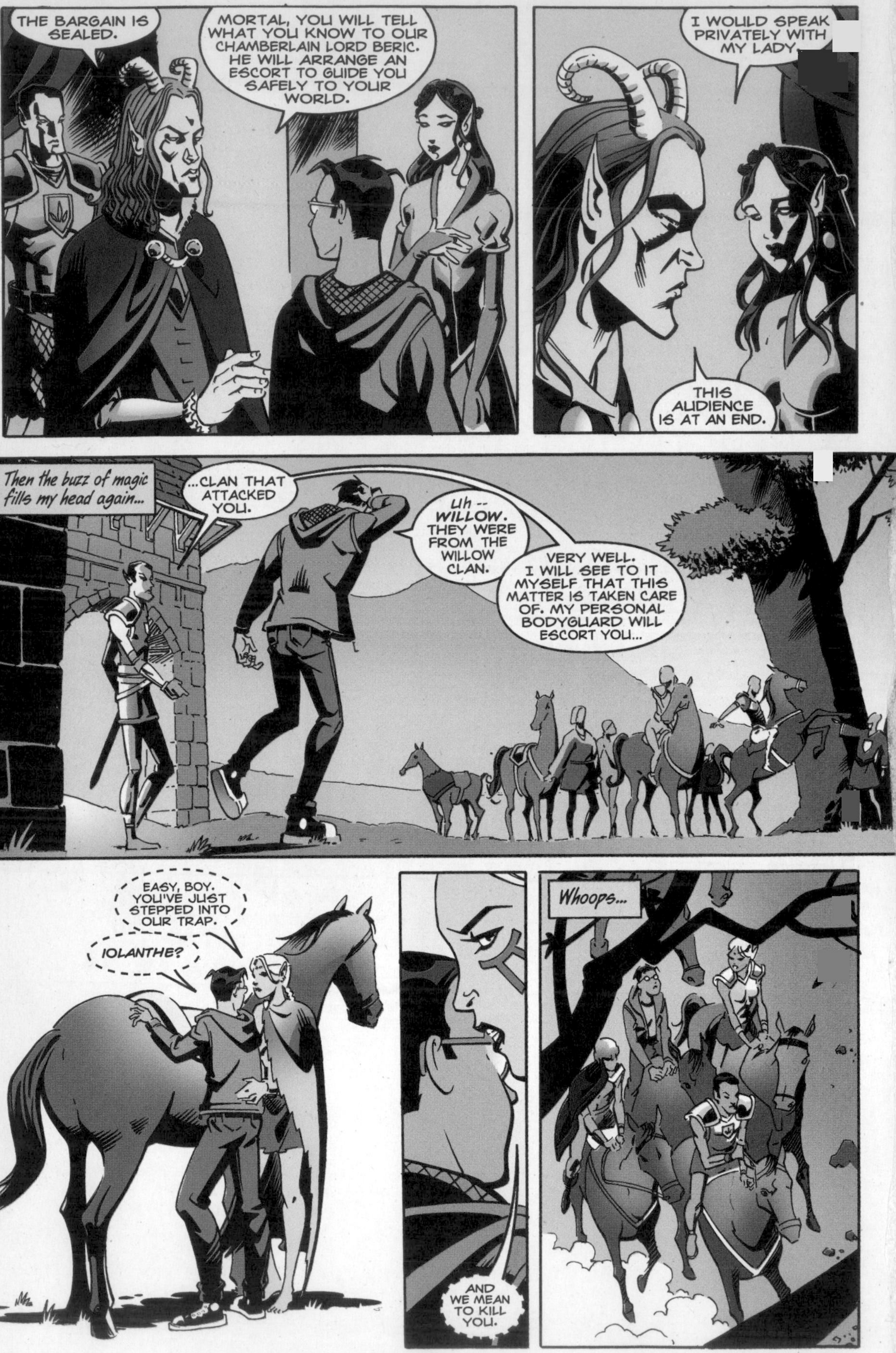
THE BARGAIN IS SEALED.
MORTAL, YOU WILL TELL WHAT YOU KNOW TO OUR CHAMBERLAIN LORD BERIC. HE WILL ARRANGE AN ESCORT TO GUIDE YOU SAFELY TO YOUR WORLD.
I WOULD SPEAK PRIVATELY WITH MY LADY.
THIS AUDIENCE IS AT AN END.
Then the buzz of magic fills my head again...
...CLAN THAT ATTACKED YOU.
Uh -- WILLOW. THEY WERE FROM THE WILLOW CLAN.
VERY WELL. I WILL SEE TO IT MYSELF THAT THIS MATTER IS TAKEN CARE OF. MY PERSONAL BODYGUARD WILL ESCORT YOU...
EASY, BOY. YOU'VE JUST STEPPED INTO OUR TRAP.
IOLANTHE?
AND WE MEAN TO KILL YOU.
Whoops...

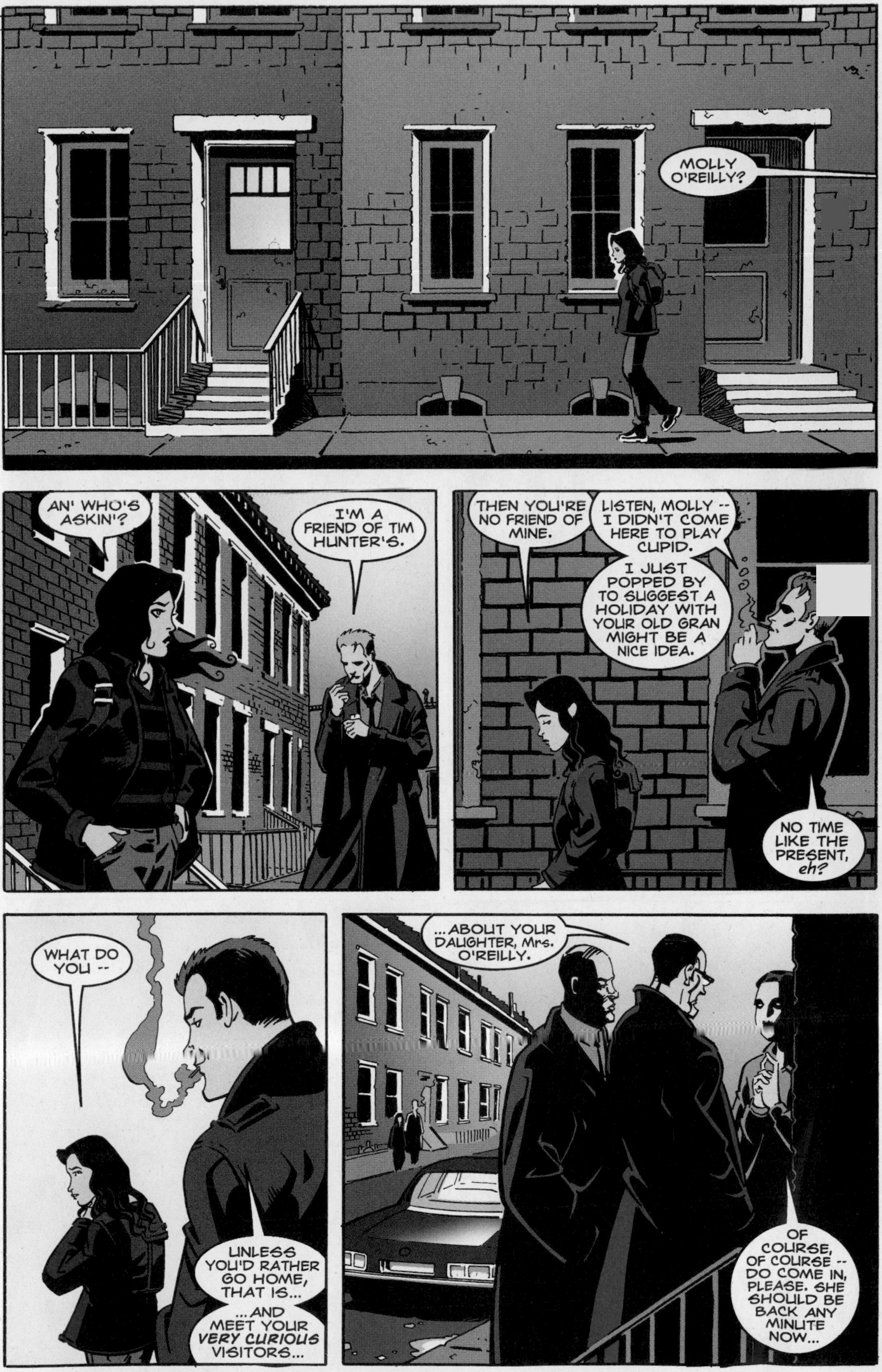
MOLLY O'REILLY?
AN' WHO'S ASKIN'?
I'M A FRIEND OF TIM HUNTER'S.
THEN YOU'RE NO FRIEND OF MINE.
LISTEN, MOLLY -- I DIDN'T COME HERE TO PLAY CUPID.
I JUST POPPED BY TO SUGGEST A HOLIDAY WITH YOUR OLD GRAN MIGHT BE A NICE IDEA.
NO TIME LIKE THE PRESENT, *eh?*
WHAT DO YOU --
UNLESS YOU'D RATHER GO HOME, THAT IS...
...AND MEET YOUR *VERY CURIOUS* VISITORS...
...ABOUT YOUR DAUGHTER, Mrs. O'REILLY.
OF COURSE, OF COURSE -- DO COME IN, PLEASE. SHE SHOULD BE BACK ANY MINUTE NOW...

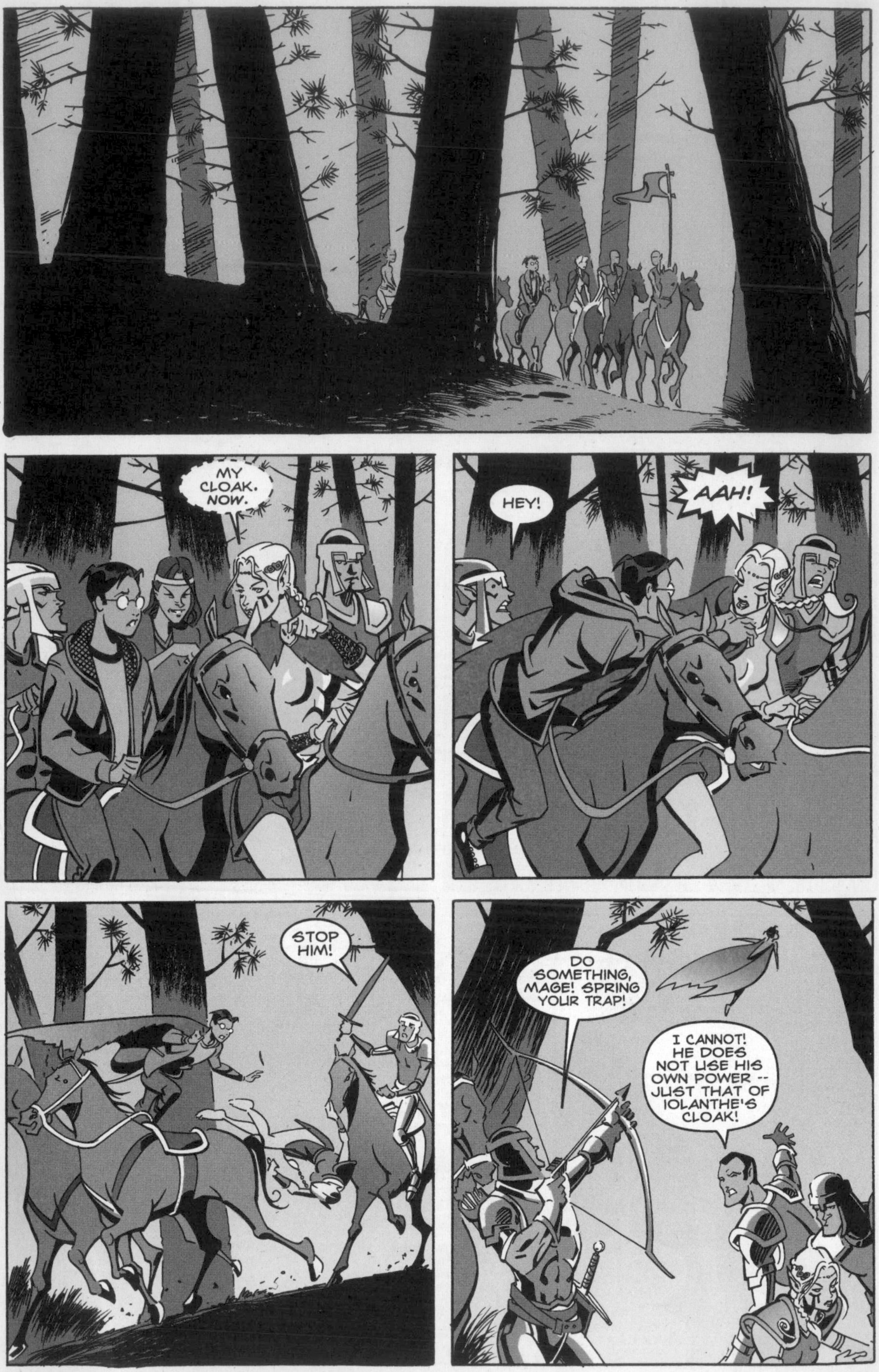
MY CLOAK. NOW.
HEY!
AAH!
STOP HIM!
DO SOMETHING, MAGE! SPRING YOUR TRAP!
I CANNOT! HE DOES NOT USE HIS OWN POWER -- JUST THAT OF IOLANTHE'S CLOAK!

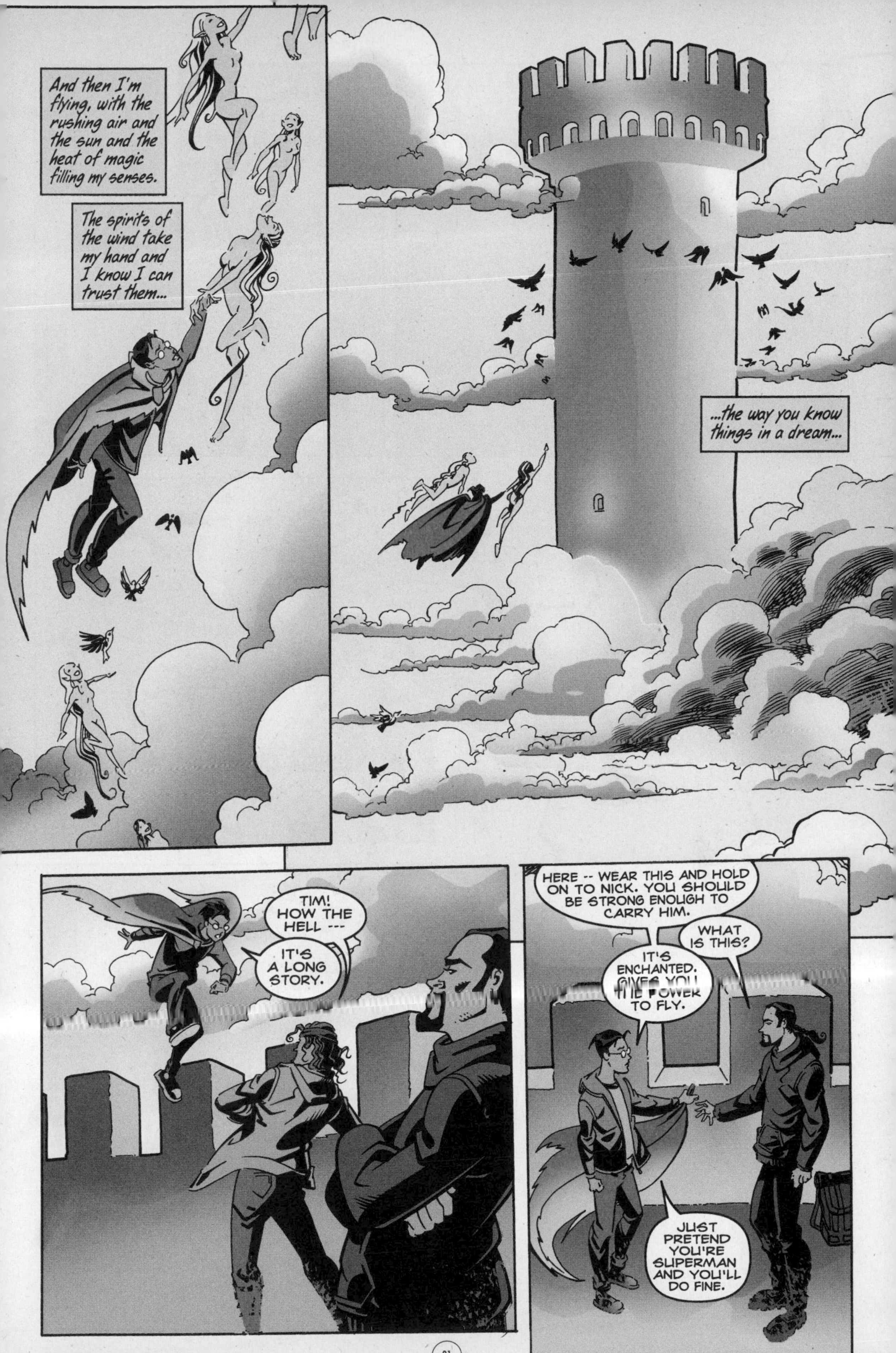
And then I'm flying, with the rushing air and the sun and the heat of magic filling my senses.
The spirits of the wind take my hand and I know I can trust them...
...the way you know things in a dream...
TIM! HOW THE HELL ---
IT'S A LONG STORY.
HERE -- WEAR THIS AND HOLD ON TO NICK. YOU SHOULD BE STRONG ENOUGH TO CARRY HIM.
WHAT IS THIS?
IT'S ENCHANTED. GIVES YOU THE POWER TO FLY.
JUST PRETEND YOU'RE SUPERMAN AND YOU'LL DO FINE.

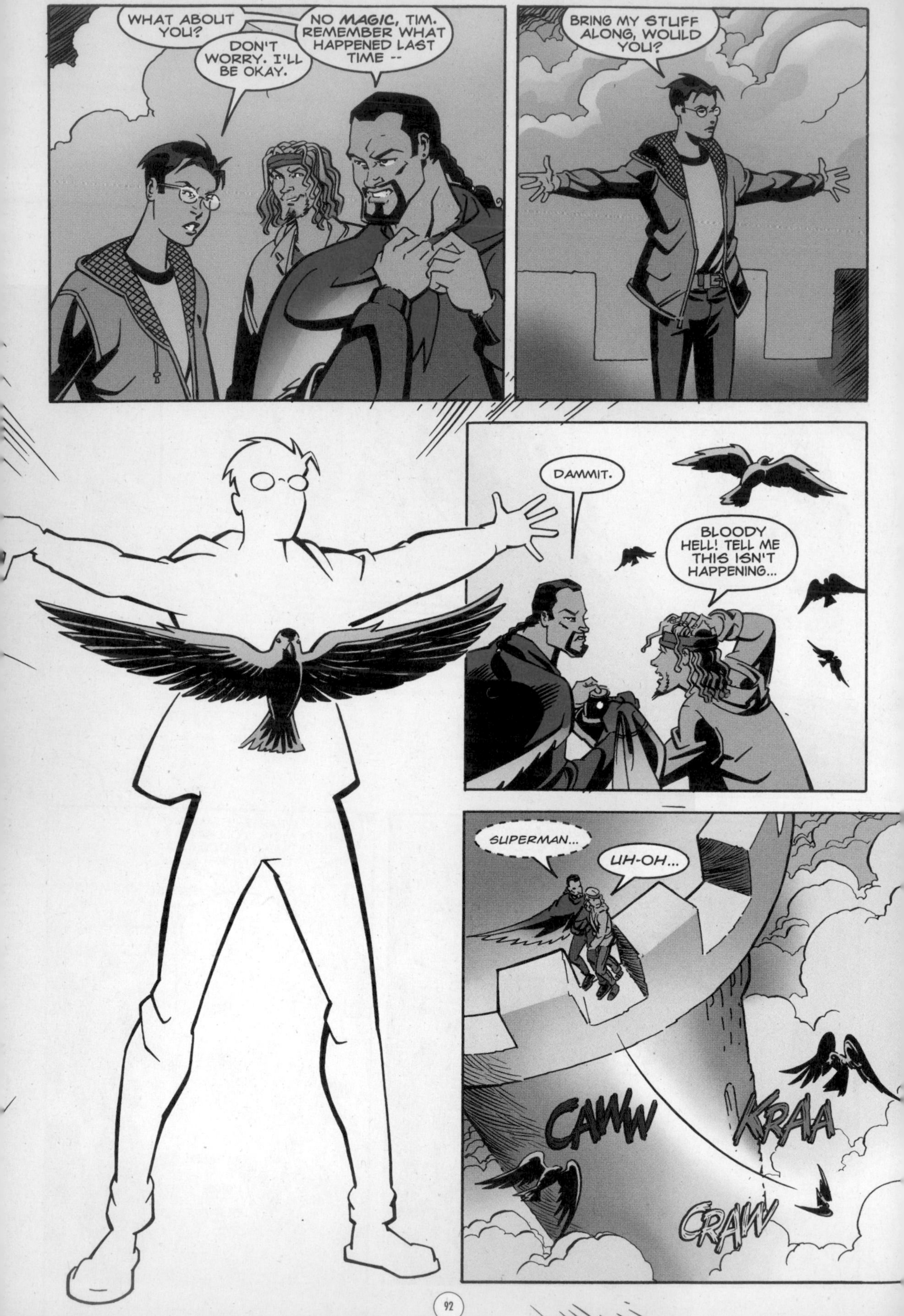
WHAT ABOUT YOU?
DON'T WORRY. I'LL BE OKAY.
NO MAGIC, TIM. REMEMBER WHAT HAPPENED LAST TIME --
BRING MY STUFF ALONG, WOULD YOU?
DAMMIT.
BLOODY HELL! TELL ME THIS ISN'T HAPPENING...
SUPERMAN...
UH-OH...
CAWW
KRAA
CRAW

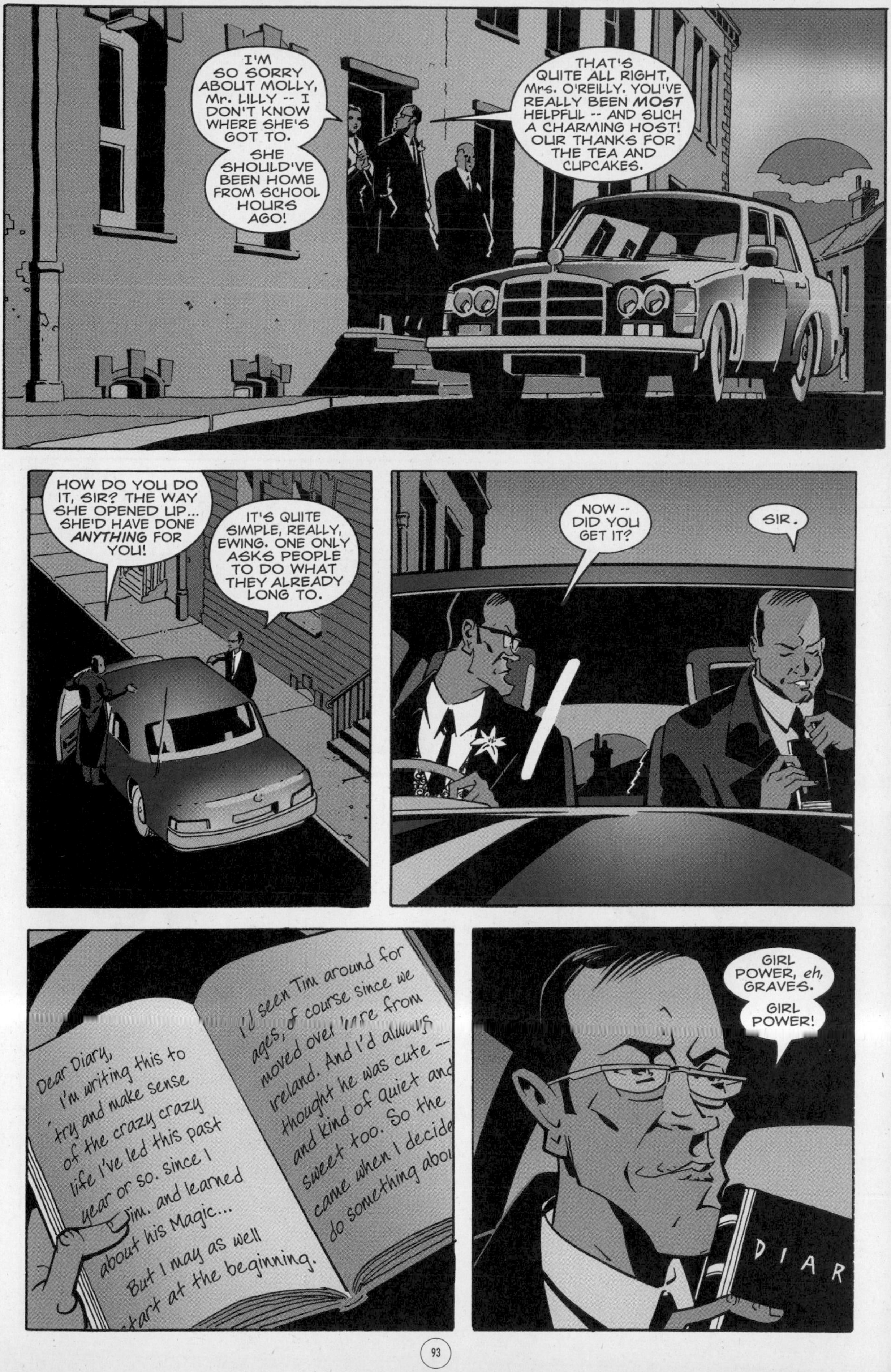
I'M SO SORRY ABOUT MOLLY, Mr. LILLY -- I DON'T KNOW WHERE SHE'S GOT TO.
SHE SHOULD'VE BEEN HOME FROM SCHOOL HOURS AGO!
THAT'S QUITE ALL RIGHT, Mrs. O'REILLY. YOU'VE REALLY BEEN MOST HELPFUL -- AND SUCH A CHARMING HOST! OUR THANKS FOR THE TEA AND CUPCAKES.
HOW DO YOU DO IT, SIR? THE WAY SHE OPENED UP... SHE'D HAVE DONE ANYTHING FOR YOU!
IT'S QUITE SIMPLE, REALLY, EWING. ONE ONLY ASKS PEOPLE TO DO WHAT THEY ALREADY LONG TO.
NOW -- DID YOU GET IT?
SIR.
Dear Diary,
I'm writing this to
try and make sense
of the crazy crazy
life I've led this past
year or so. since I
...im. and learned
about his Magic...
But I may as well
...tart at the beginning.
I'd seen Tim around for
ages, of course since we
moved over ...re from
Ireland. And I'd always
thought he was cute --
and kind of quiet and
sweet too. So the
came when I decide
do something abo
GIRL POWER, eh, GRAVES.
GIRL POWER!
DIAR

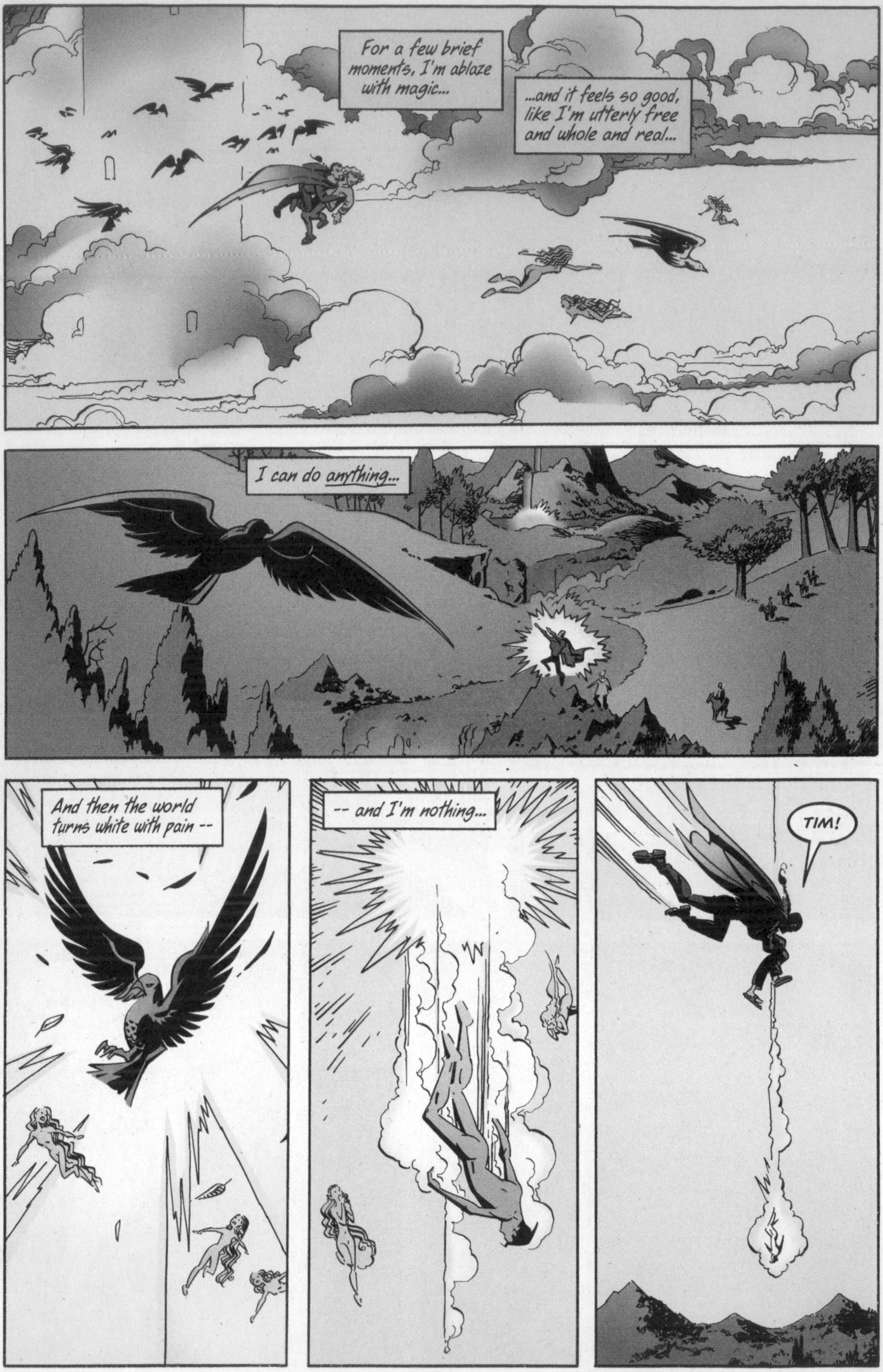
For a few brief moments, I'm ablaze with magic...
...and it feels so good, like I'm utterly free and whole and real...
I can do anything...
And then the world turns white with pain --
-- and I'm nothing...
TIM!

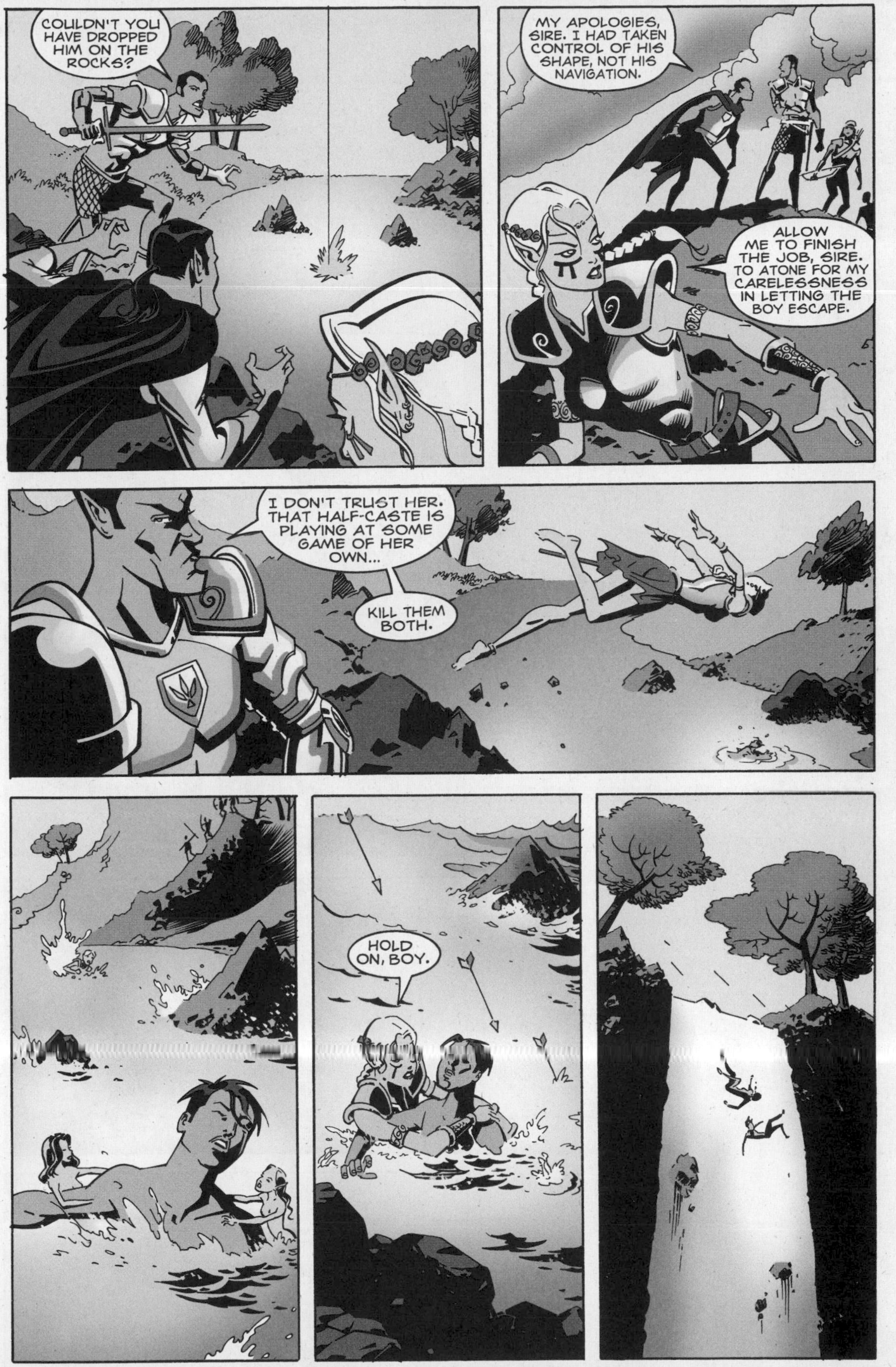
COULDN'T YOU HAVE DROPPED HIM ON THE ROCKS?
MY APOLOGIES, SIRE. I HAD TAKEN CONTROL OF HIS SHAPE, NOT HIS NAVIGATION.
ALLOW ME TO FINISH THE JOB, SIRE. TO ATONE FOR MY CARELESSNESS IN LETTING THE BOY ESCAPE.
I DON'T TRUST HER. THAT HALF-CASTE IS PLAYING AT SOME GAME OF HER OWN...
KILL THEM BOTH.
HOLD ON, BOY.

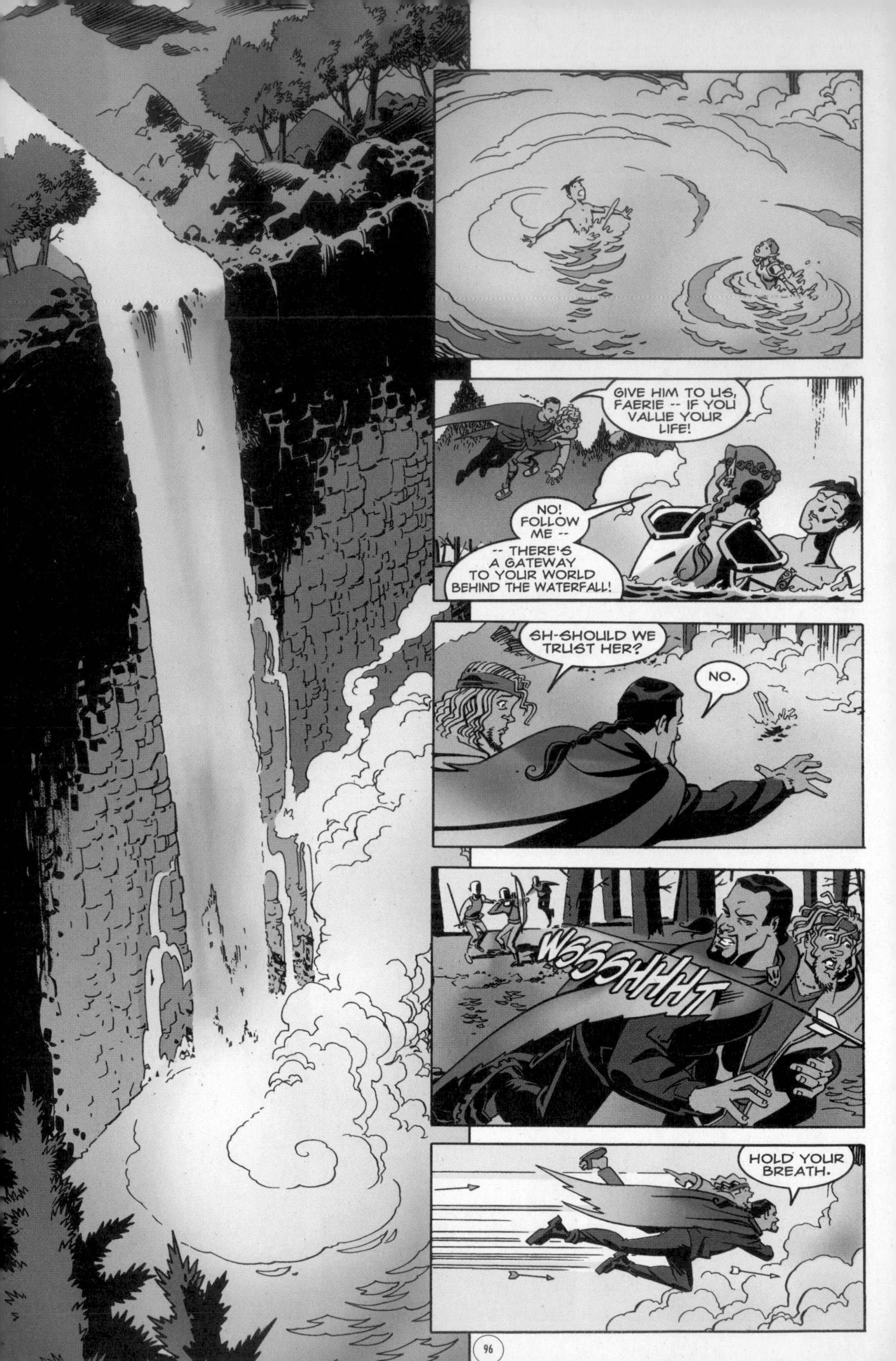
GIVE HIM TO US, FAERIE -- IF YOU VALUE YOUR LIFE!
NO! FOLLOW ME --
-- THERE'S A GATEWAY TO YOUR WORLD BEHIND THE WATERFALL!
SH-SHOULD WE TRUST HER?
NO.
WSSHHHT
HOLD YOUR BREATH.

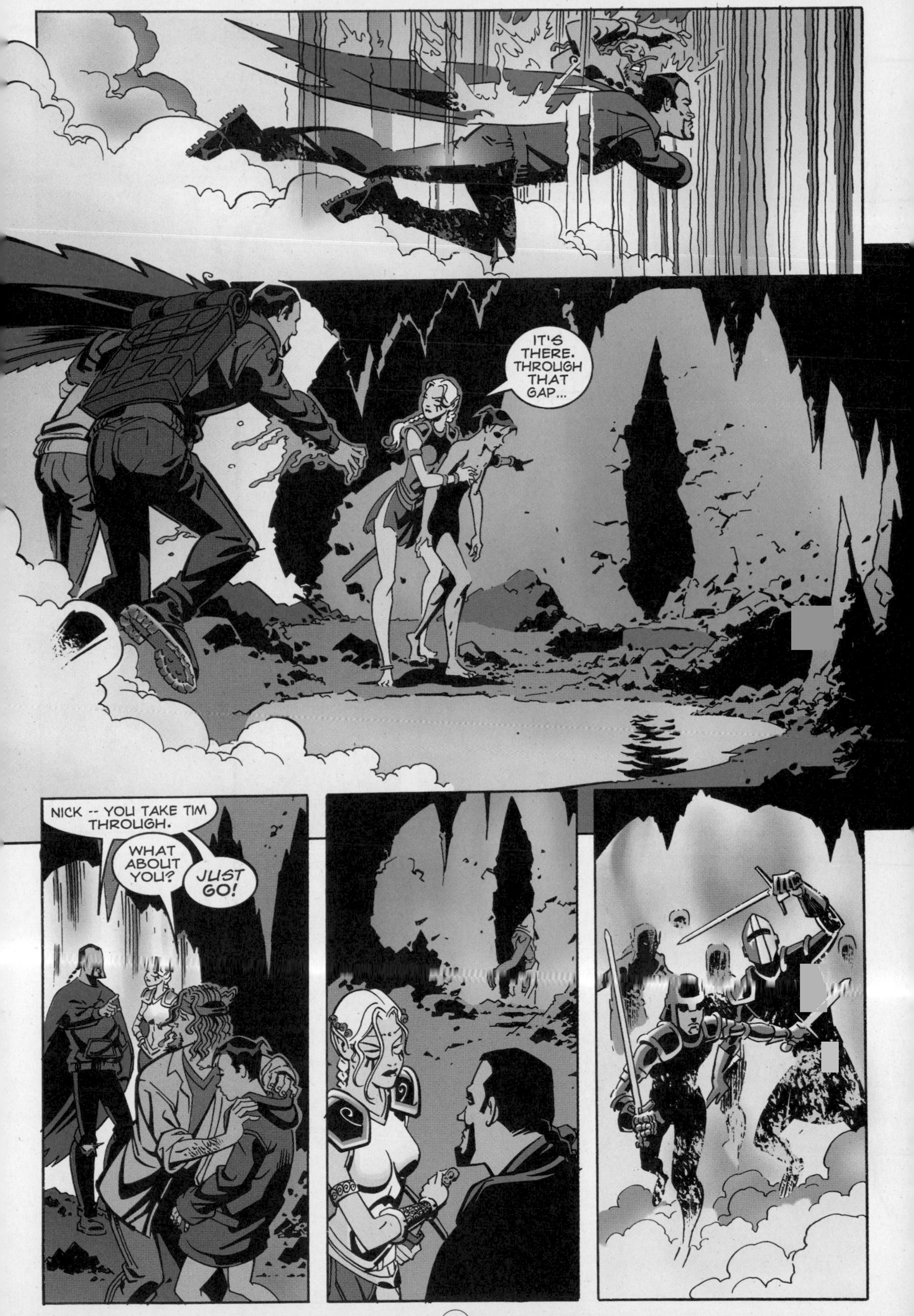
IT'S THERE. THROUGH THAT GAP...
NICK -- YOU TAKE TIM THROUGH.
WHAT ABOUT YOU?
JUST GO!

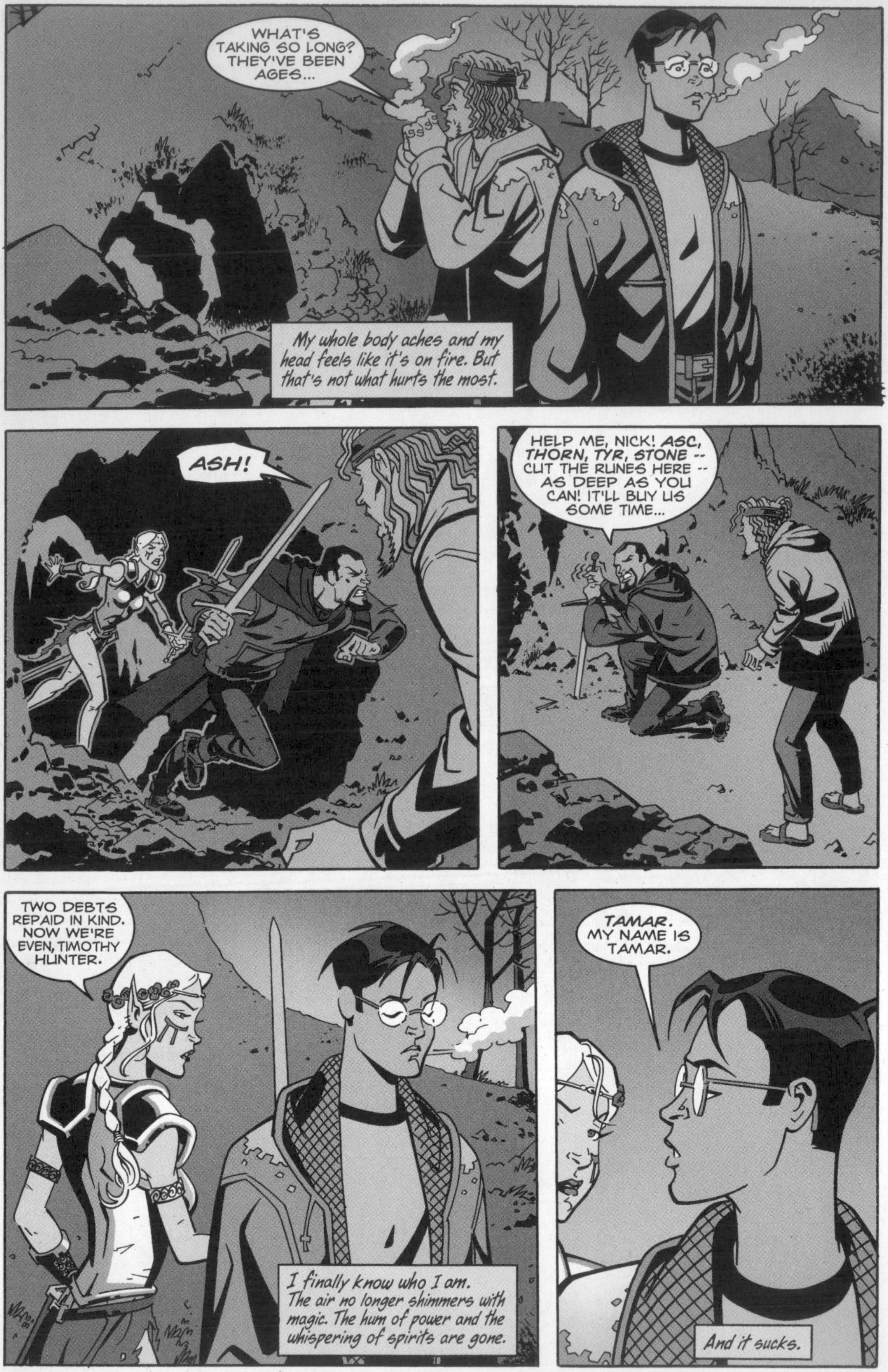
WHAT'S TAKING SO LONG? THEY'VE BEEN AGES...
SSSS
My whole body aches and my head feels like it's on fire. But that's not what hurts the most.
ASH!
HELP ME, NICK! ASC, THORN, TYR, STONE -- CUT THE RUNES HERE -- AS DEEP AS YOU CAN! IT'LL BUY US SOME TIME...
TWO DEBTS REPAID IN KIND. NOW WE'RE EVEN, TIMOTHY HUNTER.
I finally know who I am. The air no longer shimmers with magic. The hum of power and the whispering of spirits are gone.
TAMAR. MY NAME IS TAMAR.
And it sucks.

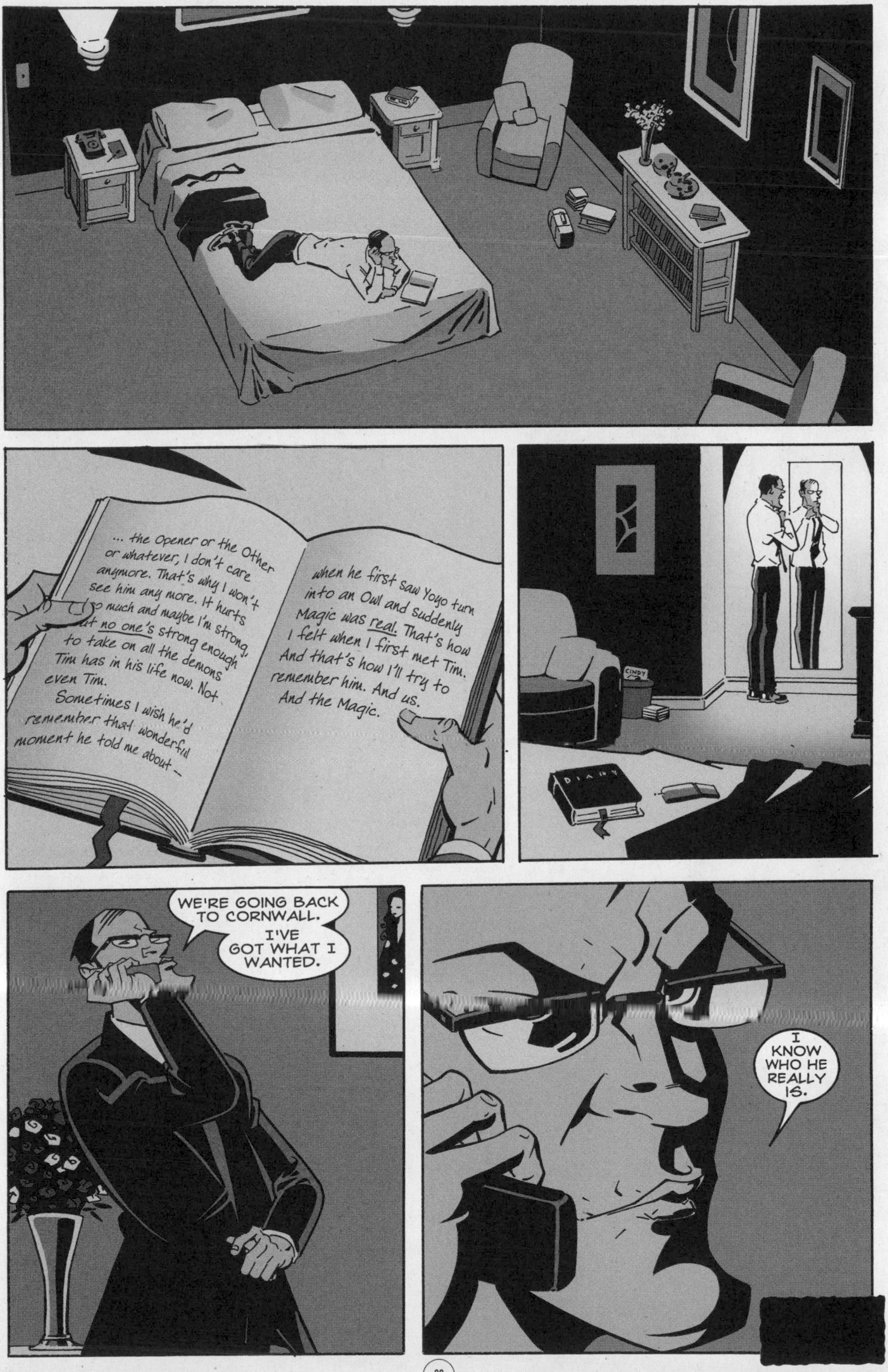
... the Opener or the Other or whatever, I don't care anymore. That's why I won't see him any more. It hurts so much and maybe I'm strong, but no one's strong enough to take on all the demons Tim has in his life now. Not even Tim.
Sometimes I wish he'd remember that wonderful moment he told me about -
when he first saw Yoyo turn into an Owl and suddenly Magic was real. That's how I felt when I first met Tim. And that's how I'll try to remember him. And us. And the Magic.
DIARY
CINDY
WE'RE GOING BACK TO CORNWALL.
I'VE GOT WHAT I WANTED.
I KNOW WHO HE REALLY IS.

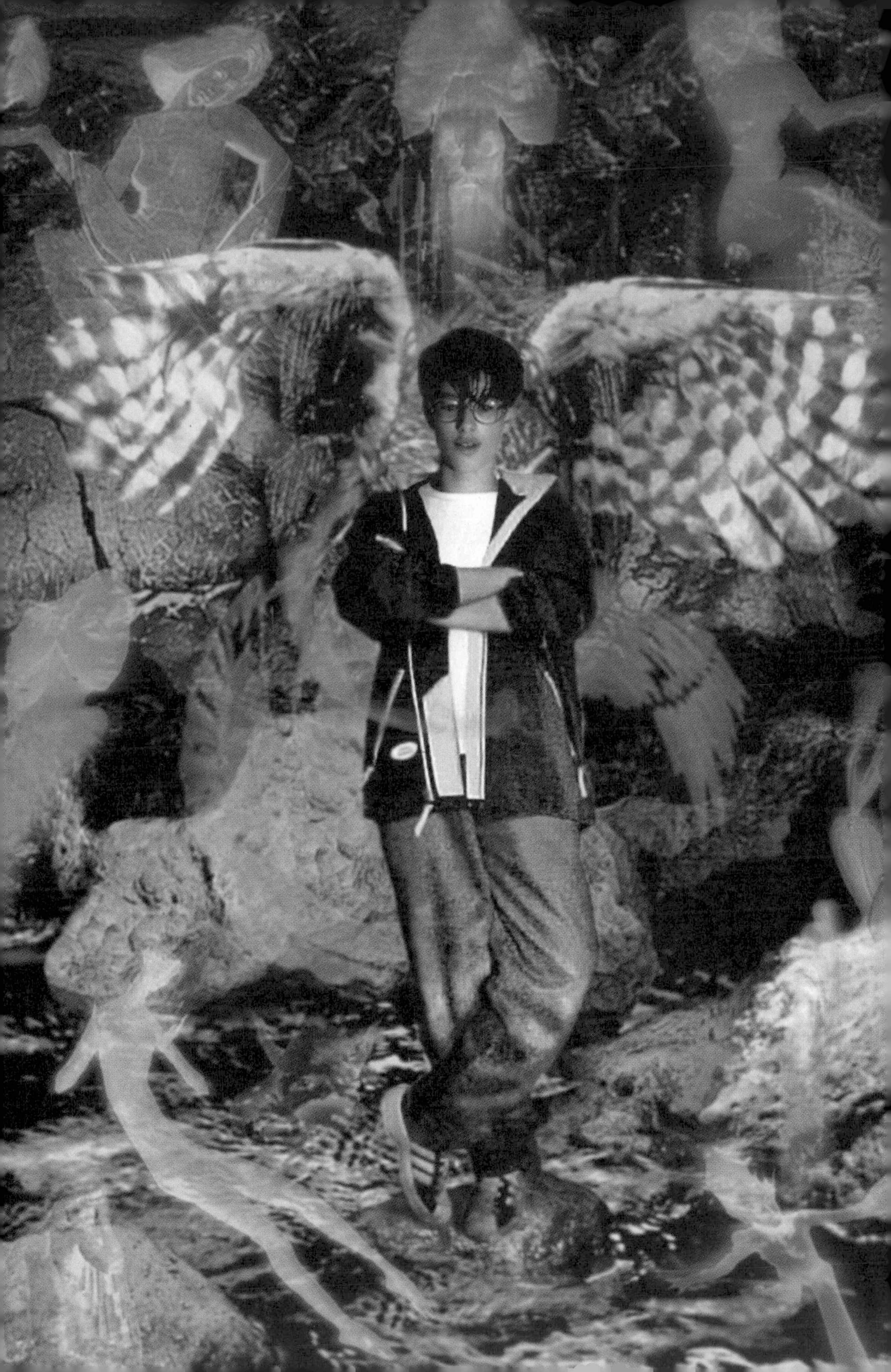

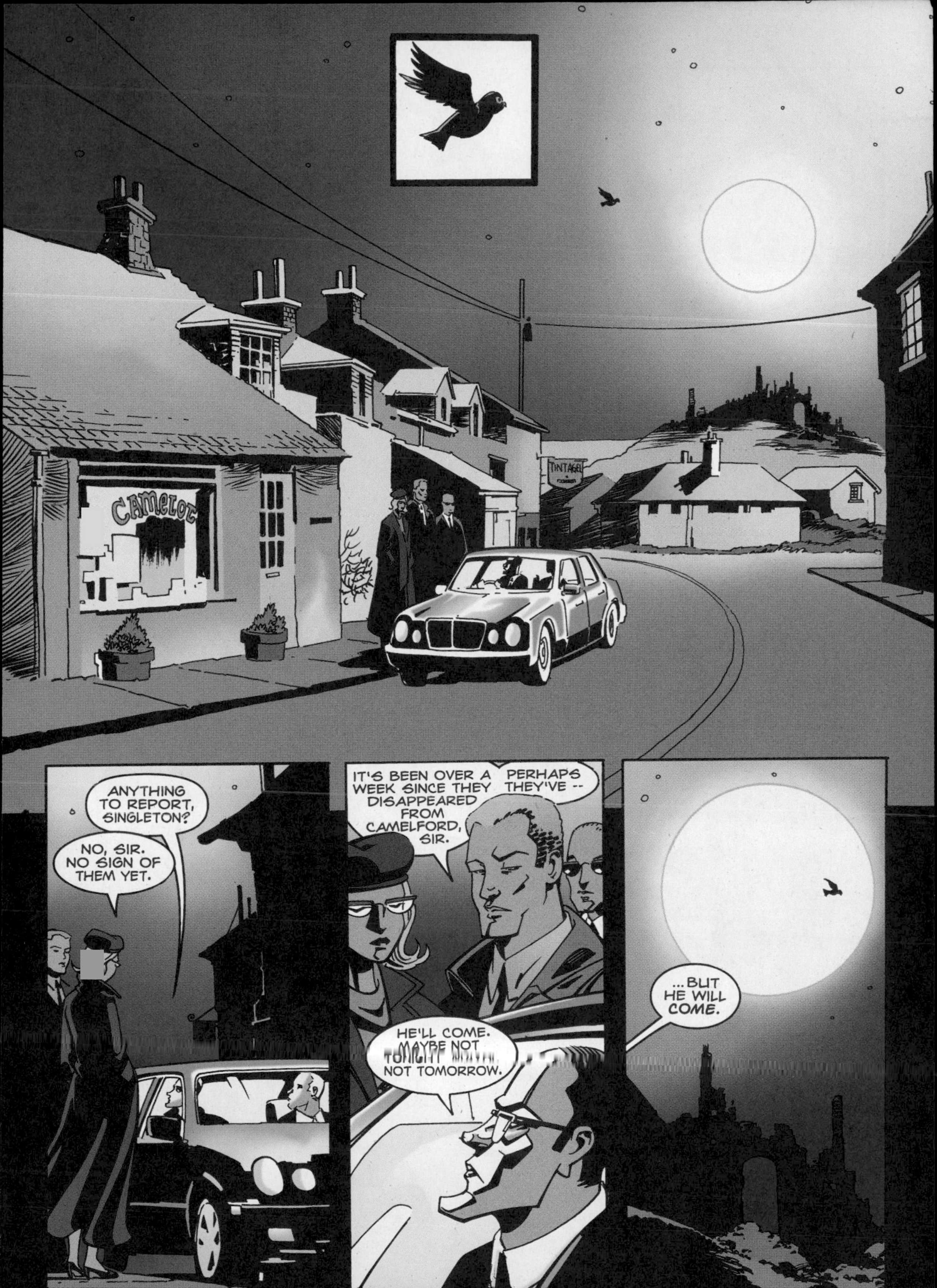
CAMELOT
TINTAGEL
ANYTHING TO REPORT, SINGLETON?
NO, SIR. NO SIGN OF THEM YET.
IT'S BEEN OVER A WEEK SINCE THEY DISAPPEARED FROM CAMELFORD, SIR.
PERHAPS THEY'VE --
HE'LL COME. MAYBE NOT TONIGHT
NOT TOMORROW.
...BUT HE WILL COME.

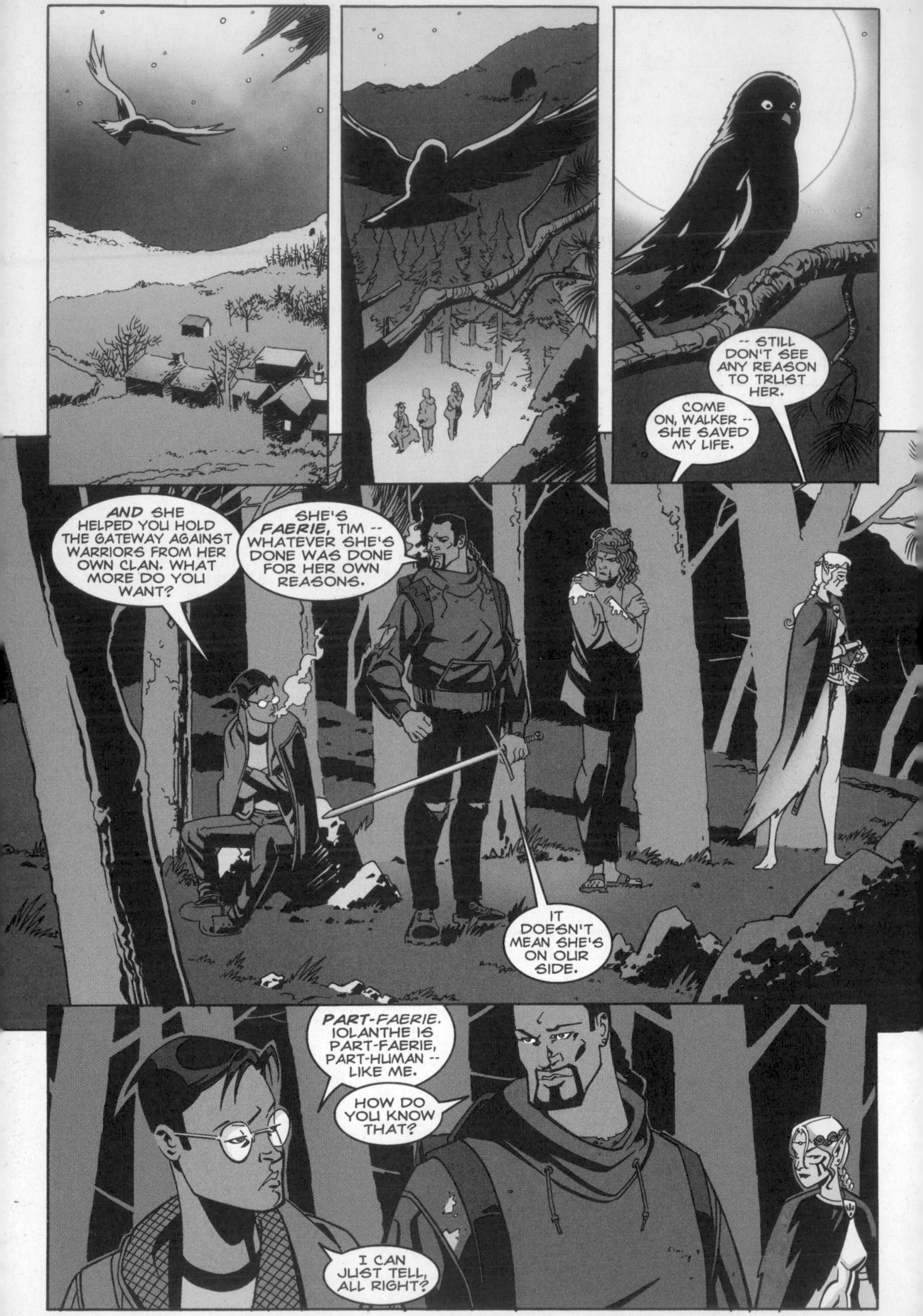
-- STILL DON'T SEE ANY REASON TO TRUST HER.
COME ON, WALKER -- SHE SAVED MY LIFE.
AND SHE HELPED YOU HOLD THE GATEWAY AGAINST WARRIORS FROM HER OWN CLAN. WHAT MORE DO YOU WANT?
SHE'S FAERIE, TIM -- WHATEVER SHE'S DONE WAS DONE FOR HER OWN REASONS.
IT DOESN'T MEAN SHE'S ON OUR SIDE.
PART-FAERIE. IOLANTHE IS PART-FAERIE, PART-HUMAN -- LIKE ME.
HOW DO YOU KNOW THAT?
I CAN JUST TELL, ALL RIGHT?

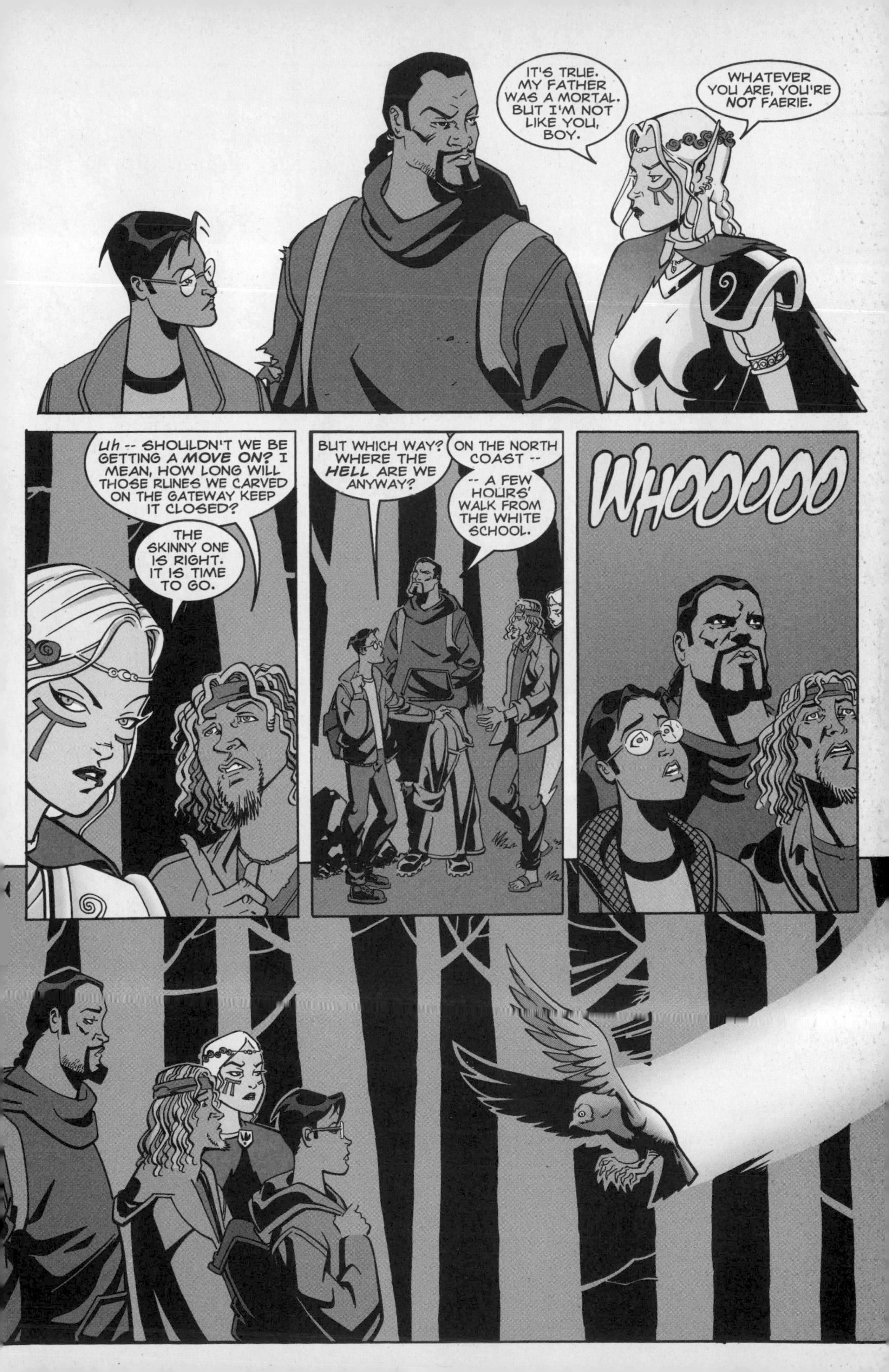
IT'S TRUE. MY FATHER WAS A MORTAL. BUT I'M NOT LIKE YOU, BOY.
WHATEVER YOU ARE, YOU'RE *NOT* FAERIE.
UH -- SHOULDN'T WE BE GETTING A *MOVE ON?* I MEAN, HOW LONG WILL THOSE RUNES WE CARVED ON THE GATEWAY KEEP IT CLOSED?
THE SKINNY ONE IS RIGHT. IT IS TIME TO GO.
BUT WHICH WAY? WHERE THE *HELL* ARE WE ANYWAY?
ON THE NORTH COAST --
-- A FEW HOURS' WALK FROM THE WHITE SCHOOL.
WHOOOOO

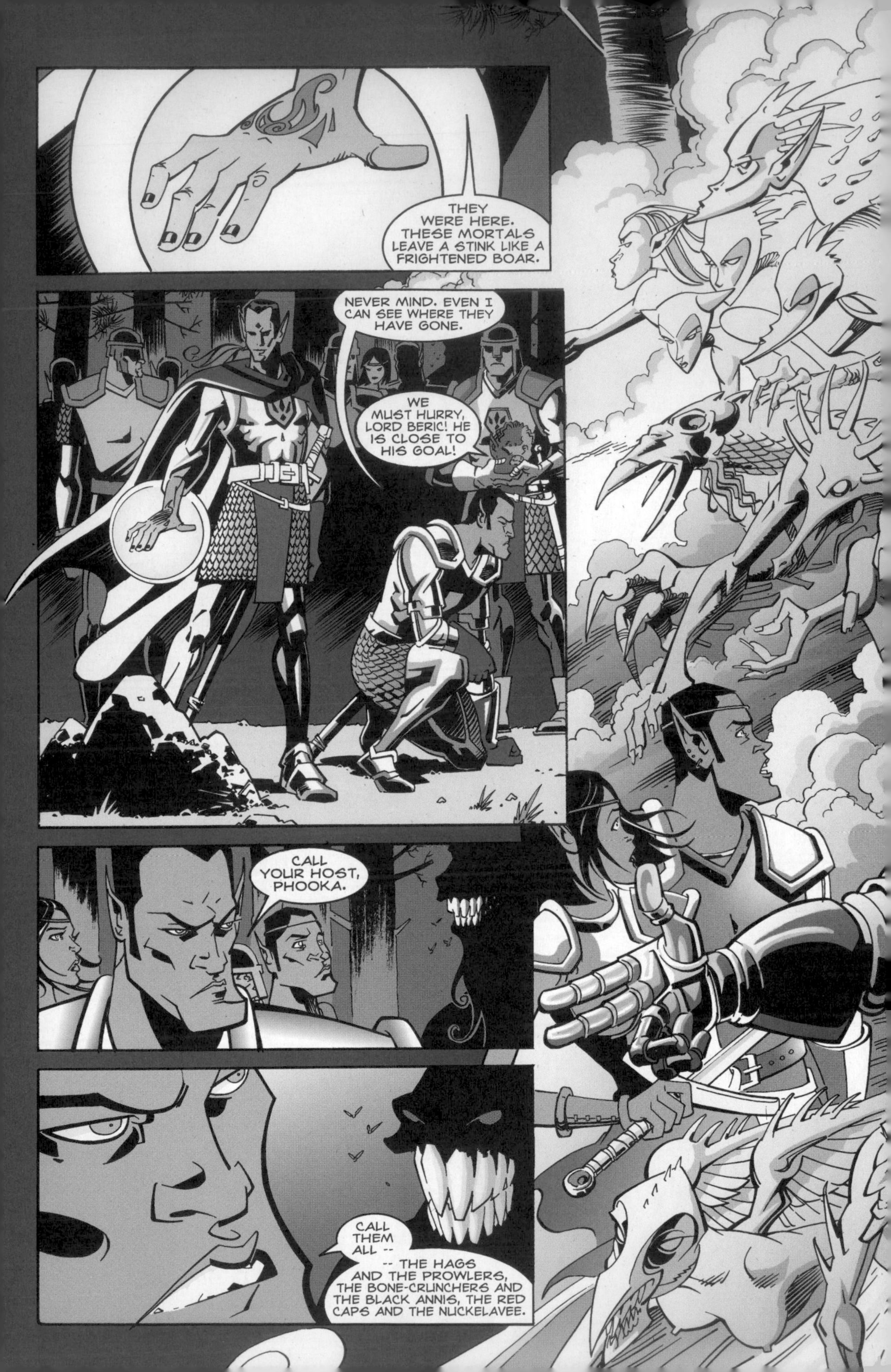
THEY WERE HERE. THESE MORTALS LEAVE A STINK LIKE A FRIGHTENED BOAR.
NEVER MIND. EVEN I CAN SEE WHERE THEY HAVE GONE.
WE MUST HURRY, LORD BERIC! HE IS CLOSE TO HIS GOAL!
CALL YOUR HOST, PHOOKA.
CALL THEM ALL --
-- THE HAGS AND THE PROWLERS, THE BONE-CRUNCHERS AND THE BLACK ANNIS, THE RED CAPS AND THE NUCKELAVEE.

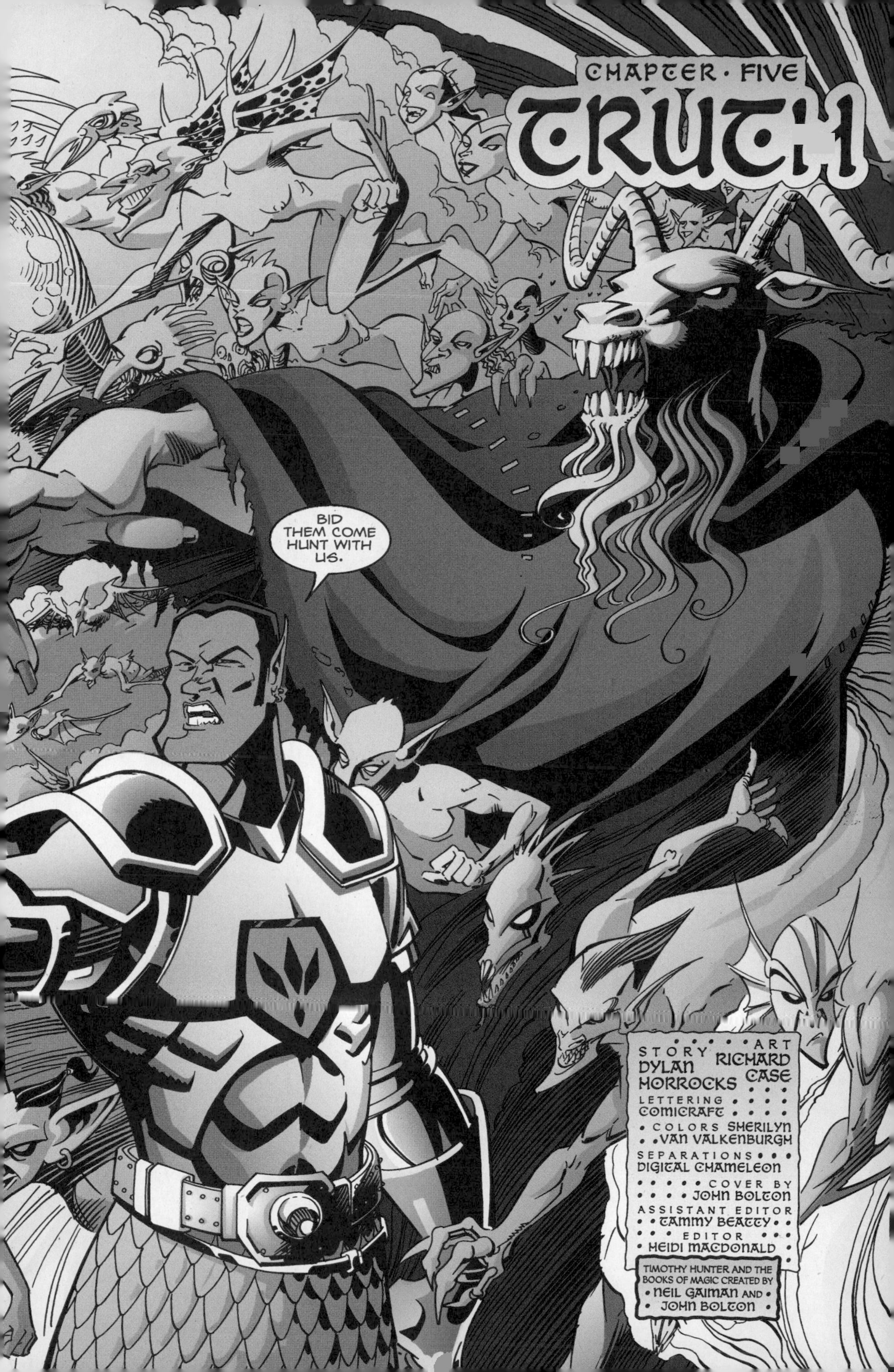
CHAPTER · FIVE
TRUTH
BID THEM COME HUNT WITH US.
STORY DYLAN HORROCKS
ART RICHARD CASE
LETTERING COMICRAFT
COLORS SHERILYN VAN VALKENBURGH
SEPARATIONS DIGITAL CHAMELEON
COVER BY JOHN BOLTON
ASSISTANT EDITOR TAMMY BEATTY
EDITOR HEIDI MACDONALD
TIMOTHY HUNTER AND THE BOOKS OF MAGIC CREATED BY NEIL GAIMAN AND JOHN BOLTON

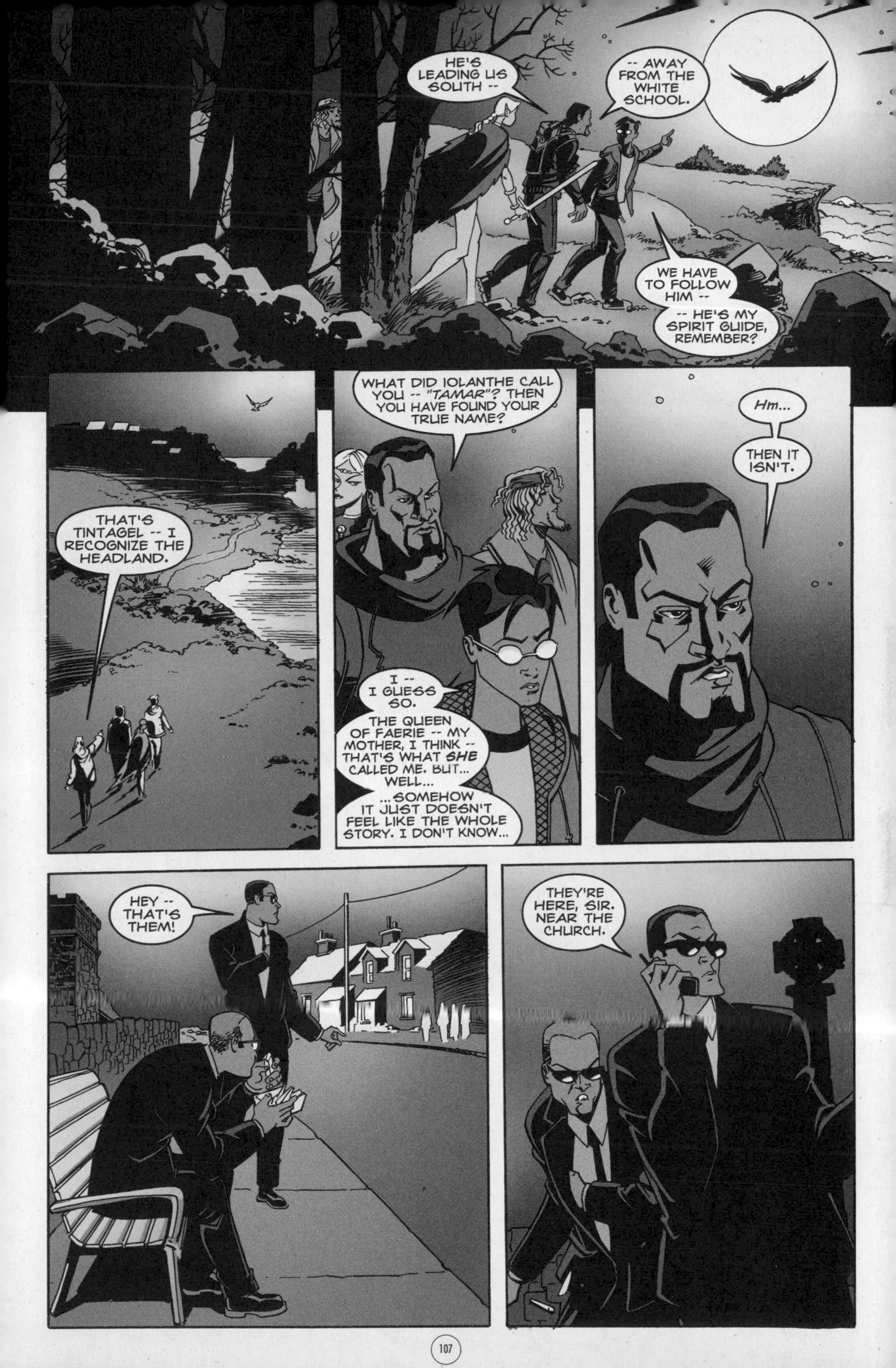
HE'S LEADING US SOUTH --
-- AWAY FROM THE WHITE SCHOOL.
WE HAVE TO FOLLOW HIM --
-- HE'S MY SPIRIT GUIDE, REMEMBER?
THAT'S TINTAGEL -- I RECOGNIZE THE HEADLAND.
WHAT DID IOLANTHE CALL YOU -- "TAMAR"? THEN YOU HAVE FOUND YOUR TRUE NAME?
I -- I GUESS SO.
THE QUEEN OF FAERIE -- MY MOTHER, I THINK -- THAT'S WHAT SHE CALLED ME. BUT... WELL...
...SOMEHOW IT JUST DOESN'T FEEL LIKE THE WHOLE STORY. I DON'T KNOW...
Hm...
THEN IT ISN'T.
HEY -- THAT'S THEM!
THEY'RE HERE, SIR. NEAR THE CHURCH.

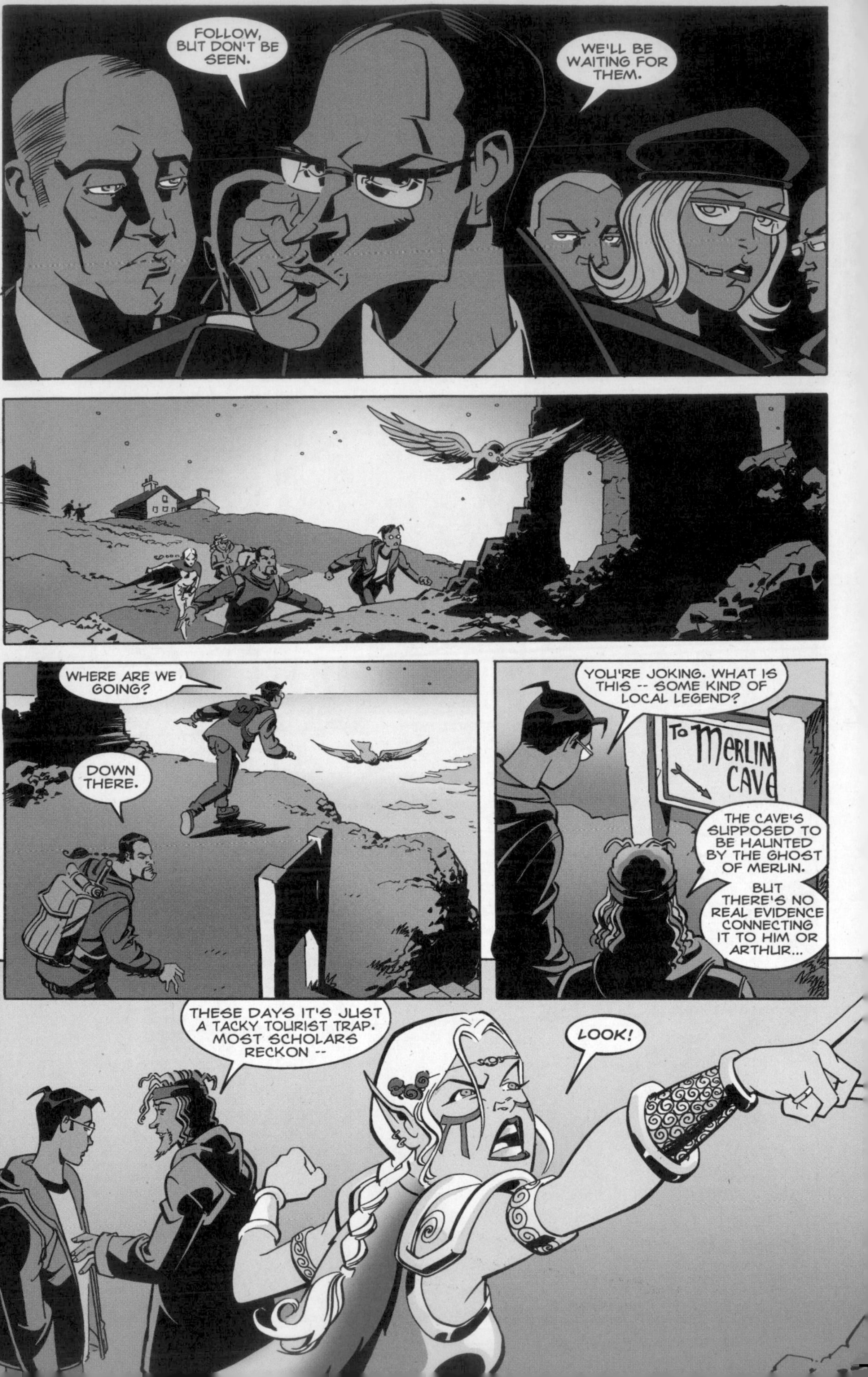
FOLLOW, BUT DON'T BE SEEN.
WE'LL BE WAITING FOR THEM.
WHERE ARE WE GOING?
DOWN THERE.
YOU'RE JOKING. WHAT IS THIS -- SOME KIND OF LOCAL LEGEND?
To Merlin Cave
THE CAVE'S SUPPOSED TO BE HAUNTED BY THE GHOST OF MERLIN.
BUT THERE'S NO REAL EVIDENCE CONNECTING IT TO HIM OR ARTHUR...
THESE DAYS IT'S JUST A TACKY TOURIST TRAP. MOST SCHOLARS RECKON --
LOOK!

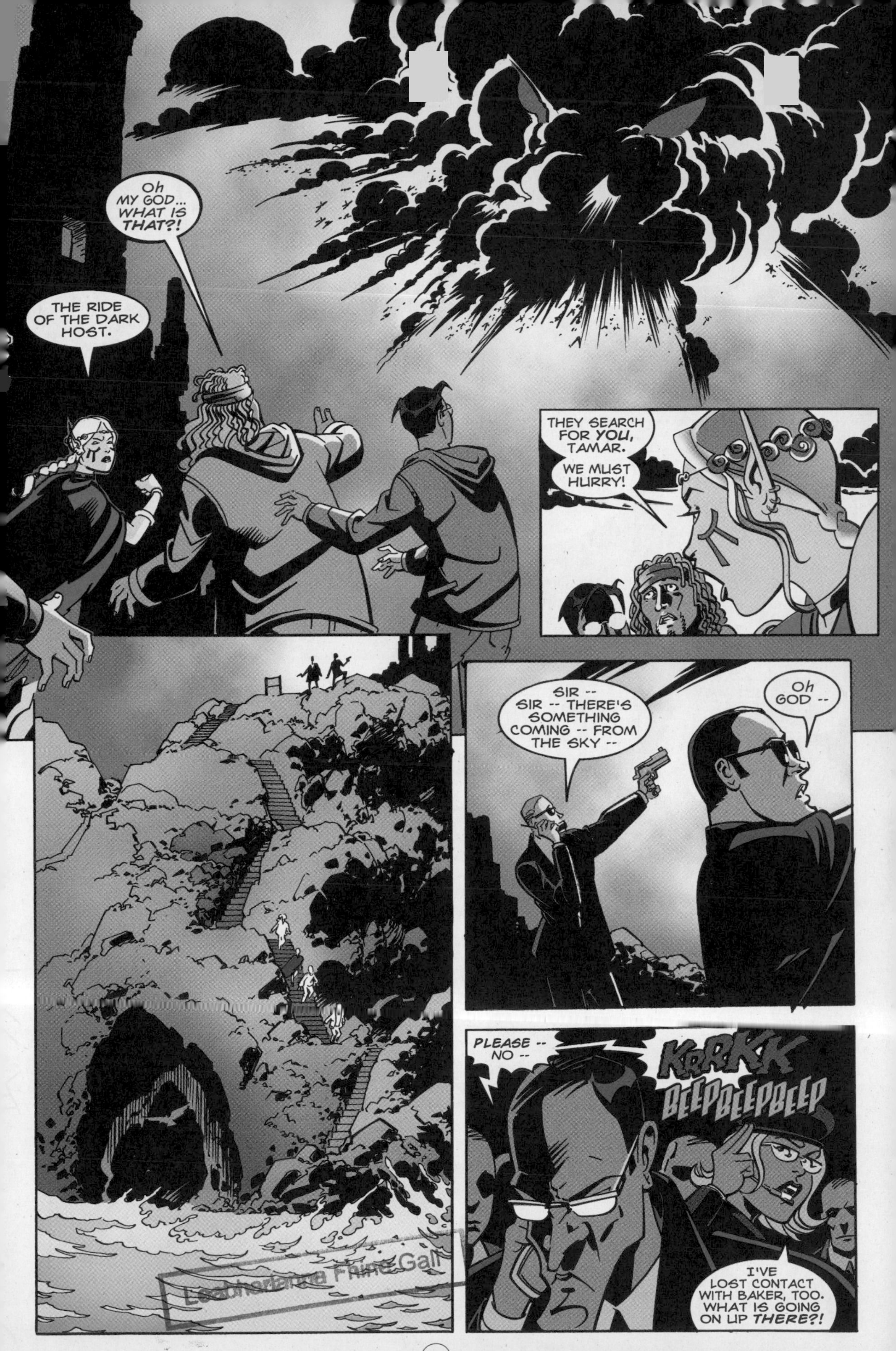
Oh MY GOD... WHAT IS THAT?!
THE RIDE OF THE DARK HOST.
THEY SEARCH FOR YOU, TAMAR.
WE MUST HURRY!
SIR -- SIR -- THERE'S SOMETHING COMING -- FROM THE SKY --
Oh GOD --
PLEASE -- NO --
KRRKK
BEEPBEEPBEEP
I'VE LOST CONTACT WITH BAKER, TOO. WHAT IS GOING ON UP THERE?!

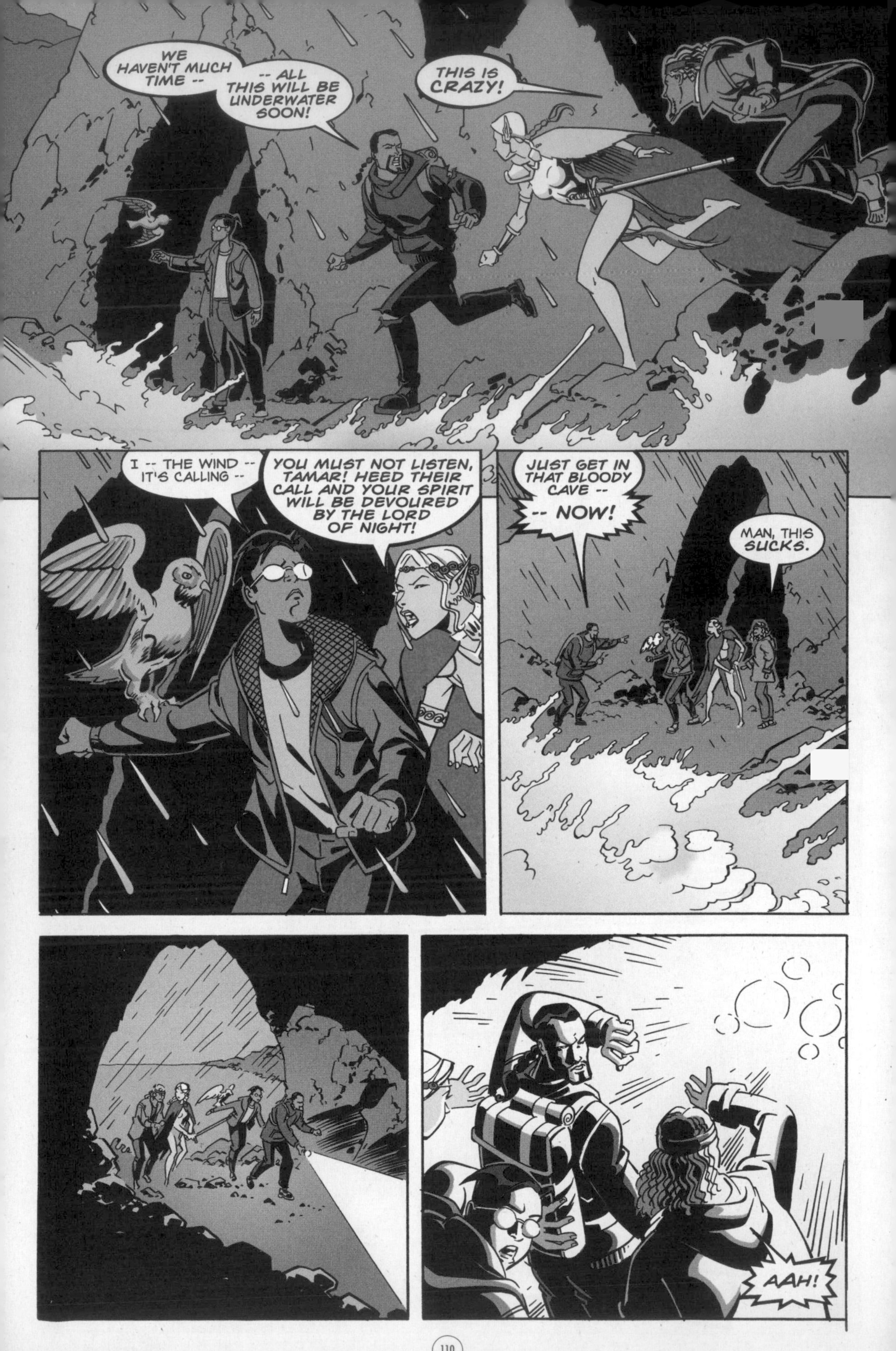

WE HAVEN'T MUCH TIME --
-- ALL THIS WILL BE UNDERWATER SOON!
THIS IS CRAZY!
I -- THE WIND -- IT'S CALLING --
YOU MUST NOT LISTEN, TAMAR! HEED THEIR CALL AND YOUR SPIRIT WILL BE DEVOURED BY THE LORD OF NIGHT!
JUST GET IN THAT BLOODY CAVE --
-- NOW!
MAN, THIS SUCKS.
AAH!

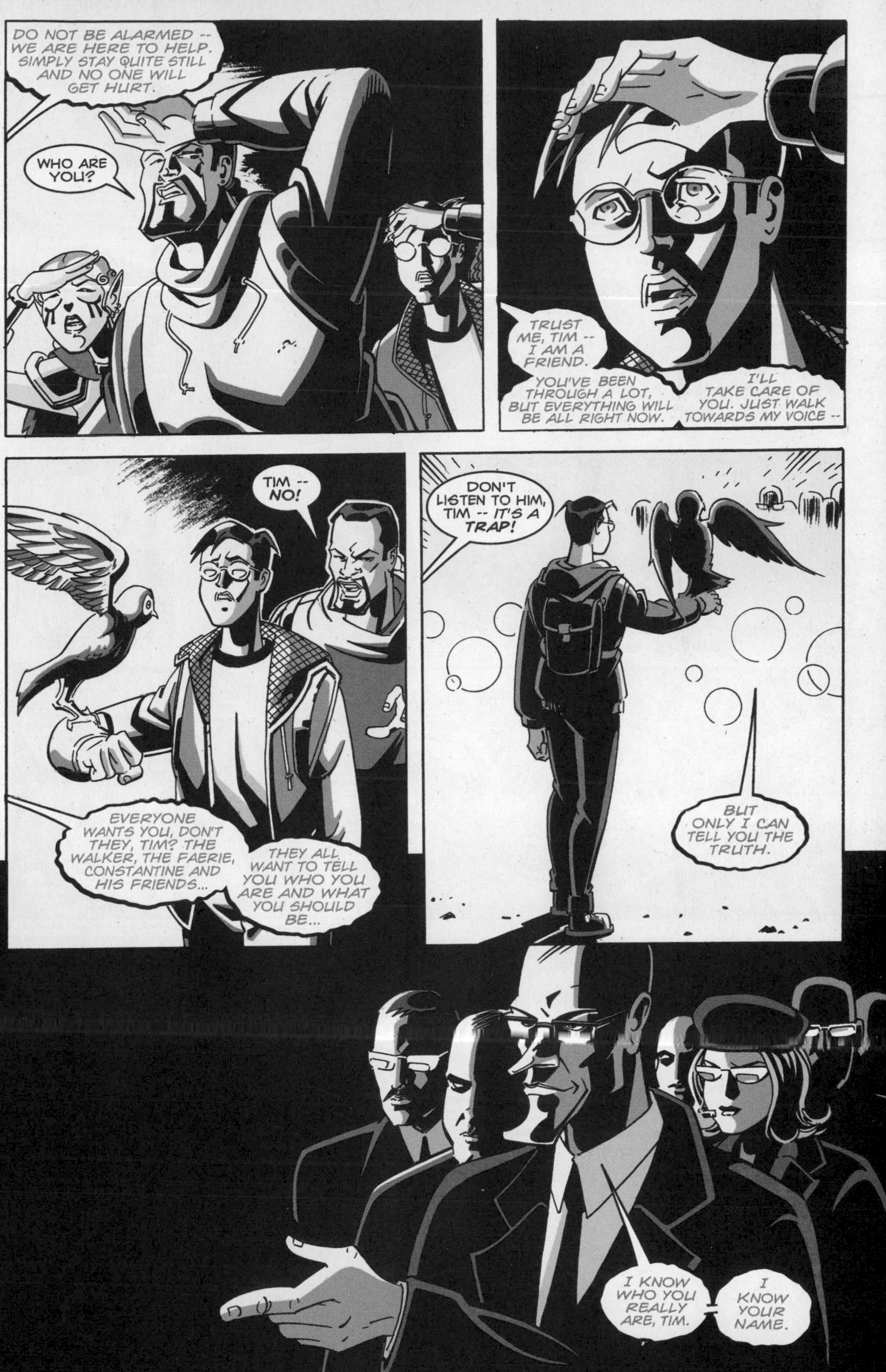
DO NOT BE ALARMED -- WE ARE HERE TO HELP. SIMPLY STAY QUITE STILL AND NO ONE WILL GET HURT.
WHO ARE YOU?
TRUST ME, TIM -- I AM A FRIEND.
YOU'VE BEEN THROUGH A LOT, BUT EVERYTHING WILL BE ALL RIGHT NOW.
I'LL TAKE CARE OF YOU. JUST WALK TOWARDS MY VOICE --
TIM -- NO!
EVERYONE WANTS YOU, DON'T THEY, TIM? THE WALKER, THE FAERIE, CONSTANTINE AND HIS FRIENDS...
THEY ALL WANT TO TELL YOU WHO YOU ARE AND WHAT YOU SHOULD BE...
DON'T LISTEN TO HIM, TIM -- IT'S A TRAP!
BUT ONLY I CAN TELL YOU THE TRUTH.
I KNOW WHO YOU REALLY ARE, TIM.
I KNOW YOUR NAME.

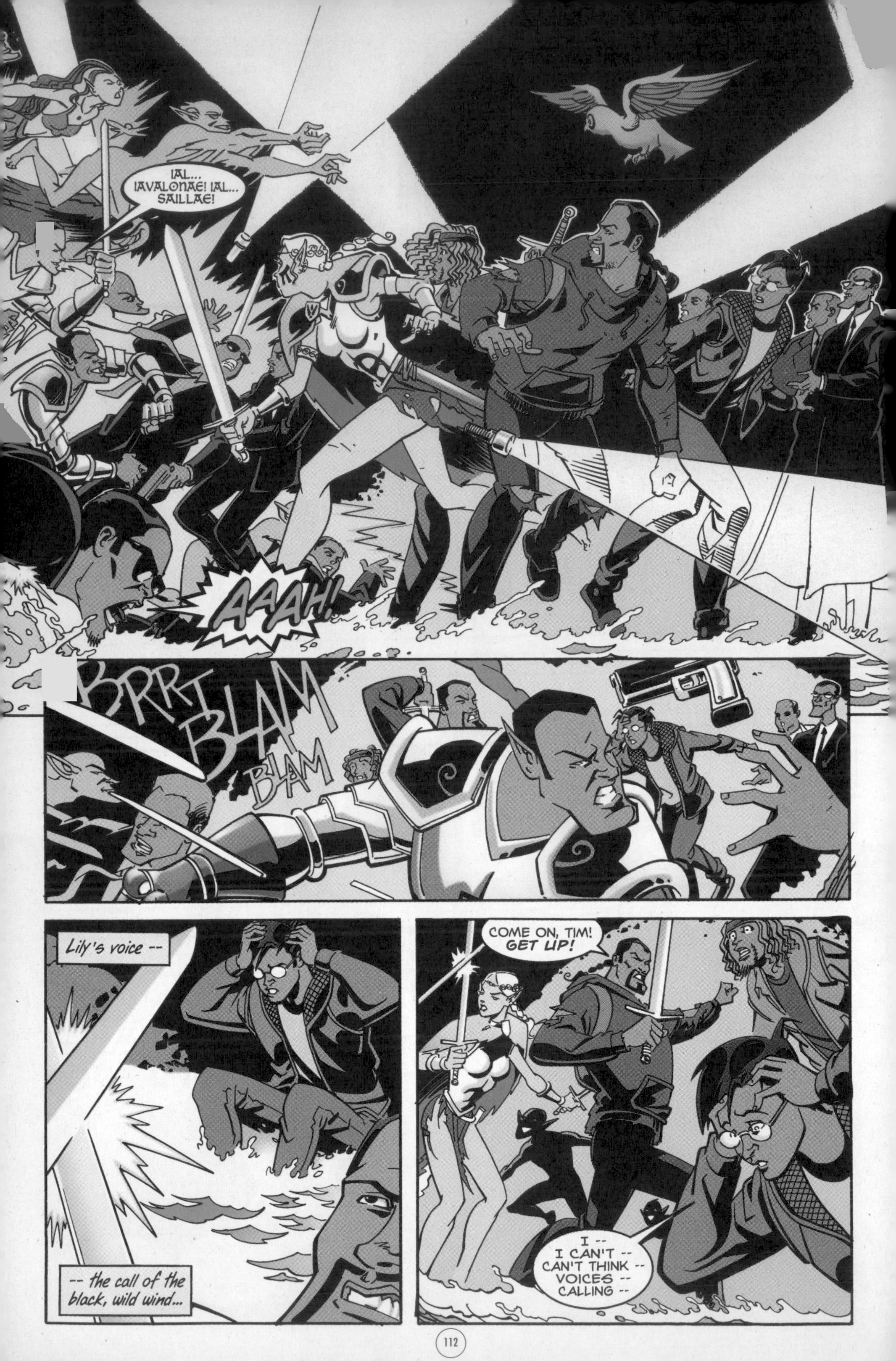

¡AL... ¡AVALONAE! ¡AL... SAILLAE!
AAAH!
BRRT BLAM BLAM
Lily's voice --
-- the call of the black, wild wind...
COME ON, TIM! GET UP!
I -- I CAN'T -- CAN'T THINK -- VOICES -- CALLING --

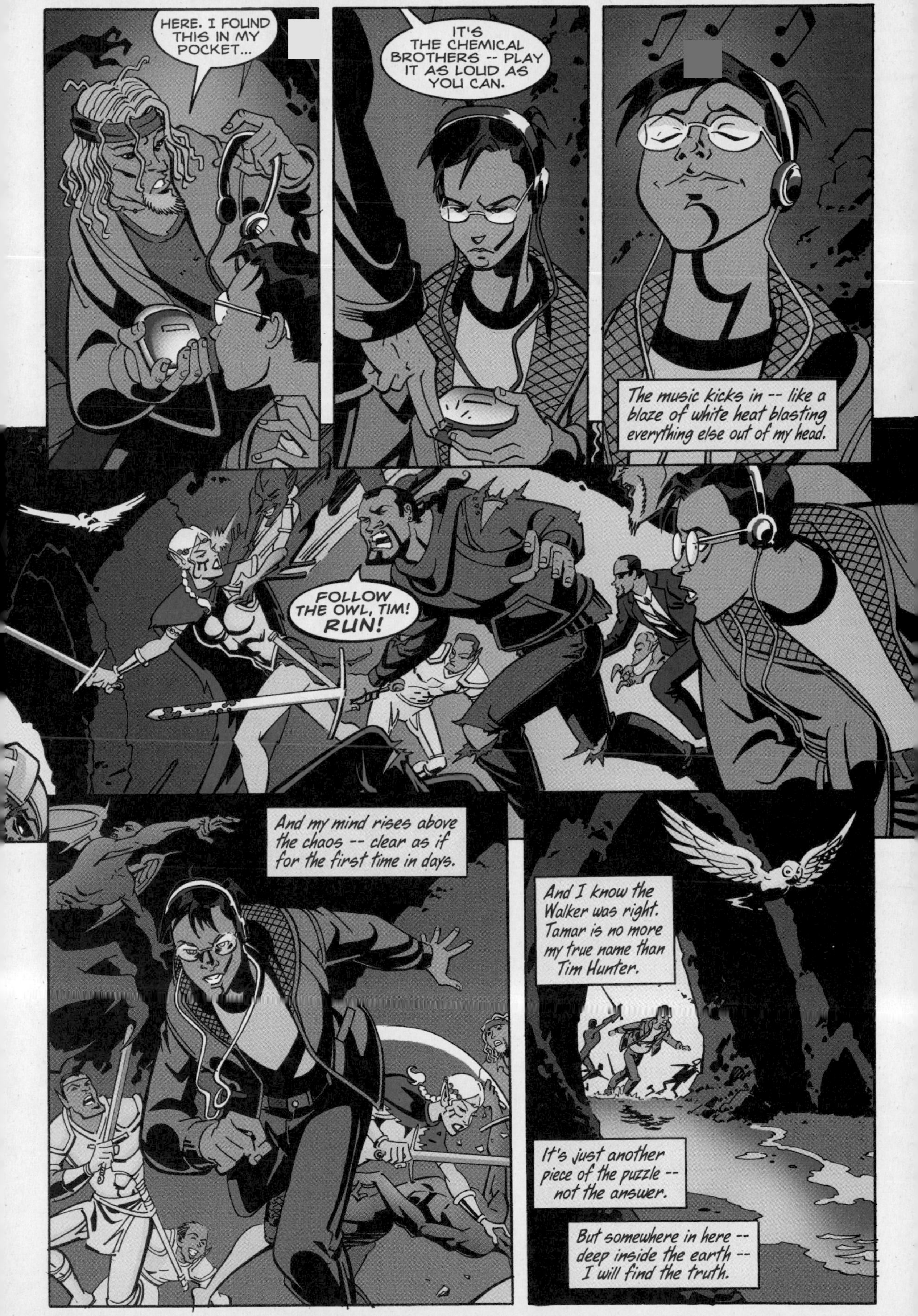
HERE. I FOUND THIS IN MY POCKET...
IT'S THE CHEMICAL BROTHERS -- PLAY IT AS LOUD AS YOU CAN.
The music kicks in -- like a blaze of white heat blasting everything else out of my head.
FOLLOW THE OWL, TIM! RUN!
And my mind rises above the chaos -- clear as if for the first time in days.
And I know the Walker was right. Tamar is no more my true name than Tim Hunter.
It's just another piece of the puzzle -- not the answer.
But somewhere in here -- deep inside the earth -- I will find the truth.

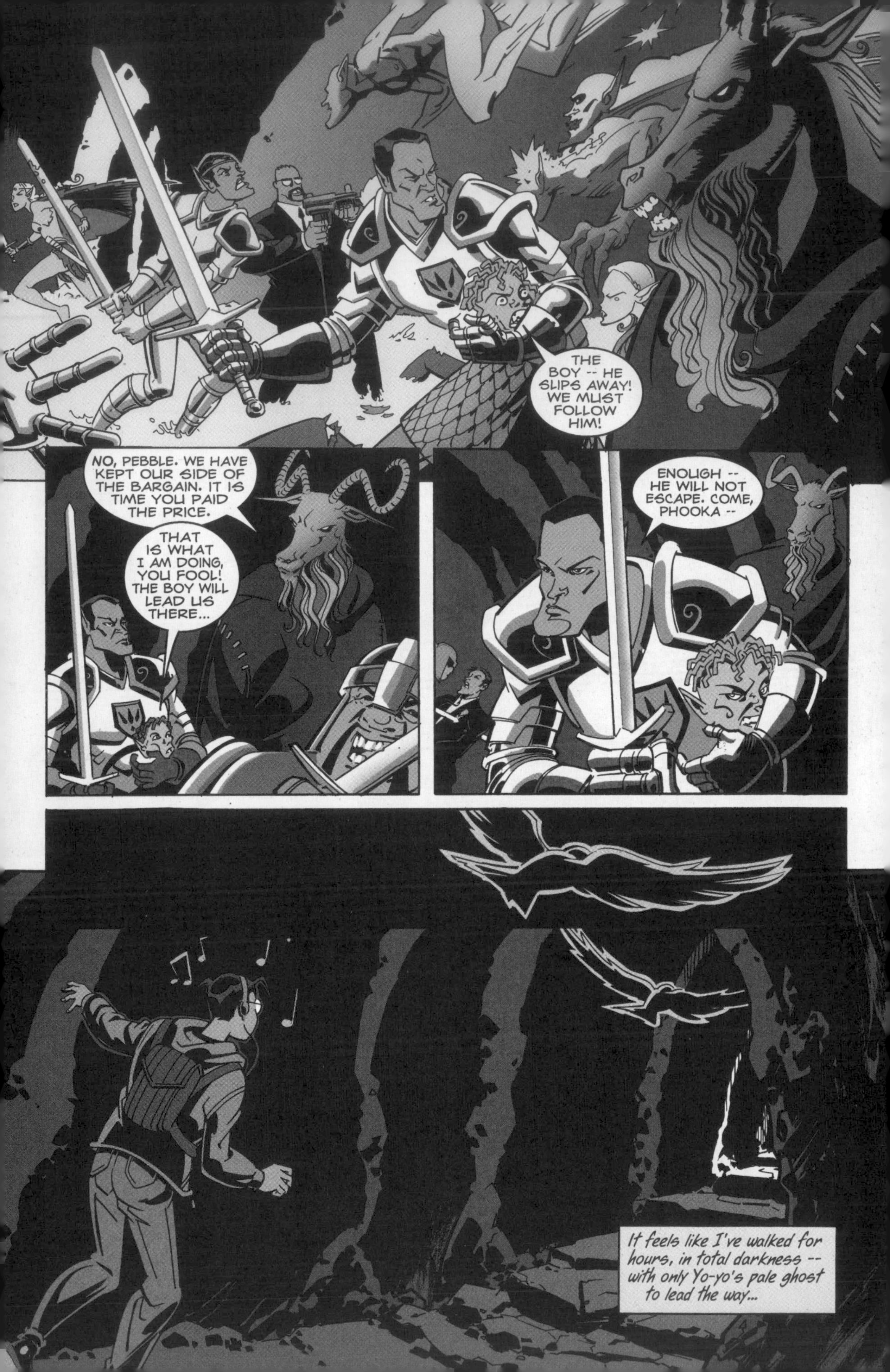
THE BOY -- HE SLIPS AWAY! WE MUST FOLLOW HIM!
NO, PEBBLE. WE HAVE KEPT OUR SIDE OF THE BARGAIN. IT IS TIME YOU PAID THE PRICE.
THAT IS WHAT I AM DOING, YOU FOOL! THE BOY WILL LEAD US THERE...
ENOUGH -- HE WILL NOT ESCAPE. COME, PHOOKA --
It feels like I've walked for hours, in total darkness -- with only Yo-yo's pale ghost to lead the way...

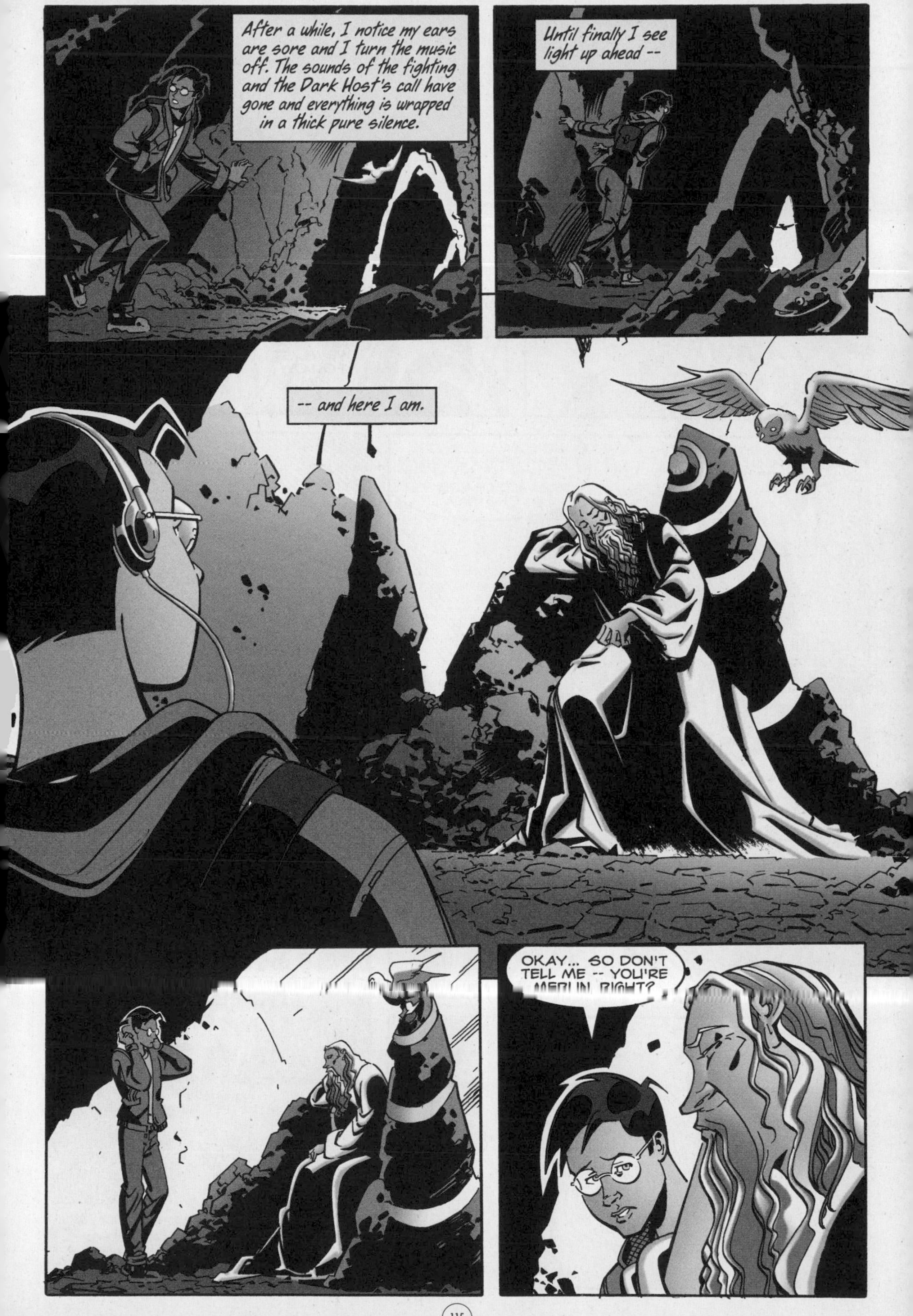
After a while, I notice my ears are sore and I turn the music off. The sounds of the fighting and the Dark Host's call have gone and everything is wrapped in a thick pure silence.
Until finally I see light up ahead --
-- and here I am.
OKAY... SO DON'T TELL ME -- YOU'RE MERLIN, RIGHT?

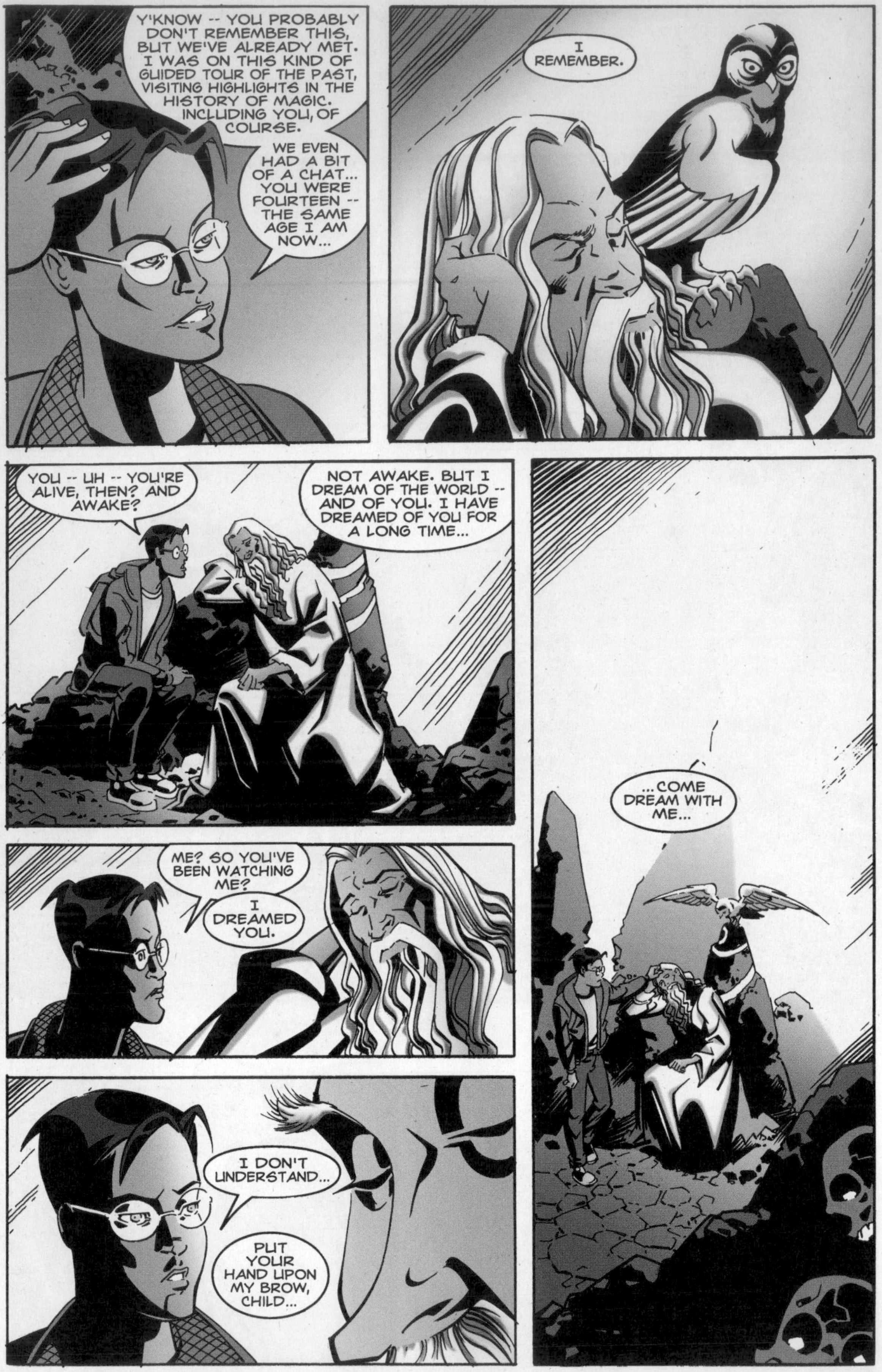
Y'KNOW -- YOU PROBABLY DON'T REMEMBER THIS, BUT WE'VE ALREADY MET. I WAS ON THIS KIND OF GUIDED TOUR OF THE PAST, VISITING HIGHLIGHTS IN THE HISTORY OF MAGIC. INCLUDING YOU, OF COURSE.
WE EVEN HAD A BIT OF A CHAT... YOU WERE FOURTEEN -- THE SAME AGE I AM NOW...
I REMEMBER.
YOU -- UH -- YOU'RE ALIVE, THEN? AND AWAKE?
NOT AWAKE. BUT I DREAM OF THE WORLD -- AND OF YOU. I HAVE DREAMED OF YOU FOR A LONG TIME...
ME? SO YOU'VE BEEN WATCHING ME?
I DREAMED YOU.
I DON'T UNDERSTAND...
PUT YOUR HAND UPON MY BROW, CHILD...
...COME DREAM WITH ME...

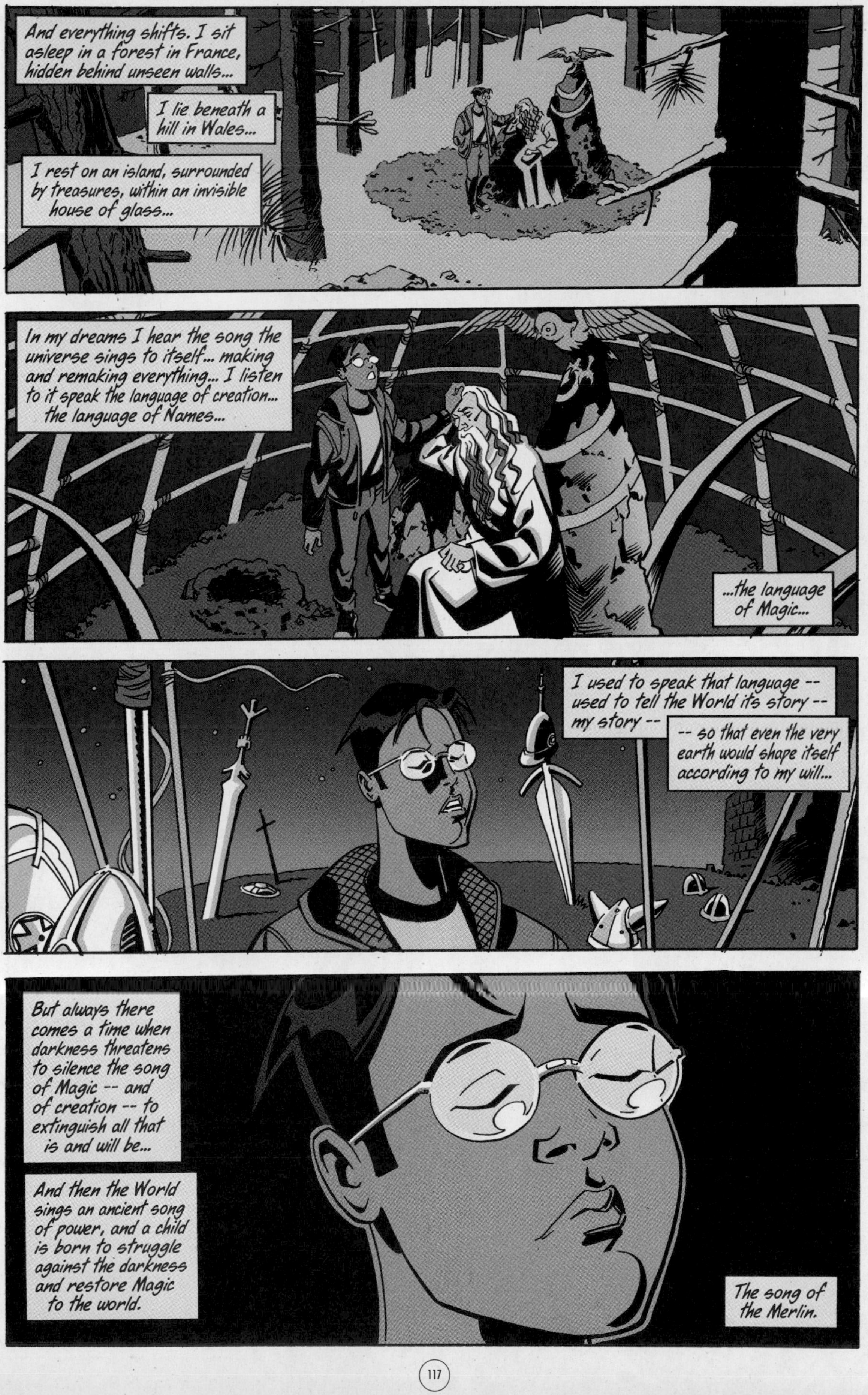

And everything shifts. I sit asleep in a forest in France, hidden behind unseen walls...
I lie beneath a hill in Wales...
I rest on an island, surrounded by treasures, within an invisible house of glass...
In my dreams I hear the song the universe sings to itself... making and remaking everything... I listen to it speak the language of creation... the language of Names...
...the language of Magic...
I used to speak that language -- used to tell the World its story -- my story --
-- so that even the very earth would shape itself according to my will...
But always there comes a time when darkness threatens to silence the song of Magic -- and of creation -- to extinguish all that is and will be...
And then the World sings an ancient song of power, and a child is born to struggle against the darkness and restore Magic to the world.
The song of the Merlin.

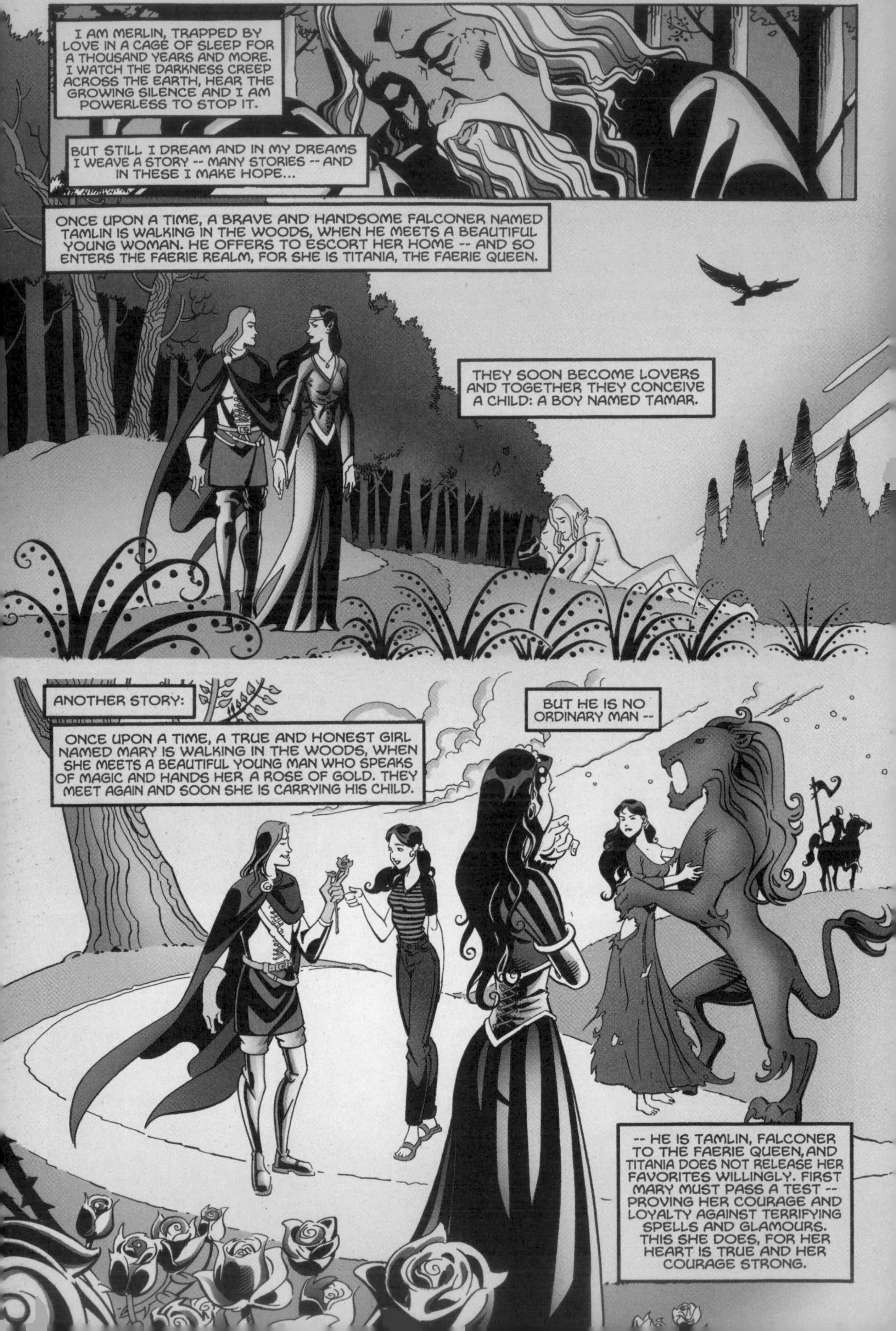
I AM MERLIN, TRAPPED BY LOVE IN A CAGE OF SLEEP FOR A THOUSAND YEARS AND MORE. I WATCH THE DARKNESS CREEP ACROSS THE EARTH, HEAR THE GROWING SILENCE AND I AM POWERLESS TO STOP IT.
BUT STILL I DREAM AND IN MY DREAMS I WEAVE A STORY -- MANY STORIES -- AND IN THESE I MAKE HOPE...
ONCE UPON A TIME, A BRAVE AND HANDSOME FALCONER NAMED TAMLIN IS WALKING IN THE WOODS, WHEN HE MEETS A BEAUTIFUL YOUNG WOMAN. HE OFFERS TO ESCORT HER HOME -- AND SO ENTERS THE FAERIE REALM, FOR SHE IS TITANIA, THE FAERIE QUEEN.
THEY SOON BECOME LOVERS AND TOGETHER THEY CONCEIVE A CHILD: A BOY NAMED TAMAR.
ANOTHER STORY:
ONCE UPON A TIME, A TRUE AND HONEST GIRL NAMED MARY IS WALKING IN THE WOODS, WHEN SHE MEETS A BEAUTIFUL YOUNG MAN WHO SPEAKS OF MAGIC AND HANDS HER A ROSE OF GOLD. THEY MEET AGAIN AND SOON SHE IS CARRYING HIS CHILD.
BUT HE IS NO ORDINARY MAN --
-- HE IS TAMLIN, FALCONER TO THE FAERIE QUEEN, AND TITANIA DOES NOT RELEASE HER FAVORITES WILLINGLY. FIRST MARY MUST PASS A TEST -- PROVING HER COURAGE AND LOYALTY AGAINST TERRIFYING SPELLS AND GLAMOURS. THIS SHE DOES, FOR HER HEART IS TRUE AND HER COURAGE STRONG.

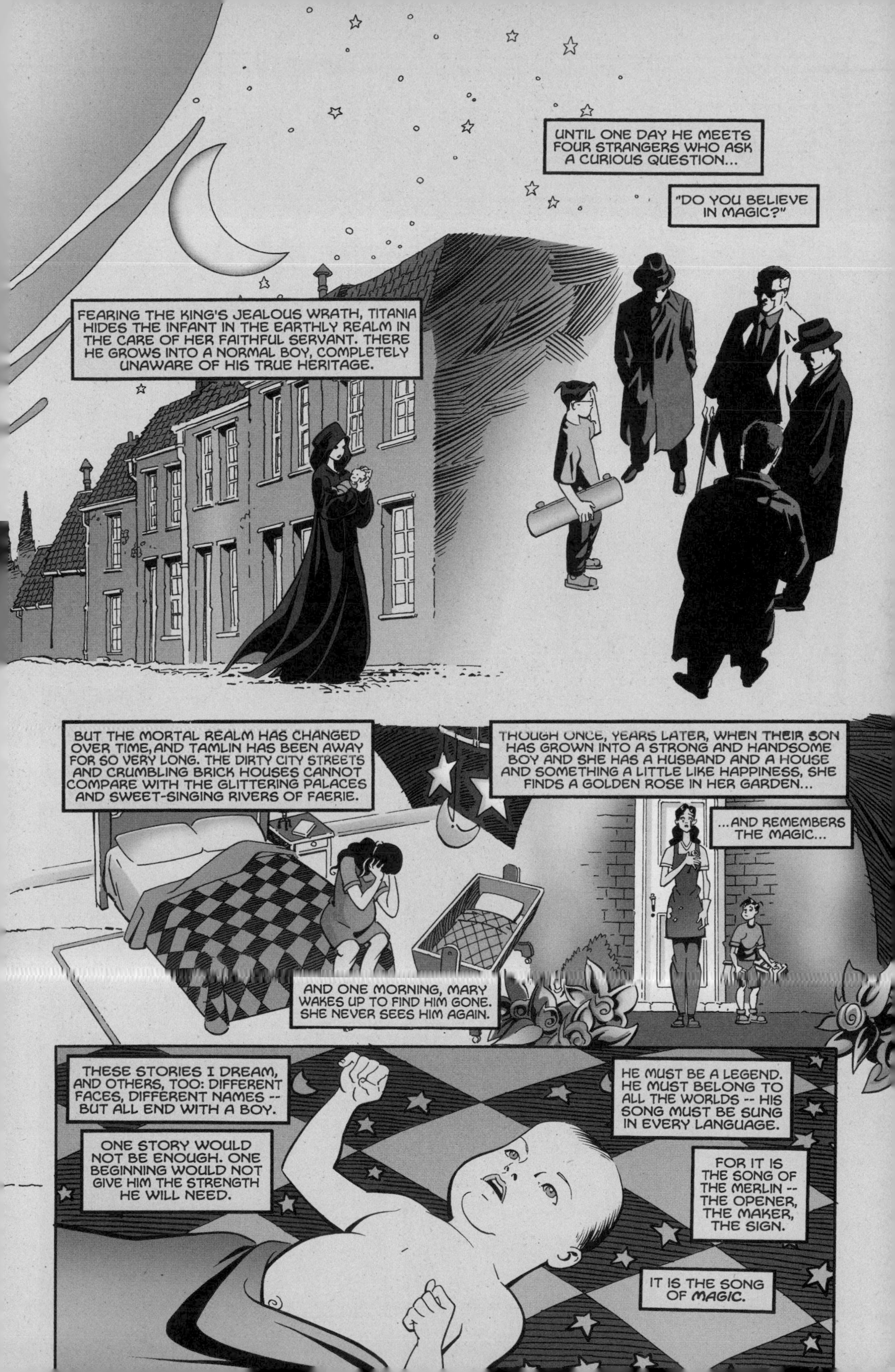
UNTIL ONE DAY HE MEETS FOUR STRANGERS WHO ASK A CURIOUS QUESTION...
"DO YOU BELIEVE IN MAGIC?"
FEARING THE KING'S JEALOUS WRATH, TITANIA HIDES THE INFANT IN THE EARTHLY REALM IN THE CARE OF HER FAITHFUL SERVANT. THERE HE GROWS INTO A NORMAL BOY, COMPLETELY UNAWARE OF HIS TRUE HERITAGE.
BUT THE MORTAL REALM HAS CHANGED OVER TIME, AND TAMLIN HAS BEEN AWAY FOR SO VERY LONG. THE DIRTY CITY STREETS AND CRUMBLING BRICK HOUSES CANNOT COMPARE WITH THE GLITTERING PALACES AND SWEET-SINGING RIVERS OF FAERIE.
AND ONE MORNING, MARY WAKES UP TO FIND HIM GONE. SHE NEVER SEES HIM AGAIN.
THOUGH ONCE, YEARS LATER, WHEN THEIR SON HAS GROWN INTO A STRONG AND HANDSOME BOY AND SHE HAS A HUSBAND AND A HOUSE AND SOMETHING A LITTLE LIKE HAPPINESS, SHE FINDS A GOLDEN ROSE IN HER GARDEN...
...AND REMEMBERS THE MAGIC...
THESE STORIES I DREAM, AND OTHERS, TOO: DIFFERENT FACES, DIFFERENT NAMES -- BUT ALL END WITH A BOY.
ONE STORY WOULD NOT BE ENOUGH. ONE BEGINNING WOULD NOT GIVE HIM THE STRENGTH HE WILL NEED.
HE MUST BE A LEGEND. HE MUST BELONG TO ALL THE WORLDS -- HIS SONG MUST BE SUNG IN EVERY LANGUAGE.
FOR IT IS THE SONG OF THE MERLIN -- THE OPENER, THE MAKER, THE SIGN.
IT IS THE SONG OF MAGIC.

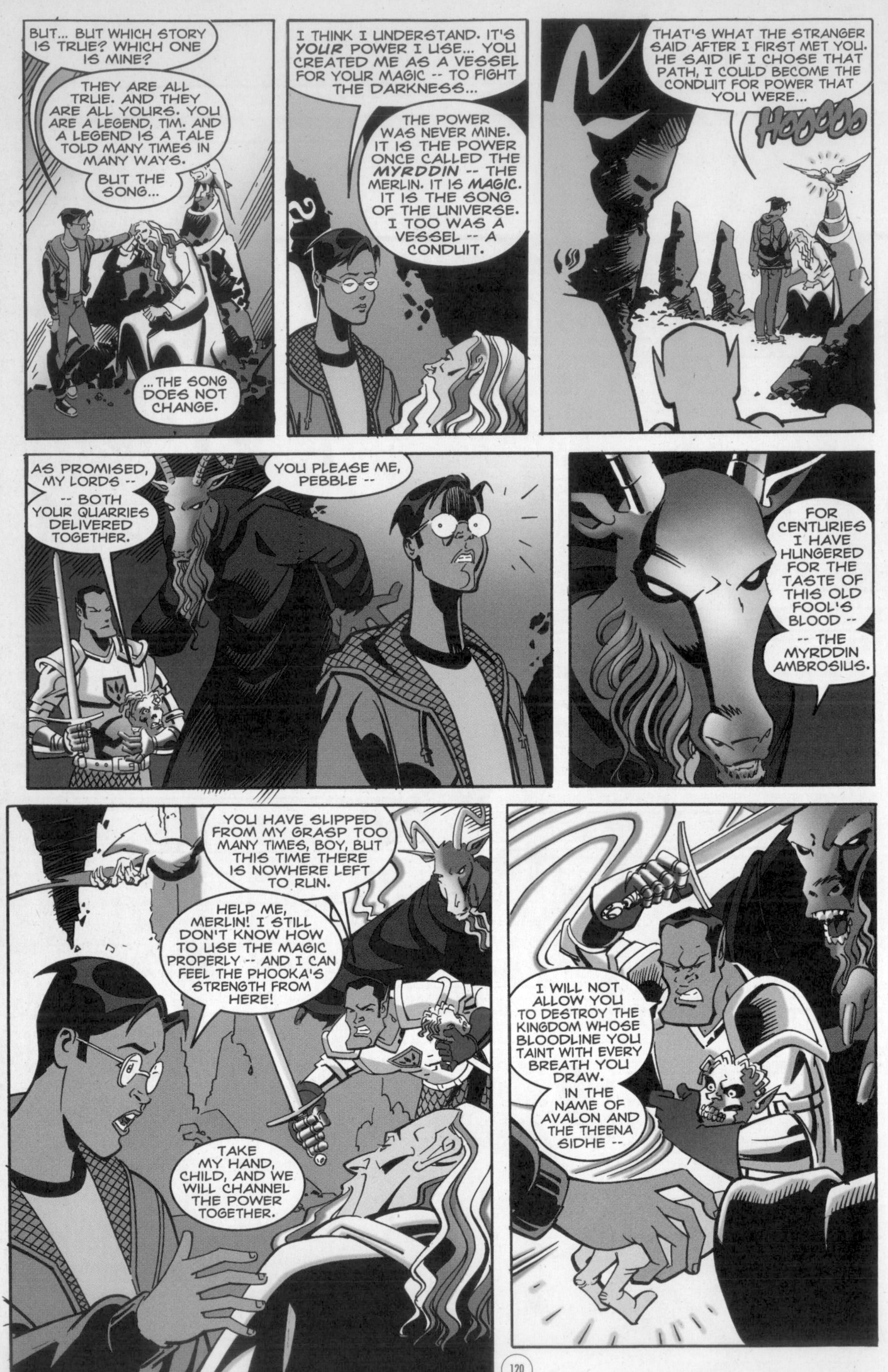
BUT... BUT WHICH STORY IS TRUE? WHICH ONE IS MINE?
THEY ARE ALL TRUE. AND THEY ARE ALL YOURS. YOU ARE A LEGEND, TIM. AND A LEGEND IS A TALE TOLD MANY TIMES IN MANY WAYS.
BUT THE SONG...
...THE SONG DOES NOT CHANGE.
I THINK I UNDERSTAND. IT'S YOUR POWER I USE... YOU CREATED ME AS A VESSEL FOR YOUR MAGIC -- TO FIGHT THE DARKNESS...
THE POWER WAS NEVER MINE. IT IS THE POWER ONCE CALLED THE MYRDDIN -- THE MERLIN. IT IS MAGIC. IT IS THE SONG OF THE UNIVERSE. I TOO WAS A VESSEL -- A CONDUIT.
THAT'S WHAT THE STRANGER SAID AFTER I FIRST MET YOU. HE SAID IF I CHOSE THAT PATH, I COULD BECOME THE CONDUIT FOR POWER THAT YOU WERE...
HOOOOo
AS PROMISED, MY LORDS --
-- BOTH YOUR QUARRIES DELIVERED TOGETHER.
YOU PLEASE ME, PEBBLE --
FOR CENTURIES I HAVE HUNGERED FOR THE TASTE OF THIS OLD FOOL'S BLOOD --
-- THE MYRDDIN AMBROSIUS.
YOU HAVE SLIPPED FROM MY GRASP TOO MANY TIMES, BOY, BUT THIS TIME THERE IS NOWHERE LEFT TO RUN.
HELP ME, MERLIN! I STILL DON'T KNOW HOW TO USE THE MAGIC PROPERLY -- AND I CAN FEEL THE PHOOKA'S STRENGTH FROM HERE!
TAKE MY HAND, CHILD, AND WE WILL CHANNEL THE POWER TOGETHER.
I WILL NOT ALLOW YOU TO DESTROY THE KINGDOM WHOSE BLOODLINE YOU TAINT WITH EVERY BREATH YOU DRAW.
IN THE NAME OF AVALON AND THE THEENA SIDHE --

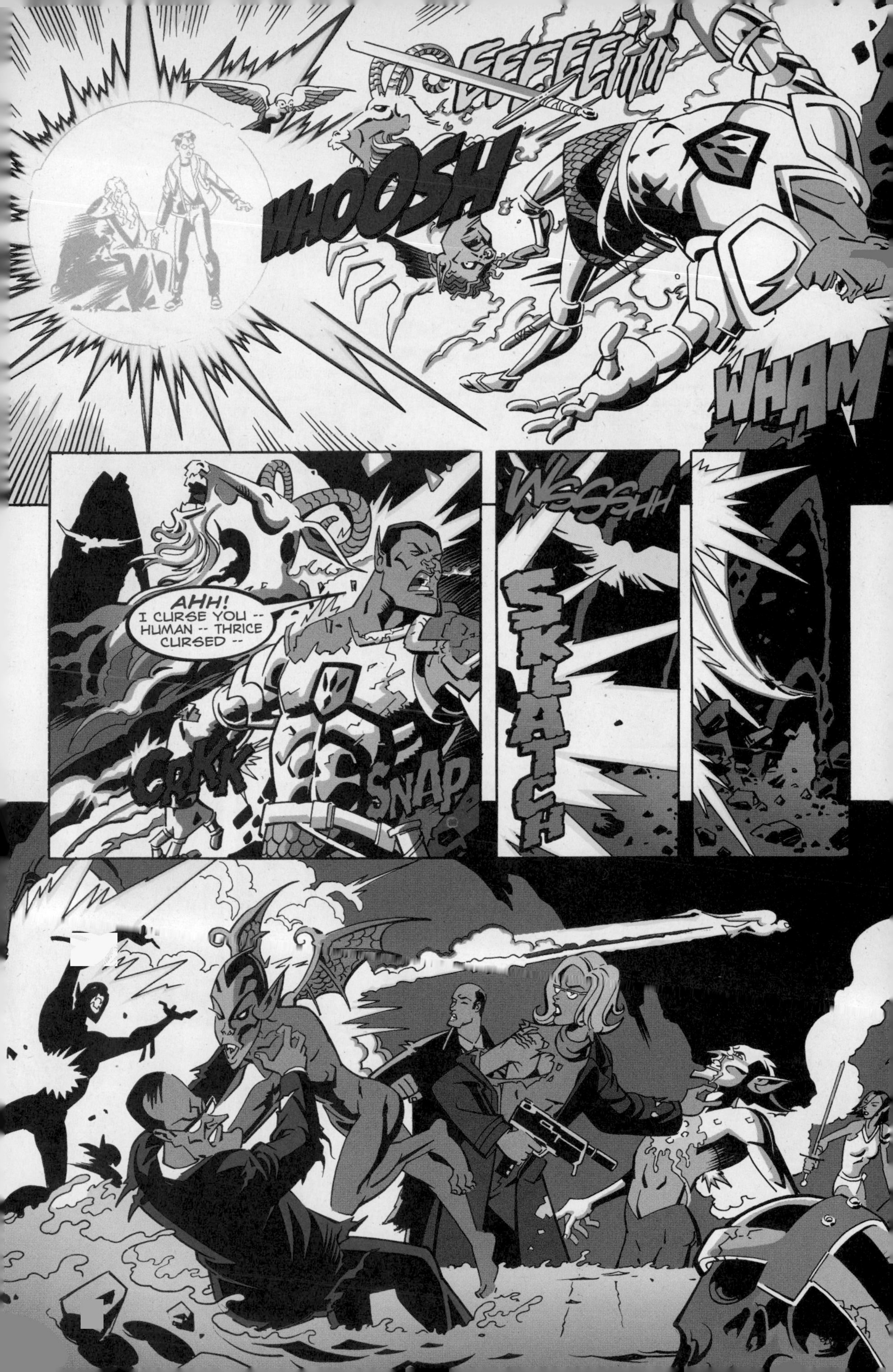
EEEEEEEIIIII
WHOOSH
WHAM
AHH! I CURSE YOU -- HUMAN -- THRICE CURSED --
CRKK
SNAP
WSSSHH
SKLATCH

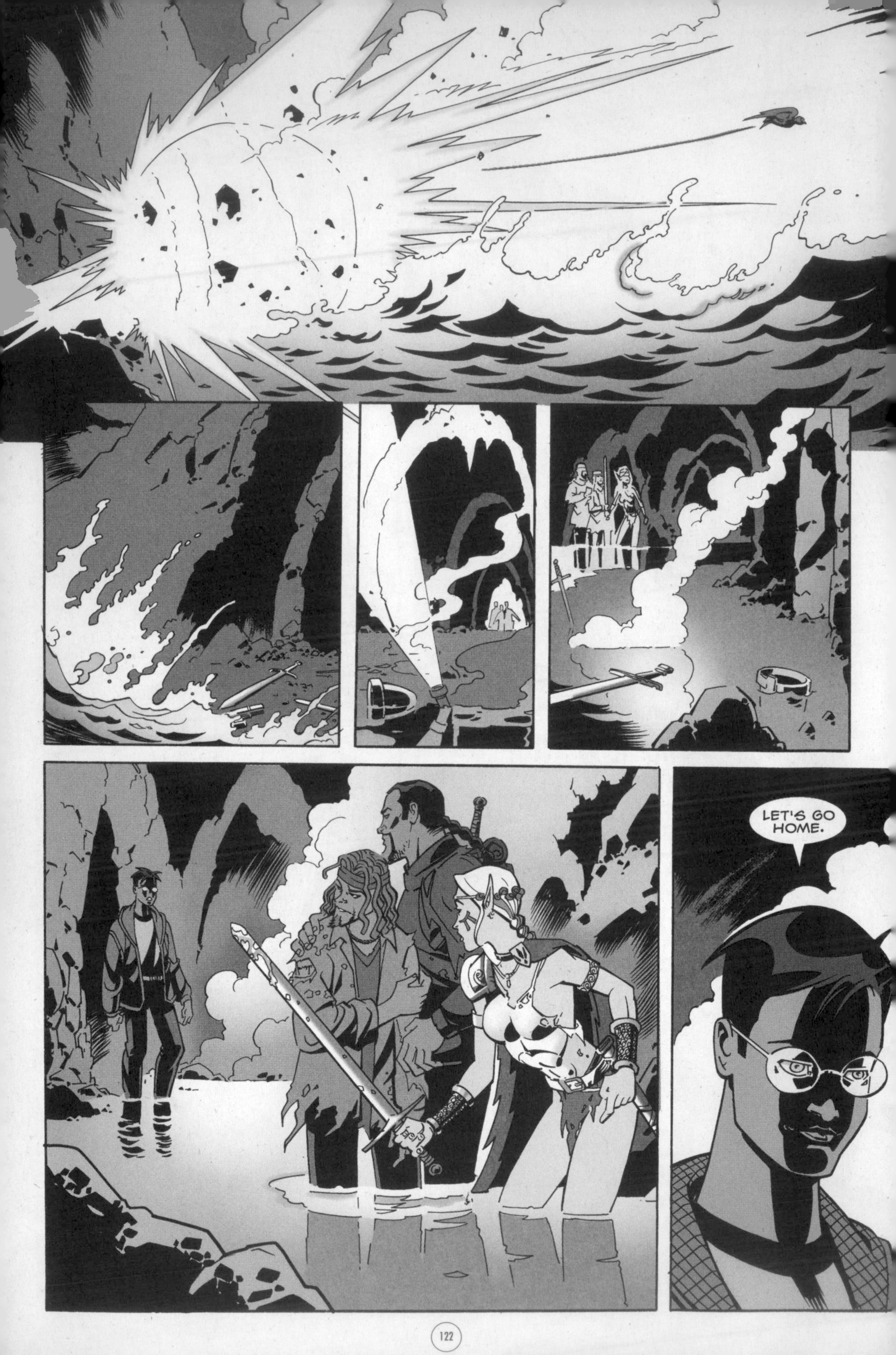
LET'S GO HOME.

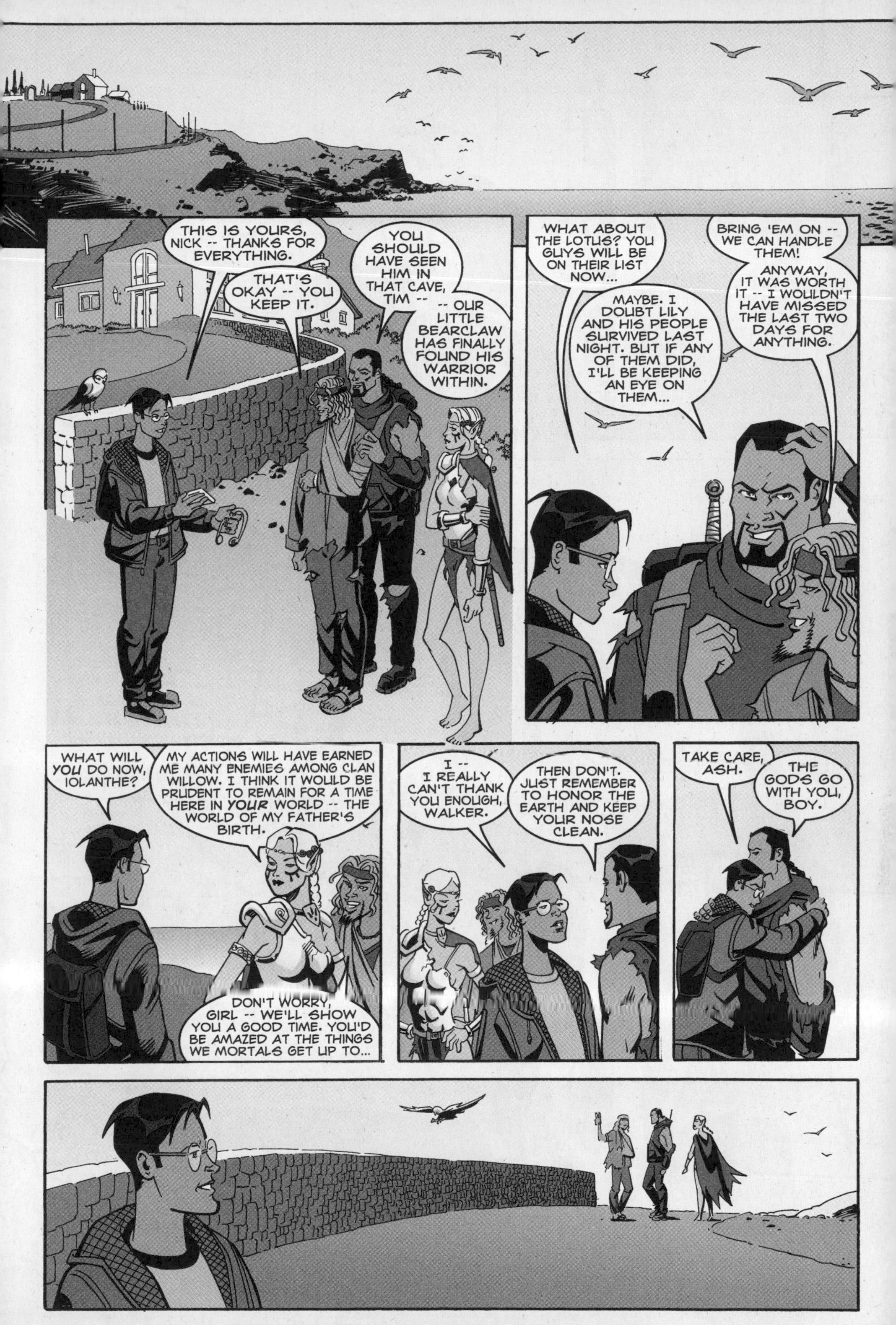
THIS IS YOURS, NICK -- THANKS FOR EVERYTHING.
THAT'S OKAY -- YOU KEEP IT.
YOU SHOULD HAVE SEEN HIM IN THAT CAVE, TIM --
-- OUR LITTLE BEARCLAW HAS FINALLY FOUND HIS WARRIOR WITHIN.
WHAT ABOUT THE LOTUS? YOU GUYS WILL BE ON THEIR LIST NOW...
MAYBE. I DOUBT LILY AND HIS PEOPLE SURVIVED LAST NIGHT. BUT IF ANY OF THEM DID, I'LL BE KEEPING AN EYE ON THEM...
BRING 'EM ON -- WE CAN HANDLE THEM!
ANYWAY, IT WAS WORTH IT -- I WOULDN'T HAVE MISSED THE LAST TWO DAYS FOR ANYTHING.
WHAT WILL YOU DO NOW, IOLANTHE?
MY ACTIONS WILL HAVE EARNED ME MANY ENEMIES AMONG CLAN WILLOW. I THINK IT WOULD BE PRUDENT TO REMAIN FOR A TIME HERE IN YOUR WORLD -- THE WORLD OF MY FATHER'S BIRTH.
DON'T WORRY, GIRL -- WE'LL SHOW YOU A GOOD TIME. YOU'D BE AMAZED AT THE THINGS WE MORTALS GET UP TO...
I -- I REALLY CAN'T THANK YOU ENOUGH, WALKER.
THEN DON'T. JUST REMEMBER TO HONOR THE EARTH AND KEEP YOUR NOSE CLEAN.
TAKE CARE, ASH.
THE GODS GO WITH YOU, BOY.

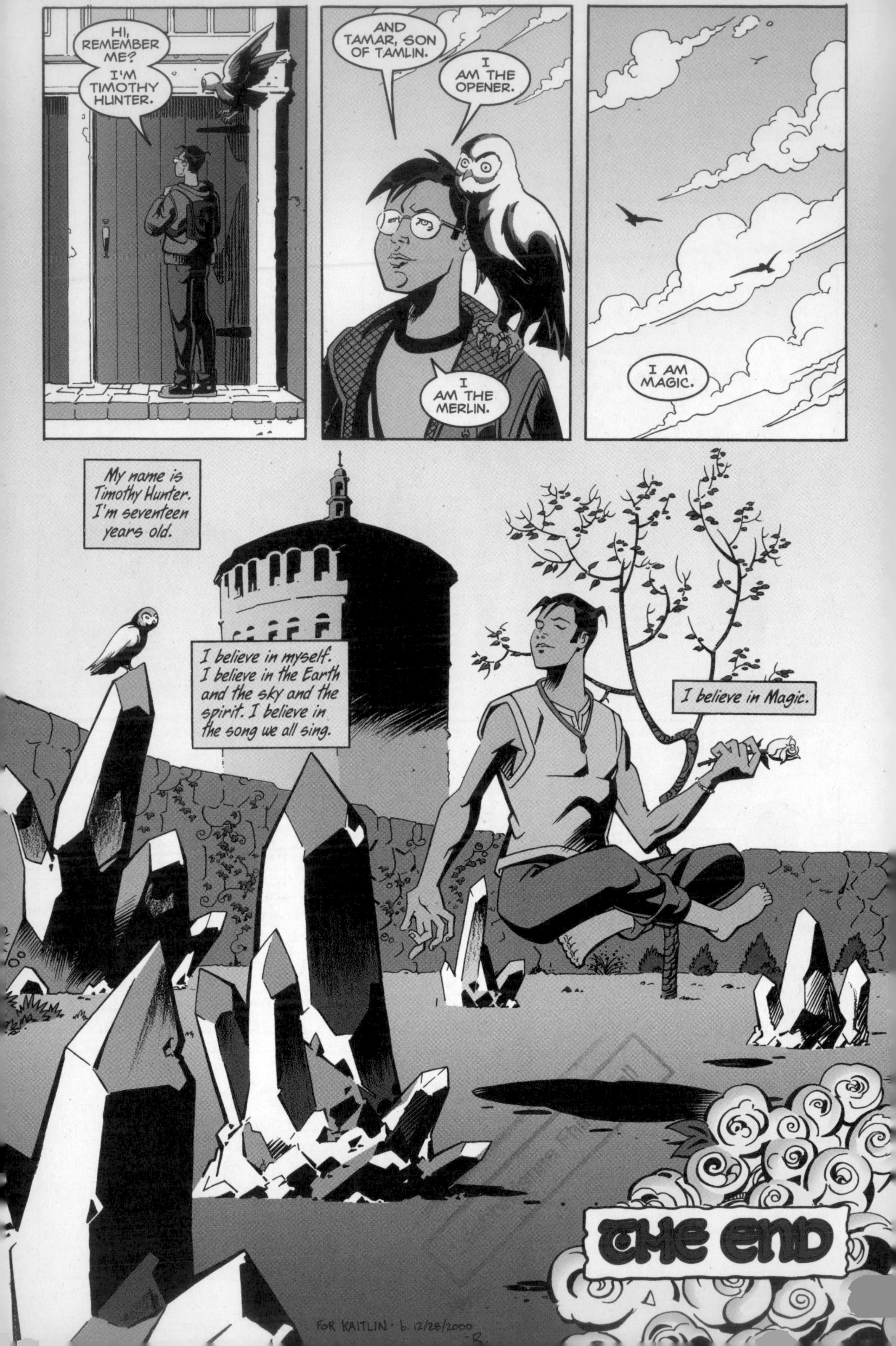
HI, REMEMBER ME? I'M TIMOTHY HUNTER.
AND TAMAR, SON OF TAMLIN.
I AM THE OPENER.
I AM THE MERLIN.
I AM MAGIC.
My name is Timothy Hunter. I'm seventeen years old.
I believe in myself. I believe in the Earth and the sky and the spirit. I believe in the song we all sing.
I believe in Magic.
THE END
FOR KAITLIN · b. 12/28/2000 -R

For Brian Rimoldi (1965-1998)

Thanks to Brad! Brooks,
Matthew Chappory and
David Billinghurst for help
with the research and to
Terry Fleming for --
well, for everything.
           — *Dylan*

Dedicated to my
grandmother Genevia,
who left us,
and daughter Kaitlin,
who arrived,
during the creation
of this book.
— *Richard*

Dedicated to James,
the real Timothy Hunter.
— *John*

THE INVISIBLES: KISSING MR. QUIMPER
G. Morrison/C. Weston/I. Reis/various

MICHAEL MOORCOCK'S MULTIVERSE
M. Moorcock/W. Simonson/J. Ridgway/M. Reeve

MERCY
J.M. DeMatteis/Paul Johnson

NEIL GAIMAN & CHARLES VESS' STARDUST
Neil Gaiman/Charles Vess

NEIL GAIMAN'S MIDNIGHT DAYS
N. Gaiman/T. Kristiansen/S. Bissette/J. Totleben/M. Mignola/various

NEVADA
S. Gerber/P. Winslade/S. Leialoha/D. Giordano

PREACHER: GONE TO TEXAS
Garth Ennis/Steve Dillon

PREACHER: UNTIL THE END OF THE WORLD
Garth Ennis/Steve Dillon

PREACHER: PROUD AMERICANS
Garth Ennis/Steve Dillon

PREACHER: ANCIENT HISTORY
G. Ennis/S. Pugh/C. Ezquerra/R. Case

PREACHER: DIXIE FRIED
Garth Ennis/Steve Dillon

PREACHER: SALVATION
Garth Ennis/Steve Dillon

PREACHER: WAR IN THE SUN
Garth Ennis/Steve Dillon/Peter Snejbjerg

THE SYSTEM
Peter Kuper

SWAMP THING: SAGA OF THE SWAMP THING
Alan Moore/Steve Bissette/John Totleben

SWAMP THING: LOVE AND DEATH
A. Moore/S. Bissette/J. Totleben/S. McManus

SWAMP THING: ROOTS
Jon J Muth

TERMINAL CITY
Dean Motter/Michael Lark

TRANSMETROPOLITAN: BACK ON THE STREET
Warren Ellis/Darick Robertson/various

TRANSMETROPOLITAN: LUST FOR LIFE
Warren Ellis/Darick Robertson/various

TRANSMETROPOLITAN: YEAR OF THE BASTARD
Warren Ellis/Darick Robertson/Rodney Ramos

TRUE FAITH
Garth Ennis/Warren Pleece

UNCLE SAM
Steve Darnall/Alex Ross

UNKNOWN SOLDIER
Garth Ennis/Kilian Plunkett

V FOR VENDETTA
Alan Moore/David Lloyd

VAMPS
Elaine Lee/William Simpson

WITCHCRAFT
J. Robinson/P. Snejbjerg/M. Zulli/S. Yeowell/T. Kristiansen

the Sandman library

THE SANDMAN: PRELUDES & NOCTURNES
N. Gaiman/S. Kieth/M. Dringenberg/M. Jones

THE SANDMAN: THE DOLL'S HOUSE
N. Gaiman/M. Dringenberg/M. Jones/C. Bachalo/M. Zulli/S. Parkhouse

THE SANDMAN: DREAM COUNTRY
N. Gaiman/K. Jones/C. Vess/C. Doran/M. Jones

THE SANDMAN: THE DREAM HUNTERS
Neil Gaiman/Yoshitaka Amano

THE SANDMAN: SEASON OF MISTS
N. Gaiman/K. Jones/M. Dringenberg/M. Jones/various

THE SANDMAN: A GAME OF YOU
Neil Gaiman/Shawn McManus/various

THE SANDMAN: FABLES AND REFLECTIONS
Neil Gaiman/various

THE SANDMAN: BRIEF LIVES
Neil Gaiman/Jill Thompson/Vince Locke

THE SANDMAN: WORLDS' END
Neil Gaiman/various

THE SANDMAN: THE KINDLY ONES
N. Gaiman/M. Hempel/R. Case/various

THE SANDMAN: THE WAKE
N. Gaiman/M. Zulli/J. Muth/C. Vess

DUSTCOVERS-THE COLLECTED SANDMAN COVERS 1989 - 1997
Dave McKean/Neil Gaiman

THE SANDMAN COMPANION
Hy Bender

To find more collected editions and monthly comic books from DC Comics, call 1-888-COMIC BOOK for the nearest comics shop or go to your local book store.

Visit us at www.dccomics.com

VER0011